TREES

of ONTARIO

Including Tall Shrubs

Linda Kershaw

Lone Pine Publishing

The Publisher: Lone Pine Publishing

10145 – 81 Avenue	1901 Raymond Ave. SW
Edmonton, AB T6E 1W9	Suite C, Renton, WA 98055
Canada	USA

Website: http://www.lonepinepublishing.com

National Library of Canada Cataloguing in Publication Data

Kershaw, Linda J., 1951–
 Trees of Ontario, including tall shrubs

Includes bibliographical references and index.
ISBN 1-55105-274-1

 1. Trees—Ontario—Identification. 2. Shrubs—Ontario—Identification. I. Title.
QK203.O5K47 2001   582.16'09713   C2001-910667-X

Editorial Director: Nancy Foulds
Project Editor: Dawn Loewen
Editorial: Dawn Loewen, Shelagh Kubish
Technical Review: Don Sutherland
Illustrations Coordinator: Carol Woo
Production Manager: Jody Reekie
Book Design, Layout & Production: Heather Markham
Cover Design: Robert Weidemann
Tree Habit Illustrations: Ian Sheldon, except pp. 189, 199 and 214 by Linda Kershaw
Other Botanical Illustrations: Linda Kershaw
Header Artwork & Vegetation Map: Elliot Engley
Range Maps: Heather Markham, Arlana Hale-Anderson
Scanning, Separations & Film: Elite Lithographers Co.

Cover photo by Hans Blohm/Masterfile

DISCLAIMER: This guide is not meant to be a 'how-to' reference guide for food or medicinal uses of plants. We do not recommend experimentation by readers, and we caution that a number of woody plants in Ontario, including some used traditionally as medicines, are poisonous and harmful.

We acknowledge the financial support of the Government of Canada through the Book Publishing Industry Development Program (BPIDP) for our publishing activities.

PC: P4

Contents

*This book is dedicated to my parents,
George and Marjorie Stewart, who introduced me
to the beauty of Ontario's forests and gave
me the freedom to go exploring.*

Acknowledgements

Many people have helped with the preparation and production of this book. In particular, I thank Don Sutherland (Ontario Natural Heritage Information Centre), who reviewed the text and provided valuable criticism and suggestions. Several people examined the species list and made suggestions regarding additions and deletions. These included Don Sutherland, Wasyl Bakowsky, George Argus, Dan Brunton and Bill Crins. Thanks also to the friendly, helpful people I met during photographic visits to parks and gardens in Ontario. A special thank-you to Rob Guthrie and Alan Watson at the University of Guelph Arboretum, and to Brian Douglas, who provided information about the Dominion Arboretum.

Photographs and other illustrations add to the beauty and usefulness of the guide. Thanks to Ian Sheldon, whose watercolour paintings illustrate the form of most species. Many people searched through their slide collections and provided excellent photos. Thanks to George Argus, Wasyl Bakowsky, Bill Crins, Mary Gartshore, Erich Haber, Glen Lumis, Jim Pojar, Robert Ritchie, Anna Roberts, Don Sutherland and John Worrall for your photographic contributions. As well, Chris Graham kindly provided photos from the Royal Botanical Gardens, and Lone Pine Publishing lent some photos from its horticultural collection. A full list of photo credits can be found on p. 215.

At Lone Pine, Dawn Loewen patiently and meticulously edited the text and coordinated the project. Carol Woo located and organized scores of photographs. Heather Markham designed the book and spent many hours bringing text and illustrations together. Thanks to everyone at Lone Pine for your hard work and creative ideas.

Pictorial Guide

NEEDLE LEAVES

Balsam fir
p. 52

Norway spruce
p. 53

White spruce
p. 54

Black spruce
p. 55

Red spruce
p. 56

Tamarack
p. 57

Eastern hemlock
p. 58

Eastern white pine
p. 59

Other pines
pp. 60–63

Eastern red-cedar
p. 64

Eastern white-cedar
p. 65

ALTERNATE BROAD LEAVES

Tulip-tree
p. 66

Cucumber-tree
p. 67

Pawpaw
p. 68

Sassafras
p. 69

American sycamore
p. 70

American witch-hazel
p. 71

Elms
pp. 73–77

Common hackberry
p. 78

Pictorial Guide

Osage-orange p. 79	Mulberries pp. 80–81	Butternut p. 83	Black walnut p. 84
Hickories pp. 85–88	American beech p. 91	American chestnut p. 92	Oaks pp. 93–102
Oaks, cont. pp. 93–102		Hop-hornbeam p. 105	Blue-beech p. 106
Birches pp. 107–113		Alders pp. 114–116	White poplar p. 120

Large-toothed aspen
p. 121

Trembling aspen
p. 122

Balsam poplar
p. 123

Eastern cottonwood
p. 124

Pictorial Guide

ALTERNATE BROAD LEAVES

Willows
pp. 125–138

Cherries
pp. 144–146, 148–149

Peach
p. 147

Plums
pp. 150–152

Common pear
p. 153

Wild crabapple
p. 154

Siberian crabapple
p. 155

Common apple
p. 156

Mountain-ashes
pp. 157–159

Hawthorns
pp. 160–168

Pictorial Guide

Downy serviceberry
p. 169

Smooth serviceberry
p. 170

Redbud
p. 171

Honey-locust
p. 172

Kentucky coffee-tree
p. 173

Black locust
p. 174

Staghorn sumac
p. 175

Poison-sumac
p. 176

Tree-of-heaven
p. 177

Common hop-tree
p. 178

American basswood
p. 179

Littleleaf linden
p. 180

Russian-olive
p. 181

Black tupelo
p. 182

Glossy buckthorn
p. 183

European buckthorn
p. 184

Alternate-leaf dogwood
p. 185

Pictorial Guide

Eastern flowering dogwood, p. 186

Euonymus pp. 187–188

American bladdernut p. 189

Horsechestnut p. 190

Ohio buckeye p. 191

Maples pp. 193–201

Maples, cont. pp. 193–201

Common lilac p. 203

Ashes pp. 204–209

Northern catalpa p. 210

Nannyberry p. 212

Wayfaring-tree p. 213

Highbush cranberry p. 214

9

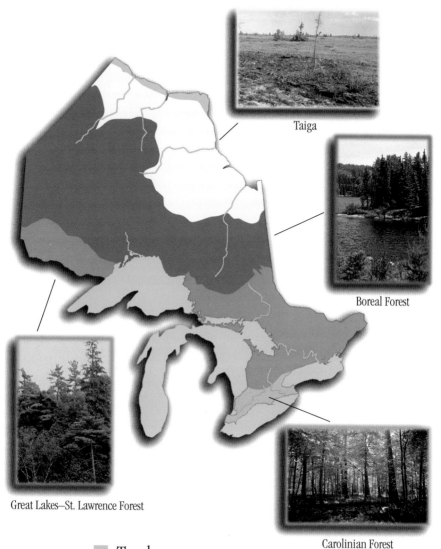

Taiga

Boreal Forest

Great Lakes–St. Lawrence Forest

Carolinian Forest

Tundra
Taiga
Boreal Forest
Great Lakes–St. Lawrence Forest
Carolinian Forest

ONTARIO WOULD BE A DIFFERENT PLACE without trees. Each spring, trees are among the first plants to bring a flush of green, often accompanied by sprays of fragrant flowers. In summer, trees shade our parks and yards, giving shelter from hot sun or drenching downpours and providing homes for birds and squirrels. In autumn, the red and golden leaves of some trees create a beautiful patchwork of colour, and the fruits of others provide delicious treats. In winter, evergreen trees shelter us from wind and snow and add colour to a drab landscape.

Trees are our largest plants, and they dominate many ecological systems. Some plants require the shelter of a forest canopy for survival, while others need the partial protection of open-grown trees in sunnier sites to become established. Beneath the canopy, light levels are lower, humidity is higher and the immediate impacts of wind and rain are muted.

Trees are also important ecosystem producers. They create large quantities of carbohydrates and oxygen, and they store huge amounts of nutrients in their massive trunks and branches. Their leaves, flowers, fruits, bark and twigs provide food for insects, birds and mammals, and their trunks and boughs provide shelter and nesting sites.

Through the ages, trees have also been important to human survival. Bark has been used for covering canoes, roofs and walls, for tanning leather, for making dyes and even for producing soft fibres that could be woven into blankets and clothing. Sap has provided food, glue, caulking and waterproofing. Fruits and nuts are still an important source of food, and many parts of different trees have been used as medicines. Fine roots have been split and spun to make thread and cord, and the knees and elbows of some larger roots were highly valued in shipbuilding. Most notably, however, trees have provided wood. This strong, light, versatile material is still widely used for building homes and other structures; for making boats, tools, utensils and other small items; for carving works of art; for producing paper, cellophane, turpentine, charcoal and countless other products; and for fuel. Without the food, shelter and fuel provided by trees, settlement in Ontario would have been difficult at best.

Many collections of trees have been established in parks and gardens throughout Ontario. An **arboretum** is a place where trees and other plants are cultivated for their beauty and for scientific and educational purposes. If you would like to learn more about trees by viewing living specimens, try visiting some of the collections listed in the appendix (p. 216).

Plants can also be studied using dried, pressed specimens. A **herbarium** is a large collection of such specimens that have been mounted, labelled and filed systematically. See the appendix (p. 217) for the names and locations of herbaria in Ontario.

What Is a Tree?

Most of us have a fairly clear idea of what a tree is. Trees are tall, long-lived plants with stout, woody trunks and spreading canopies. A giant sugar maple or perhaps a towering spruce might come to mind with the word 'tree.' Many small trees, however, fall into the grey area between trees and shrubs. Robust specimens would be considered trees, but younger or less robust individuals might be called shrubs. These species have also been included in this guide in an effort to include all species that could possibly be viewed as 'trees.'

For the purposes of this guide, a tree or tall shrub is defined as an erect, perennial, woody plant reaching **over 4 m** in height, with a distinct crown and with a trunk (one or more of the trunks on a multi-stemmed specimen) reaching **at least 7.5 cm** in diameter. The trunk diameter is the DBH (diameter at breast height), measured 1.3 m from the ground.

Some definitions stipulate that a true tree must have a single trunk that divides into branches well above the ground, so that the tree has a clearly defined bole (main stem). However, many trees, such as some willows, have trunks that divide at or near the ground. Other species, such as the birches and native chestnuts, often coppice (form bushy clumps from sprouting stumps).

Trees are our longest-lived and largest organisms. Most live about 100–200 years, but some survive much longer. For example, eastern hemlock can live 600 or even almost 1000 years. Smaller trees are usually shorter-lived, typically surviving about 60–80 years. Most trees reach 15–25 m in height, but some grow even taller. For example, eastern white pine can reach 30 m; American sycamore, tulip-tree and white oak can reach 35 m; and wych elm may tower to 40 m. At the other end of the spectrum, small trees such as pussy willow, mountain maple and poison-sumac rarely exceed 5 m.

In order to support the large trunks and branches of a tree, many cells are gradually transformed into non-living supportive tissues, such as wood and cork. These dead cells account for about 80% of a mature tree, and the remaining 20% are live cells that maintain vital functions.

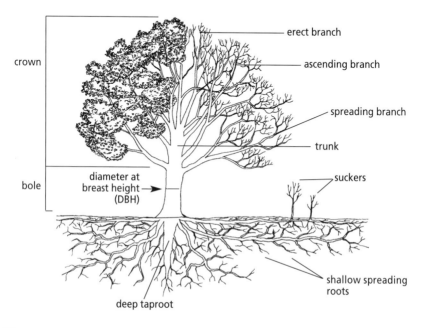

crown

bole

diameter at breast height → (DBH)

deep taproot

erect branch

ascending branch

spreading branch

trunk

suckers

shallow spreading roots

Trunks

The sturdy, woody trunk of a tree supports the weight of the aboveground mass, and it supplies the living tissues with water and nutrients from the ground and with food from the leaves. A trunk is made up of several distinct layers, each with a different function.

The outermost layer is the **bark.** Tree bark forms a protective, waterproof layer that can shield the tree from fire damage, insect or fungal attack and the stress of sudden temperature changes. Not all types of bark offer the same protection. For example, trees with thick, corky bark may survive a fire that would seriously damage or kill trees with thin, papery bark.

All bark has small, round or vertically or horizontally elongated pores called **lenticels,** which allow the trunk to breathe. Lenticels are often difficult to see, but in some trees they are very conspicuous and distinctive, with raised edges that roughen the bark. Often, trees with thin, smooth bark (e.g., birches, cherries) have large, conspicuous lenticels.

Acer saccharum, sugar maple

Bark is sometimes very distinctive (e.g., in beeches and sycamores), but often it is not a useful identifying feature. Bark characteristics can also change greatly with age. Young bark is usually smooth, with visible pores, but as a tree ages, its bark becomes thicker and rougher, and the pores are obscured in many corky layers.

Bark cells grow from a special thin layer of living cells on the inner side of the bark, called the **cork cambium** or bark cambium. Each year, the cork cambium lays down another successive layer of bark to cover the ever-expanding trunk or branch. As growth continues, the oldest, outermost layers of bark are forced either to split into corky ridges or scales (as in maple bark) or to peel away from the tree (as in birch bark).

To the inner side of the cork cambium lies the **phloem** or bast. This thin, inconspicuous layer of cells is very important to the tree because it carries the food (carbohydrates) produced by the leaves to all other living tissues. Trees are killed by 'girdling,' i.e., removing or cutting through the bark, cork cambium and phloem in a complete band around the trunk. The roots of a girdled tree no longer receive food and eventually die, along with the rest of the tree. Some roots may persist for a time using stored reserves, but the final effect of girdling is inevitable.

Trunk cross-section

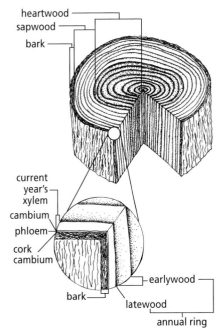

heartwood
sapwood
bark

current year's xylem
cambium
phloem
cork cambium

bark

earlywood
latewood
annual ring

Fagus grandifolia, American beech

On the inner side of the phloem lies an even narrower ring of cells, too thin to see, called the **cambium.** The cambium is responsible for increases in the diameter of a trunk or branch. Cambium cells produce phloem cells along the outer surface of the ring and xylem cells along the inner surface. The **xylem** transports water and nutrients up from the roots to the branches and leaves, where the tree produces food and energy. The thick-walled, cylindrical cells of the xylem join end to end, forming thousands of capillary tubes that extend up the trunk like tiny, elongated drinking straws. The xylem cells soon die, but their firm hollow tubes continue to function, often for many years.

Within its bark, then, the trunk of a tree has a thin outer ring of living tissue composed of the phloem and cambium, and a narrow ring of living xylem. Most of the rest of the trunk, which we call **wood,** is made up of dead xylem cells. With time, these may gradually become plugged with resins, tannins and other compounds and eventually cease to transport fluids altogether, but by then many younger xylem cells have been laid down around them to take their place. As long as xylem cells continue to transport fluids, they are part of the tree's **sapwood,** but once they clog and cease to function, they become part of the **heartwood.** Heartwood is often darker and harder than sapwood because of the resins and other compounds that fill its cells. Heartwood helps support the trunk but otherwise is not important to the general health of the tree. A tree's heartwood can burn or rot away almost completely, leaving a hollow trunk, while the branches and leaves continue to flourish.

Trees growing in temperate regions, where there are definite seasonal changes in growth, develop patterns in their wood called **annual rings.** Each year, after the first flush of spring growth, the trees set down large, relatively thin-walled, light-coloured xylem cells. As the season progresses, growth slows and the xylem cells become smaller and thicker-walled. Eventually, trunk growth stops almost completely in late summer, as trees begin to store nutrients for the coming winter and following spring. Consequently, the ring of wood that is laid down each year gradually changes from pale, large-pored **earlywood** or springwood to harder, darker, small-pored **latewood** or summerwood. The following spring, a new layer of pale springwood is laid down, often in sharp contrast with the darker adjacent summerwood of the previous season. As a result, each year's growth forms a distinct annual ring. The rings can be observed as concentric circles across a log or stump when a tree is cut down, or as a series of light and dark bands along a cylinder when a core is taken from the trunk.

Close examination of annual rings reveals much about the history of a tree. Because a new ring is created each year, counting the rings reveals the age of the tree. We can also learn much about the tree's health and environment because many factors affect the growth rate and subsequent ring widths of a tree. Droughts, unusually cold years, ash deposits from volcanic eruptions, insect infestations, diseases and pollution can all make a tree produce narrow annual rings. Alternatively, increased light (perhaps as a result of an opening in the canopy), influxes of nutrients and unusually warm years can result in wider annual rings. Scars from forest fire or avalanche damage may eventually be overgrown by new wood but will remain hidden in the trunk as a permanent record of the event.

Branches and Twigs

Branches develop the same woody structure as trunks. In young twigs, however, the soft central core of early growth, called the **pith,** is more obvious. In some trees, the pith is quite distinctive. For example, in pawpaw twigs, the pith is marked with horizontal bands, and in hackberry twigs, it has a series of horizontal chambers; both patterns are visible in longitudinal section (cut lengthwise down the middle of the twig). In oaks, the pith is five-pointed when viewed in cross-section (cut across the twig).

Acer rubrum, red maple

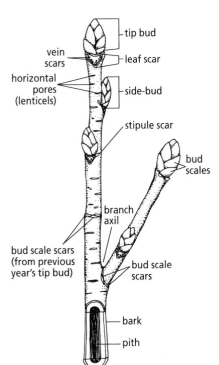

tip bud
vein scars
leaf scar
horizontal pores (lenticels)
side-bud
stipule scar
bud scales
branch axil
bud scale scars (from previous year's tip bud)
bud scale scars
bark
pith

Unlike the trunk, branch tips and twigs grow lengthwise as well as widthwise. The history of recent growth can often be observed through a series of leaf or bud scars on young branches. Each summer, small branches produce buds along their lengths and (usually) at their tips. By autumn, each bud contains all of the rudimentary cells necessary to produce a new structure. The **tip bud** or terminal bud is often much larger than the lower **side-buds** or lateral buds, and it produces a new extension of the shoot the following year. Most side-buds produce leaves and sometimes flowers, but a few send out new branches.

Buds develop gradually over the summer. Usually they are covered by one or more tough, overlapping **bud scales,** which protect the tender, developing tissues from insect and fungal attacks and from drying out. A few trees have **naked buds,** which lack bud scales.

Each bud contains embryonic tissues of the part that it will produce the following year. These tissues remain dormant over winter, but in spring rapid growth resumes, and the new shoots, leaves and flowers expand to emerge from their buds. As the buds open, the scales are shed, but scars remain to show the scales were attached to the branch. Buds at the twig tips are encircled by scales, which leave a ring of scars around the twig, and each successive ring or **annual node** along a branch indicates one year's growth.

15

Picea glauca, white spruce

Leaves

Leaves come in all shapes and sizes, from the tiny, simple scales on cedar boughs to the giant, compound leaves almost a metre long on the Kentucky coffee-tree. (See pp. 28–29 for further discussion of leaf shapes, structures and arrangements.)

Leaves house the food factories and breathing devices of the tree. A leaf produces food by first capturing the sun's energy with the green pigment **chlorophyll,** concentrated in the outer leaf tissues. The leaf then uses the trapped energy in a process called **photosynthesis** to combine carbon dioxide and water and produce sugars (the direct or indirect source of energy for animals) and oxygen (also essential to animal life).

Most trees that have needle-like leaves are **evergreen,** shedding leaves gradually throughout the year and always retaining some green needles for photosynthesis. In Ontario, most trees have broad, **deciduous** leaves, which are produced each spring and shed each autumn.

Leaves breathe through many tiny pores called **stomata.** During the day, leaves take in carbon dioxide and give off moisture and oxygen through their stomata. At night, photosynthesis stops, but the tree continues to respire, expelling carbon dioxide. On broad, deciduous leaves, stomata are usually concentrated on the lower surface of the leaf, and a thin, waxy coating called the **cuticle** protects the upper surface and reduces water loss. On evergreen needles, all sides of the leaf are coated with a cuticle, and the stomata are scattered over the needle surface or concentrated in bands or lines on the lower side. The more extensive cuticle of evergreen needles helps to reduce water loss in winter, when water supply is limited by below-freezing temperatures.

Reproductive Structures

Most tree species reproduce sexually, but the reproductive structures are not always present on every tree. Male and female structures are produced on mature trees in cones or in flowers. In cones these parts are hidden behind protective scales, but in most Ontario trees male and/or female structures are readily visible in flowers.

Flowers may consist of several series of structures. Usually the female organs, or **pistil**(s), are

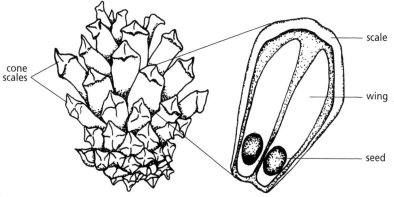

cone scales

scale

wing

seed

at the centre, surrounded by a ring of male organs, or **stamens,** and then rings of floral leaves (petals and sepals). **Petals,** which collectively form the **corolla,** are usually much larger and showier than sepals. Most showy tree flowers in Ontario have white petals, but some are brightly coloured or marked with contrasting spots or stripes. **Sepals,** which collectively form the outer ring or **calyx,** tend to be small and green, serving primarily to protect immature flowers in much the same way as bud scales. Sometimes the petals and sepals look alike and are then collectively called **tepals.**

When all four sets of organs are present, the flower is called **complete,** but in most cases, one or more are absent. **Bisexual** or perfect flowers have both female and male organs (pistils and stamens); **unisexual** flowers have either male or female parts. Unisexual flowers of each sex may be borne on the same **(monoecious)** or separate **(dioecious)** trees.

A flower's main function is to transfer viable **pollen** from its **anthers** (pollen-producing organs of the stamens) to the receptive **stigma** (pollen-receiving organ of the pistil) of another flower, preferably on another plant. When transfer to another plant succeeds, **cross-pollination** occurs.

Many tree flowers are small, greenish and inconspicuous, with minute petals or no petals at all. These flowers usually appear early in the year

Malus cultivar, crabapple

and are wind pollinated (the pollen is carried from one flower to another by the wind). Other trees have insect-pollinated flowers, with showy petals that attract insects and sometimes provide them with handy landing platforms. Often flowers also have special glands called **nectaries,** which produce a sugary liquid **(nectar)** that attracts numerous insects. Many flowers also produce strong odours. Usually these are sweet and fragrant, attracting bees and other nectar-seeking

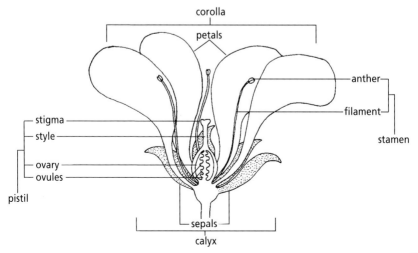

Introduction

Acer ginnala, Amur maple

providing moisture and nutrients for the developing seedlings. Fleshy fruits such as **drupes** (cherries, plums, nannyberries), **pomes** (apples, serviceberries, mountain-ash fruits), and true **berries** (pawpaw fruits) are often juicy and rich in sugars. These fruits attract fruit-eating birds and mammals that swallow the seeds along with the flesh and later deposit the seeds in their droppings at new sites. Similarly, many animals eagerly seek the oil-rich meat of many **nuts** (walnuts, butternuts, hickory nuts, oak acorns). In fleshy fruits, the seed is often protected by woody or bony structures within the fruit (e.g., cores or stones), but in nuts the edible part of the fruit is encased in a hard protective covering.

Many animals also feed on non-fleshy fruits, but these fruits often have special structures that promote seed dispersal without animal assistance. Trees such as ashes, maples and elms produce **samaras** with broad wings that help to carry the seeds through the air or on water to new sites. **Capsules** (willows, American witch-hazel, common lilac), **follicles** (magnolias) and **legumes** (redbud, honey-locust, Kentucky coffee-tree, black locust) are all dry fruits with protective coverings that eventually **dehisce** (split open) to release the seeds.

Seeds vary greatly in size from one species to the next, but all have a dry, often hard covering, the **seed coat,** which protects the developing **embryo** and its food reserves. Seeds with thin, papery seed coats usually germinate as soon as they are shed, whereas those with thick, hard seed coats may persist for several years before developing. Many Ontario trees have seeds that must experience a cold, dormant period before they can germinate. Once germination begins, food reserves in the seed sustain the seedling while it develops roots and leaves for producing its own food. Large seeds, such as those of chestnuts and oaks, may have enough stored energy to allow the seedling to survive for many days. Small seeds have limited reserves, so the seedlings must develop quickly.

Although trees may produce many thousands of seeds each year, very few survive predation and disease, and even fewer find their way to suitable sites where they can grow into new trees.

insects, but sometimes flowers have a fetid odour that is irresistible to flies in search of carrion. When an insect visits a flower it is first directed over the stigma, where it deposits pollen from the previous flower, and then past the anthers, where it picks up pollen to carry to the next blossom.

When pollen fertilizes an **ovule** in a female cone or flower, the ovule develops into a **seed.** In conifers, the seeds are naked but remain protected behind the scales of the cones. Other trees produce flowers with ovules in **ovaries,** which develop into **fruits.** Fruits generally have a protective outer skin, but the inner layer surrounding the seeds can vary from thick and fleshy to dry and fibrous or even hard and bony. In most cases, **simple fruits** are produced from the fertilization of a single ovary. However, in some trees (e.g., cucumber-tree, tulip-tree), dense clusters of many fertilized ovaries produce **aggregate fruits.** Occasionally, compact flower clusters produce very dense clusters of fruits (e.g., mulberries). These **multiple fruits** resemble aggregate fruits, but each part of the group is produced by an individual flower.

Fruits can serve many functions, including protecting the seeds, aiding in seed dispersal and

Forest Regions of Ontario

Many of the dominant plants in Ontario's natural vegetation are trees, and as such, trees define most biological zones in the province. Four major forest regions, along with tundra, are found in Ontario; see the map of vegetation zones on p. 10, based on information in Rowe (1972).

In Ontario, the **Taiga** or Forest and Barren Region covers the Hudson Bay Lowlands, a broad, low region reaching a maximum elevation of 150 m above sea level. Most areas in this forest zone are accessible only by boat or plane. The cold, flat, poorly drained land supports some of the most extensive freshwater wetlands in the world (swamps, bogs and patterned fens) over deposits of marine clay and beach sand on sedimentary bedrock. Soils are usually organic, and some are frozen year-round. Vegetation typically consists of scattered black spruce and tamarack trees in muskeg. In raised, slightly warmer sites such as river levees, broad-leaved trees such as balsam poplar, trembling aspen and paper birch may be found. At the northern edge of this region, near Hudson Bay and James Bay, black spruce is replaced by white spruce, which is better adapted to seashore environments.

The **Boreal Forest Region** is the largest forest region in Canada, covering a broad band from Newfoundland and Labrador to the Yukon Territory. The ecosystems of this young landscape have developed during the short time (9000–10,000 years) since the retreat of the last continental glaciers. Soils are generally poorly developed and the flora and fauna are much less diverse than in southern forests. Snow blankets the land for eight to nine months of the year, and summer days, though long, seldom warm to more than 25° C. Much of the Boreal Forest Region is inaccessible by road and has yet to be described in detail. White spruce and black spruce are the characteristic trees. Jack pine covers vast tracts of well-drained land with stands maintained by fire, and balsam fir flourishes in moist, rarely burned sites. Broad-leaved trees such as paper birch, trembling aspen and balsam poplar are also common, usually growing mixed with spruce. In southern sections, trees of the Great Lakes–St. Lawrence Forest (e.g., yellow birch, sugar maple, black ash, eastern white-cedar) become increasingly common. To the north, black spruce and tamarack become more dominant as stands grow more open and gradually merge with the Taiga.

Picea glauca, white spruce

Boreal forest

Acer saccharum, sugar maple (above)

The **Great Lakes–St. Lawrence Forest Region** or Transition Forest is a broad transitional zone. The northern needle-leaved trees extend south and the southern broad-leaved deciduous trees extend north as far as the adaptations of each species permit. This overlap produces a complex mosaic of communities controlled in large part by local climate and soils. More precipitation falls here than in the Boreal Forest Region, with well-distributed summer rainfall and high winter snowfall. The Great Lakes influence climate in many areas, increasing precipitation and moderating temperatures. Although many parts of the Great Lakes–St. Lawrence Forest Region have been cleared and settled, large sections of forest still remain intact, especially in the north. Logged areas now support secondary or tertiary growth. The mixed stands characteristic of this forest region are dominated by conifers such as eastern white pine, red pine, eastern hemlock and eastern white-cedar, interspersed with broad-leaved trees such as yellow birch, sugar maple, red maple, red oak, American beech and American basswood. Boreal species (e.g., white spruce, black spruce, balsam fir, jack pine, trembling aspen, balsam poplar, paper birch) become increasingly important to the north.

Trillium grandiflorum, white trillium, with sugar maple

The **Carolinian Forest Region** or Deciduous Forest is widespread in the eastern U.S. but extends into Canada only in southernmost Ontario. Here, winters are relatively short and mild, and summer days can be hot and muggy. Each season lasts about three months, and with each the character of the forest changes dramatically as leaves of the dominant deciduous trees come and go. Rich soils and a favourable climate foster diverse ecosystems, with a great variety of both overstorey and understorey trees. Unfortunately, most of the forest in this densely populated region has been cleared for settlement and agriculture, and the few small stands that remain are threatened by further development and by the invasion of aggressive introduced species. Broad-leaved trees typical of the Great Lakes–St. Lawrence Forest Region (primarily sugar maple and American beech, with some American basswood, red ash, white oak and butternut) dominate, and coniferous trees are uncommon. The trees that set this region apart from the others usually grow scattered through the forest, persevering at the northern limit of their range. Most of these Carolinian species grow nowhere else in Canada, and they include tulip-tree, cucumber-tree, pawpaw, red mulberry, Kentucky coffee-tree, honey-locust, black tupelo, blue ash, sassafras, pignut hickory, shellbark hickory, black oak, Shumard oak, pumpkin ash, Ohio buckeye, pin oak, swamp white oak, black walnut and American sycamore.

Liriodendron tulipifera, tulip-tree (above)

Carolinian forest, Rondeau Provincial Park

Rare Trees

Many of Ontario's native tree and tall shrub species are rare, threatened or endangered in the province and/or in Canada. Lists of Ontario's rare plants have been published, including the comprehensive *Atlas of the Rare Vascular Plants of Ontario* (Argus et al. 1982–87), but the status of these species is continually changing. Today, rare plants in Ontario are monitored by the Ontario Ministry of Natural Resource's Ontario Natural Heritage Information Centre (ONHIC). The centre maintains computerized databases and supporting manual files with information on rare species, plant community occurrences and natural areas in the province. Up-to-date information about rare, threatened and endangered species and spaces is stored centrally in Peterborough and is accessible through the ONHIC website at <http://www.mnr.gov.on.ca/MNR/nhic/nhic.html>.

One of the primary functions of the ONHIC is to assess the relative conservation priority of all species in the province. Employing methods developed in the U.S. by The Nature Conservancy, global ranks (GRANKs) and sub-national (provincial) ranks (SRANKs) are assigned for each species in the province. These ranks are not legal designations, but they are used to assess species' rarity and conservation status and thereby assist in setting protection priorities for species and natural communities. Occurrence information is gathered only for those species and communities deemed rare or extirpated in the province, i.e., ranked S1, S2, S3, SH or SX.

Although a number of factors are considered in assigning a rank, the most important single factor is the estimated number of occurrences. Definitions for the rank levels are provided below. For more information on global and sub-national ranks, consult either the ONHIC website or NatureServe via the Association for Biodiversity Information website at <http://www.abi.org>.

The number in each rank denotes the following:

1. Extremely rare; usually 5 or fewer occurrences or very few remaining individuals; often especially vulnerable to extirpation.
2. Very rare; usually between 5 and 20 occurrences or with many individuals in fewer occurrences; may be at risk of extirpation.
3. Rare to uncommon; usually between 20 and 100 occurrences; may have fewer occurrences, but with a large number of individuals in some populations; may be susceptible to large-scale disturbances.
4. Common and apparently secure; usually with more than 100 occurrences.
5. Very common and demonstrably secure.
?. If a question mark follows a ranking (e.g., S3?), the rank is questionable owing to insufficient information.

If two ranks are given, e.g., G3G5, it means the rank falls between these two categories. Occasionally, a letter (rather than a number) is used to assign an S or G rank:

H Historically known from Ontario, but not verified recently (typically not recorded in the province in the last 20 years); however, suitable habitat is thought to remain in the province and there is reasonable expectation that the species may be rediscovered.

Q Questionable taxonomic status.

X Apparently extirpated from Ontario, with little likelihood of rediscovery. Typically not seen in the province for many decades, despite searches at previously noted sites.

The provincial and global rankings of Ontario's rare trees and tall shrubs are presented in the table opposite.

Asimina triloba, pawpaw

Rare and Extirpated Trees and Tall Shrubs in Ontario

Scientific Name	Common Name	Prov.	Global	Forest Region
Aesculus glabra	Ohio buckeye	S1	G5	Carolinian
Asimina triloba	pawpaw	S3	G5	Carolinian
Betula lenta	sweet birch	S1	G5	Carolinian
Betula neoalaskana	Alaska birch	S2	G4G5	Boreal
Betula occidentalis	water birch	S3	G4G5	Boreal
Carya glabra	pignut hickory	S3	G5	Carolinian
Carya laciniosa	shellbark hickory	S3	G5	Carolinian
Castanea dentata	American chestnut	S3	G4	Carolinian
Celtis tenuifolia	dwarf hackberry	S2	G5	Carolinian
Cercis canadensis	redbud	SX	G5	Carolinian
Crataegus apiomorpha	Fort Sheridan hawthorn	S1S2	G3G4Q	Carol./Gt.Lk.St.Lawr.
Crataegus ater	Nashville hawthorn	S1?	G2G4Q	Gt.Lk.St.Lawr.
Crataegus beata	Dunbar's hawthorn	SH	G2G4Q	Carolinian
Crataegus brainerdii	Brainerd hawthorn	S2	G5	Gt.Lk.St.Lawr.
Crataegus compta	adorned hawthorn	S2?	G5?Q	Carolinian
Crataegus conspecta	hawthorn	S1	G3G4Q	Carolinian
Crataegus corusca	shiningbranch hawthorn	S2S3	G3G5	Carolinian
Crataegus dilatata	black hawthorn	S1	G4	Carolinian
Crataegus disperma	spreading hawthorn	S1?	G4?	Carolinian
Crataegus dissona	northern hawthorn	S3	G4G5	Carolinian
Crataegus foetida	hawthorn	SH	G4Q	Carolinian
Crataegus formosa	hawthorn	S2	G2G3Q	Carolinian
Crataegus fulleriana	Fuller's hawthorn	S2?	G3G5Q	Carolinian
Crataegus grandis	grand hawthorn	S1?	G3G5Q	Carolinian
Crataegus margarettiae	Margarett's hawthorn	SH	G5?	Carolinian
Crataegus nitidula	Ontario hawthorn	SH	G1G3Q	Carolinian
Crataegus perjucunda	pearthorn	S1?	G1?Q	Carolinian
Crataegus persimilis	plumleaf hawthorn	S1	G5?	Carolinian
Crataegus scabrida	rough hawthorn	S3?	G5?	Carol./Gt.Lk.St.Lawr.
Crataegus suborbiculata	Caughuawaga hawthorn	S1	G3?	Carol./Gt.Lk.St.Lawr.
Euonymus atropurpureus	eastern wahoo	S3	G5	Carolinian
Fraxinus profunda	pumpkin ash	S2	G4	Carolinian
Fraxinus quadrangulata	blue ash	S3	G5	Carolinian
Gleditsia triacanthos	honey-locust	S2	G5	Carolinian
Gymnocladus dioicus	Kentucky coffee-tree	S2	G5	Carolinian
Magnolia acuminata	cucumber-tree	S2	G5	Carolinian
Morus rubra	red mulberry	S2	G5	Carolinian
Nyssa sylvatica	black tupelo	S3	G5	Carolinian
Pinus rigida	pitch pine	S2S3	G5	Carolinian
Ptelea trifoliata	common hop-tree	S3	G5	Carolinian
Quercus ellipsoidalis	northern pin oak	S3	G4	Gt.Lk.St.Lawr.
Quercus ilicifolia	bear oak	S1	G5	Carolinian
Quercus palustris	pin oak	S3	G5	Carolinian
Quercus prinoides	dwarf chinquapin oak	S2	G5	Carolinian
Quercus shumardii	Shumard Oak	S3	G5	Carolinian
Salix arbusculoides	littletree willow	S1	G5	Boreal
Salix pseudomonticola	false mountain willow	S3	G5?	Boreal

Information from Ontario Natural Heritage Information Centre (ONHIC 1997); published with permission

How to Use This Guide

This guide includes all of Ontario's native trees as well as many introduced species that have escaped cultivation and therefore could be mistaken for wild trees. *Assume each species is native to Ontario unless otherwise specified.*

When identifying a tree, be sure to look carefully for all available clues, both on the tree and on the ground nearby. Large features such as tree size and shape, bark patterns and leaf dimensions may be clearly visible at a glance, but a 10x hand lens can come in handy for examining smaller features such as leaf hairs, flower structures and bud scales.

The main information sources used for compiling the species descriptions in this guide are Farrar (1995), Hosie (1969), Lauriault (1992), Soper and Heimburger (1982), Gleason and Cronquist (1991) and Elias (1989). Additional sources of information are included in the reference list (p. 226).

Keys

The guide presents several illustrated keys to each genus based on different tree features—leaves (pp. 32–35), flowers and young cones (pp. 36–38), fruits and mature cones (pp. 39–41), and winter characteristics (twigs and buds, pp. 42–44). These keys are followed by a broader, conventional key (pp. 45–49) that uses combinations of characteristics (e.g., leaves and fruits) to identify all families and some genera. Throughout the rest of the book, large families are prefaced with a key for identifying each genus, as well as keys to the species for large genera. (The terms family, genus and species are discussed in the next section, 'Organization.')

If you are a novice botanist, don't feel intimidated by any of the keys. Once you have used keys a few times, they become invaluable aids to identification. You may wish to start with the illustrated keys, which are more user-friendly for beginners. All of the keys in this book are dichotomous—that is, they provide mutually exclusive, paired descriptions (e.g., 1a and 1b). Each choice leads either to another dichotomy or to the name of the group (family, genus or species) to which the tree belongs. Whenever possible, keys use everyday language and focus on readily recognizable features. Consult the glossary (p. 218) for explanations of any unfamiliar terms.

tree shape

leaf and flower detail

bark colour and texture

Organization

Trees can be divided into two main groups—the gymnosperms in Division Pinophyta and the angiosperms in Division Magnoliophyta.

Gymnosperm trees are also called **conifers** or **softwoods,** because they produce cones rather than flowers and fruits, and because their wood is typically softer than that of the flowering trees. The name gymnosperm ('naked seed') refers to the bare seeds produced at the base of protective scales in cones. All gymnosperms in Ontario have needle-like leaves and *most* are evergreen. Some people mistakenly use 'conifer' and 'evergreen' interchangeably, but larches (p. 57) are conifers with deciduous leaves.

All of the **angiosperm** trees in Ontario bear **deciduous** leaves with broad, flat blades—hence the name **broad-leaved** trees. Broad-leaved evergreens grow elsewhere in the world (e.g., arbutus trees in British Columbia) but are not now part of the Ontario flora. Angiosperm ('enclosed seed') trees are also called **flowering trees** or **hardwoods.** All species in this large, highly variable group produce flowers with ovules (immature seeds) protected by ovaries, which eventually develop into fruits. In a few cases, the flowers are reduced to tiny structures behind protective scales in cone-like clusters, but most flowers have visible petals and/or sepals as well as stamens and/or pistils. Although broad-leaved trees produce the hardest, heaviest wood, the general label 'hardwood' can be misleading, because the wood of many angiosperms (e.g., willows, poplars, basswoods) is softer than that of some softwoods (e.g., some pines).

The families, genera and species in this guide have been organized in a roughly taxonomic order, in an attempt to place the most similar, closely related species together. Minor deviations from the taxonomic sequence allow the angiosperms to be divided into two convenient groups: species with **alternate branching** (only one leaf or branch at each node) and those with **opposite branching** (two leaves or branches at each node).

Within the three broad groups—needle-leaved, alternate broad-leaved and opposite broad-leaved—trees are further divided into a hierarchy

Gymnosperms (conifers or softwoods)

Angiosperms (flowering trees or hardwoods)

alternate branching   opposite branching

of taxonomic groups, beginning with **families,** such as the rose family (Rosaceae; *look in the keys or index for the Latin equivalents of all family names*). Families are then divided into **genera** (plural of genus); for example, the rose family is made up of several genera including *Amelanchier* (serviceberries), *Prunus* (cherries, plums) and *Sorbus* (mountain-ashes). Genera,

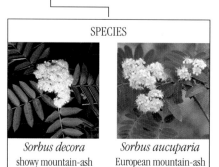

NEEDLE LEAVES

ALTERNATE BROAD LEAVES

OPPOSITE BROAD LEAVES

|
FAMILY
e.g., Rose Family (Rosaceae)
|
GENERA

Sorbus
mountain-ash

Malus
apple

SPECIES

Sorbus decora
showy mountain-ash

Sorbus aucuparia
European mountain-ash

in turn, are divided into **species;** for example, the mountain-ash genus, *Sorbus,* includes species such as *Sorbus aucuparia* (European mountain-ash) and *Sorbus decora* (showy mountain-ash).

Some species can be divided further into forms, varieties and subspecies, but these taxa are not usually described in this guide. Species in some groups of plants (e.g., spruces, poplars, willows, ashes) frequently cross-pollinate to produce **hybrids** with characteristics of both parents. In some cases (e.g., hawthorns), hybridization is so common and the characteristics of offspring are so variable that the entire genus might be best described as a highly variable complex. This guide mentions a few hybrids, but they are not described in separate entries. Similarly, horticultural variants or **cultivars,** developed by plant breeders, are also mentioned in some species accounts but are not described separately.

Species Entries

NAMES
Each species entry provides the scientific (italicized Latin) name as well as common names in both English and French. The preferred or most common name in each category is presented first, but additional common names and scientific **synonyms** (earlier names for the same species) can be found under the heading 'Also Called.'

Although common names may seem easiest to use at first, they can present problems. Most species have many different common names, some unique to different regions. Because common names originate through local usage, it is also possible for the same name to apply to different trees in different regions.

Scientific names, on the other hand, are much less confusing. All must be published in taxonomic works, which clearly describe the plant being named. If the study of a group results in a taxonomic revision, and the name of a species is changed, this change must be justified and published before the existing name can be replaced by a new one. Theoretically, a species can have only one accepted scientific name, but taxonomists, like most scientists, have been known to disagree, and in some cases different groups of botanists recognize different names. However, because all name changes must be published, it is possible to trace synonyms and reduce confusion.

Though unfamiliar to the ear, scientific names are much more consistent than common names and provide a reference point for finding and exchanging information in Ontario and around the world. The scientific names used in this guide follow treatments of the Canadian Integrated Taxonomic Information System (ITIS 2000), Gleason and Cronquist (1991) and the Biota of North America Program (BONAP n.d.).

A full scientific name is properly followed by the name, often abbreviated, of the **authority** (person or persons) who specified it. In this book, authorities can be found in the index.

NOTES

The paragraph at the top of each entry provides special points of interest for each species. The content of the notes varies from one species to the next. Ethnobotanical information is usually provided, indicating how a tree has been and is important to people. You may also find points of historical interest and notes about propagating and cultivating certain species. Trees are very important components of natural systems, and ecological factors such as common diseases and pests, and the importance of trees to wildlife, may be noted here. Also look for the derivation (etymology) of common and scientific tree names. Names often have an interesting history that can help you to understand and remember them. Finally, one or more secondary species closely related to the primary species may be described in this section. Taxonomic problems may also be addressed, particularly if the trees are sterile or frequently hybridize, and tips are provided to help distinguish commonly confused species.

ILLUSTRATIONS

Each primary species is illustrated with one or more colour photos or drawings showing diagnostic characteristics. Secondary species mentioned in the notes section may also be illustrated

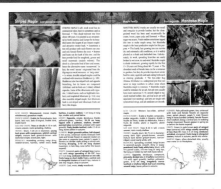

with photos, in which case a caption can be found at the end of the notes section. A watercolour silhouette at the bottom of the page shows each primary species' overall shape.

DESCRIPTIONS

The lower section of each account presents a detailed description of the tree and its parts. Diagnostic or key features are highlighted in bold text. Descriptions include size ranges based on information from Ontario or occasionally elsewhere in Canada. Most trees that you come across in the field should fall within these ranges.

Tree characteristics are described under the following headings:

Size and Shape. In addition to describing the size and shape of the tree as a whole, this section may also include the depth and expanse of the roots.

Trunks. Here you will find information on trunk shape, diameter and orientation, as well as bark characteristics. Because bark can change dramatically with age, young bark and old bark are often presented separately. Bark descriptions usually focus on colour, texture and thickness. Although bark is not always a reliable feature for identifying trees, some groups of trees (e.g., birches, sycamores, beeches) have very distinctive bark, and in some genera (e.g., the ashes), bark characteristics can be useful in distinguishing species.

The wood of different species may be recognizably distinct under a compound microscope, but wood is seldom used for identifying trees in the field. Many people, however, consider wood the most important part of the tree. Wood descriptions usually include

Gymnocladus dioicus, Kentucky coffee-tree

Acer saccharum, sugar maple

colour, hardness, weight and strength. In this book, some of these features may be mentioned in the notes section of an entry, along with a discussion of how the wood has been used.

Branches. This section begins with a description of the size, orientation and arrangement of the main branches. Spines or thorns are important diagnostic features for some species. Twigs are often very different from the larger branches and can provide helpful clues for identifying a tree. Twig descriptions usually include colour, texture, hairiness and occasionally pith characteristics (when viewed in cross- or long-section) or general twig shape (e.g., round or square). Buds can help you identify a tree during the winter, when leaves, fruits and flowers are absent (see the illustrated twig key, pp. 42–44). Important bud characteristics vary with the species, but they may include colour, texture, hairiness, size, number of scales, arrangement of buds and their scales and the presence of sticky or fragrant resins.

Leaves. Of all the parts of a tree, the leaves are most widely used for identifying species (see the illustrated leaf key, pp. 32–35). The leaf descriptions in this guide usually begin with the arrangement of leaves on the branch (opposite, whorled, alternate, spiral) and the type of leaf (simple or compound; deciduous or evergreen). In some cases, care must be taken not to confuse compound and simple leaves. The long, firm central axes of some large compound leaves (e.g., Kentucky coffee-tree) could be mistaken for a small branch and the leaflets for simple leaves. Leaflets of a compound leaf are always attached to a herbaceous (non-woody) main stalk without buds. Most branchlets, on the other hand, have developed buds in the leaf axils by midsummer. Definitions and illustrations of leaf shapes and arrangements are presented in the glossary (pp. 218–219).

Leaf characteristics can vary greatly with age and environment, so when choosing a representative sample for identification, look for healthy, mature leaves on normal branches in full sun. Disease, insect infestations, adverse climatic conditions (e.g., drought, late frost), low light levels and rapid growth spurts can all produce abnormal leaves.

Some trees are more changeable than others. The hawthorns are extremely variable, but aberrations are greatest on vegetative shoots, so choose leaves from flowering or fruiting shoots.

The most obvious part of a leaf is the blade. Important blade characteristics include size, colour (above and beneath), texture (thin, leathery, fleshy), shape (linear, oblong, round, widest above or below the middle) and edges (smooth, toothed, lobed). Leaf stalks are described separately, because they are often quite different from the blades in colour and hairiness. Some leaf stalks have distinctive characteristics such as unusual shapes (e.g., distinctly flattened), lengths (e.g., as long as the blade) or glands (usually near the junction with the blade); others have stipules at the stalk base. Leaf scars can also be useful diagnostic features, especially when identifying trees in winter (see twig key, pp. 42–44). Important leaf scar characteristics include shape, size and arrangement on the branch, and the number and arrangement of vein scars within the leaf scars.

The leaf section may also contain a few notes about seasonality (e.g., leaf colour in fall).

Prunus pensylvanica, pin cherry

Reproductive structures. Cones, flowers and fruits are usually much less variable than vegetative parts such as leaves and branches, and consequently reproductive parts are more reliable features for identifying trees. Unfortunately, not all trees have reproductive structures at any given time. Many species don't begin to produce seed until they are 30 years old, and even then, they may not flower every year. Diseases, insect infestations, droughts and other environmental stresses can all prevent trees from flowering. In most cases, only healthy, mature trees have the reserves necessary to produce abundant seed crops.

Cones are the reproductive structures of the first trees in the guide—the gymnosperms (see the illustrated keys on pp. 36–41). Although male cones and female cones usually appear on the same tree, they are very different in appearance and position, so they are described separately. Male (pollen) cones are small and soft, whereas female cones are relatively large and woody when mature. Important characteristics include colour, texture, shape, size and arrangement on the

Juglans nigra, black walnut

29

Amelanchier laevis, smooth serviceberry

Viburnum lantana, wayfaring-tree

Gymnocladus dioicus, Kentucky coffee-tree

branches. The scales of female cones are sometimes also described. The cone section ends with a short description of seasonality (the timing of cone growth and changes at maturity).

Most other Ontario tree species produce flowers and fruits. Flowers can be very distinctive and can provide essential clues to a tree's identity (see the illustrated flower key, pp. 36–38). Unfortunately, most flowers appear for short periods only and then fade or develop into fruit. Occasionally, the structure of a faded flower can be reconstructed through careful observation of parts that persist on the fruits. The flower section of the tree description indicates colour, texture, shape, size, fragrance and sexuality (e.g., bisexual or unisexual). Most trees in Ontario have unisexual flowers, so male flowers and female flowers and their clusters are often described separately. Diagnostic flower parts such as petals, sepals, stamens and stigmas are sometimes described in detail, but in many cases these components are too small or are not sufficiently distinctive to warrant description. The flower section also describes the arrangement of flowers and types of **inflorescences,** or flower clusters (e.g., racemes, panicles, corymbs, umbels; see glossary, p. 221), and the timing of their development (seasonality).

Fruits are usually more useful than flowers in tree identification, because they tend to last longer. Many fruits can be found throughout the year, either on branches or on the ground nearby, providing valuable clues to the identity of the tree (see the illustrated fruit key, pp. 39–41). The fruit section describes the colour, texture, shape, size and type of fruit (e.g., drupes, capsules, nuts, samaras; see glossary, pp. 222–223). The number, size and shape of the seeds are usually described separately. The fruit section also describes the arrangement of the fruits (hanging vs. erect; cluster shape and size) along with the characteristics of mature fruit (e.g., colour changes, dehiscence).

Habitat. This section describes the types of sites where a tree species is usually found. Habitat information, combined with the distribution (see next section), gives a general idea where to look for the tree. Almost all trees grow best on rich, deep, well-drained soils with adequate moisture, but some also do well on open, disturbed sites and others require the shade and humidity of an established forest. Trees that move in to colonize recently disturbed areas are sometimes called **pioneer species,** and those that require the protection of a forest canopy are called **climax species.** In the absence of repeated disturbances, sun-loving pioneer species are gradually replaced by shade-tolerant climax species, which eventually create relatively stable, self-perpetuating ecosystems. Usually, however, the equilibrium is upset by disturbances such as fire, windfall or insect attacks, and then the canopy opens and the cycle begins again.

DISTRIBUTION

The distributions of native tree species are presented graphically in maps. These range maps are based on information from published sources, mainly Farrar (1995), Soper and Heimberger (1982) and Phipps and Muniyamma (1980). The range of the primary species discussed on each page is shown in bright green, and if an additional native species is mentioned in the notes section, its range may be shown on the same map in pink (where sufficient information is available). Areas where the two species overlap are indicated in dark green.

Information about the ranges of introduced, wild-growing trees is not readily available, so the Ontario distribution of each of these species is simply described in general terms under the heading 'Distribution,' for primary species, or in the notes section, for additional mentioned species.

Liriodendron tulipifera, tulip-tree

The countries or regions that make up these introduced species' native ranges are also noted.

More detailed and up-to-date maps of Ontario tree distributions will soon be available in an atlas. The Ontario Tree Atlas Project has been a cooperative effort between the University of Guelph Arboretum and the Genetic Heritage Program of the Ontario Forest Research Institute, Ontario Ministry of Natural Resources. During this intensive five-year program, people throughout the province gathered detailed information about tree distributions. The database is now essentially complete, and we look forward to publication of the atlas.

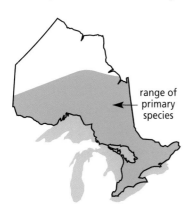

range of primary species

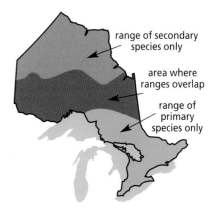

range of secondary species only

area where ranges overlap

range of primary species only

IT'S EASY TO IDENTIFY TREES using the 4 illustrated keys based on leaf, flower, fruit and twig features. Simply work your way through a key choosing between paired alternatives. Try the leaf key with a red maple, for example. The leaves have broad blades, so at lead **1** choose **1b**. This takes you to **4**. Your leaf is simple, so choose **4b** and go to **9**. Palmately lobed, toothed edges take you to **9a, 10a, 11a** and finally **12b**. This brings you to the end of your search—a group of illustrations. Choose the best fit, and go to the page or pages indicated for more information.

1a Leaves narrow, either needle-like or scale-like **2**
1b Leaves broad, with definite blades **4**

2a Leaves needle-like **3**
2b Leaves scale-like, evergreen

Thuja
(white-cedar)
p. 65

Juniperus
(red-cedar)
p. 64

3a Needles in pairs, whorls, tufts or bundles

Juniperus
(red-cedar)
p. 64

Larix
(larch)
p. 57

Pinus
(pine)
pp. 59–63

3b Needles single, alternate

Abies (flat)
(fir)
p. 52

Tsuga (flat)
(hemlock)
p. 58

Picea (3–4-sided)
(spruce)
pp. 53–56

4a Leaves divided into leaflets (compound) . . **5**
4b Leaves simple **9**

5a Leaves pinnately compound **6**
5b Leaves palmately compound or trifoliate

Aesculus
(buckeye)
pp. 190–191

Ptelea
(hop-tree)
p. 178

Staphylea
(bladdernut)
p. 189

6a Leaves once-divided **7**
6b Leaves 2–3 times divided into leaflets

Gymnocladus
(coffee-tree)
p. 173

Gleditsia
(honey-locust)
p. 172

7a Leaves alternate **8**
7b Leaves paired (opposite)

Acer
(maple)
pp. 193–201

Fraxinus
(ash)
pp. 204–209

8a Leaf edges smooth, without teeth or with 1–2 basal lobes

Toxicodendron
(poison-sumac)
p. 176

Robinia
(locust)
p. 174

Ailanthus
(tree-of-heaven)
p. 177

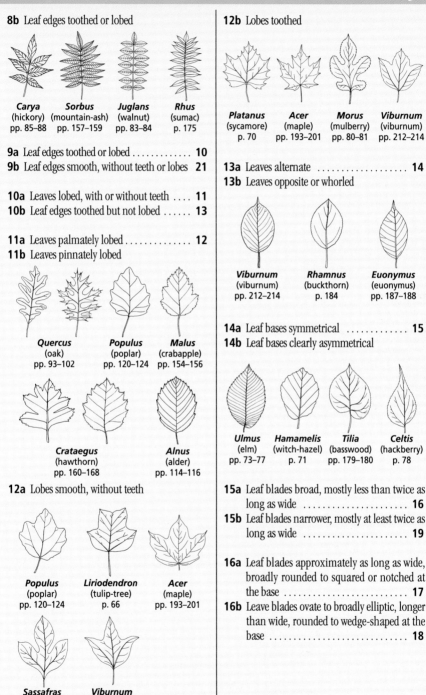

8b Leaf edges toothed or lobed

Carya
(hickory)
pp. 85–88

Sorbus
(mountain-ash)
pp. 157–159

Juglans
(walnut)
pp. 83–84

Rhus
(sumac)
p. 175

9a Leaf edges toothed or lobed **10**
9b Leaf edges smooth, without teeth or lobes **21**

10a Leaves lobed, with or without teeth **11**
10b Leaf edges toothed but not lobed **13**

11a Leaves palmately lobed **12**
11b Leaves pinnately lobed

Quercus
(oak)
pp. 93–102

Populus
(poplar)
pp. 120–124

Malus
(crabapple)
pp. 154–156

Crataegus
(hawthorn)
pp. 160–168

Alnus
(alder)
pp. 114–116

12a Lobes smooth, without teeth

Populus
(poplar)
pp. 120–124

Liriodendron
(tulip-tree)
p. 66

Acer
(maple)
pp. 193–201

Sassafras
(sassafras)
p. 69

Viburnum
(viburnum)
pp. 212–214

12b Lobes toothed

Platanus
(sycamore)
p. 70

Acer
(maple)
pp. 193–201

Morus
(mulberry)
pp. 80–81

Viburnum
(viburnum)
pp. 212–214

13a Leaves alternate **14**
13b Leaves opposite or whorled

Viburnum
(viburnum)
pp. 212–214

Rhamnus
(buckthorn)
p. 184

Euonymus
(euonymus)
pp. 187–188

14a Leaf bases symmetrical **15**
14b Leaf bases clearly asymmetrical

Ulmus
(elm)
pp. 73–77

Hamamelis
(witch-hazel)
p. 71

Tilia
(basswood)
pp. 179–180

Celtis
(hackberry)
p. 78

15a Leaf blades broad, mostly less than twice as
long as wide **16**
15b Leaf blades narrower, mostly at least twice as
long as wide **19**

16a Leaf blades approximately as long as wide,
broadly rounded to squared or notched at
the base **17**
16b Leave blades ovate to broadly elliptic, longer
than wide, rounded to wedge-shaped at the
base **18**

17a Leaf blades roughly triangular with squared bases

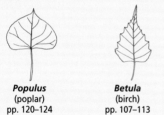

Populus
(poplar)
pp. 120–124

Betula
(birch)
pp. 107–113

17b Leaf blades rounded to round-heart-shaped

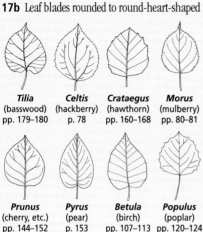

Tilia
(basswood)
pp. 179–180

Celtis
(hackberry)
p. 78

Crataegus
(hawthorn)
pp. 160–168

Morus
(mulberry)
pp. 80–81

Prunus
(cherry, etc.)
pp. 144–152

Pyrus
(pear)
p. 153

Betula
(birch)
pp. 107–113

Populus
(poplar)
pp. 120–124

18a Leaves finely and regularly toothed

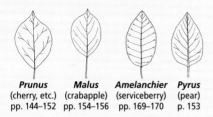

Prunus
(cherry, etc.)
pp. 144–152

Malus
(crabapple)
pp. 154–156

Amelanchier
(serviceberry)
pp. 169–170

Pyrus
(pear)
p. 153

18b Leaves sharply and often irregularly toothed

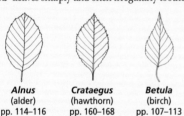

Alnus
(alder)
pp. 114–116

Crataegus
(hawthorn)
pp. 160–168

Betula
(birch)
pp. 107–113

19a Leaf edges moderately to finely toothed .. **20**
19b Leaf edges coarsely toothed, 1 tooth per vein

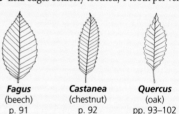

Fagus
(beech)
p. 91

Castanea
(chestnut)
p. 92

Quercus
(oak)
pp. 93–102

20a Leaf edges sharply, often irregularly saw-toothed

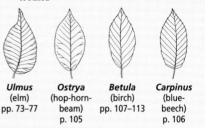

Ulmus
(elm)
pp. 73–77

Ostrya
(hop-horn-beam)
p. 105

Betula
(birch)
pp. 107–113

Carpinus
(blue-beech)
p. 106

20b Leaf edges with finer or more rounded, relatively regular teeth

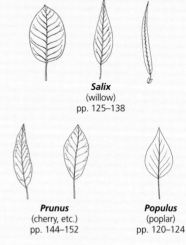

Salix
(willow)
pp. 125–138

Prunus
(cherry, etc.)
pp. 144–152

Populus
(poplar)
pp. 120–124

21a Leaf blades broad, clearly less than twice as long as wide **22**
21b Leaf blades narrower, usually at least twice as long as wide **23**

22a Leaves opposite

Syringa	**Cornus**	**Catalpa**
(lilac)	(dogwood)	(catalpa)
p. 203	p. 186	p. 210

22b Leaves alternate

Sassafras	**Cornus**
(sassafras)	(dogwood)
p. 69	p. 185

Celtis	**Cercis**
(hackberry)	(redbud)
p. 78	p. 171

23a Leaves elliptic to ovate **24**
23b Leaves narrowly oblong to linear

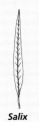 

Salix	**Elaeagnus**
(willow)	(oleaster)
pp. 125–138	p. 181

24a Leaf blades often widest above the middle

Asimina	**Nyssa**
(pawpaw)	(tupelo)
p. 68	p. 182

24b Leaf blades widest at or below the middle

Frangula	**Magnolia**	**Maclura**
(glossy buckthorn)	(magnolia)	(Osage-orange)
p. 183	p. 67	p. 79

1a Reproductive parts tiny, concealed in cones; male cones soft and relatively small; female cones with firm, often woody scales **2**

1b Reproductive parts in true flowers **3**

2a Female flowering cones small, less than 1 cm long

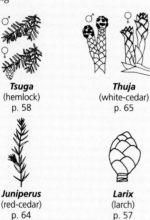

Tsuga
(hemlock)
p. 58

Thuja
(white-cedar)
p. 65

Juniperus
(red-cedar)
p. 64

Larix
(larch)
p. 57

2b Female cones larger, over 2 cm long

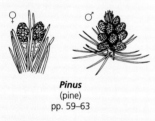

Pinus
(pine)
pp. 59–63

Picea
(spruce)
pp. 53–56

Abies
(fir)
p. 52

3a Flowers short-stalked or stalkless in dense clusters, tiny, inconspicuous, usually green-ish, unisexual, with male and female flowers in separate clusters **4**

3b Flowers clearly stalked, usually larger (over 5 mm across) and showier **7**

4a Flowers (at least male flowers) in elongated clusters (catkins) **5**

4b Flowers (at least male flowers) in spherical clusters

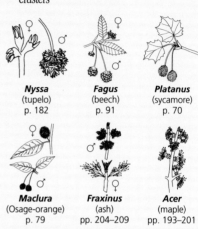

Nyssa
(tupelo)
p. 182

Fagus
(beech)
p. 91

Platanus
(sycamore)
p. 70

Maclura
(Osage-orange)
p. 79

Fraxinus
(ash)
pp. 204–209

Acer
(maple)
pp. 193–201

5a Male and female flowers on the same tree **6**

5b Male and female flowers on separate trees

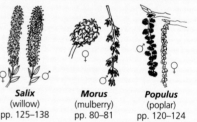

Salix
(willow)
pp. 125–138

Morus
(mulberry)
pp. 80–81

Populus
(poplar)
pp. 120–124

6a Female flowers few, in small, inconspicuous clusters of 1–7

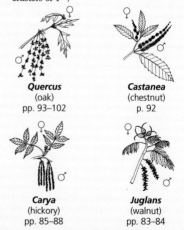

Quercus
(oak)
pp. 93–102

Castanea
(chestnut)
p. 92

Carya
(hickory)
pp. 85–88

Juglans
(walnut)
pp. 83–84

6b Female flowers numerous, usually 15 or more per cluster

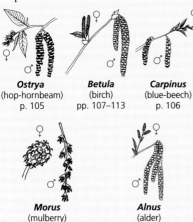

Ostrya
(hop-hornbeam)
p. 105

Betula
(birch)
pp. 107–113

Carpinus
(blue-beech)
p. 106

Morus
(mulberry)
pp. 80–81

Alnus
(alder)
pp. 114–116

7a Flowers small, less than 2 cm across, inconspicuous or in showy clusters **8**
7b Flowers large and showy, more than 2 cm across **14**

8a Flowers relatively showy, usually with petals, in branched clusters (except *Cercis* and some *Prunus*) **9**
8b Flowers inconspicuous, greenish or yellowish, with minute or no petals, single or in small, tassel-like clusters (sometimes elongated in *Ulmus*)

Rhamnus/Frangula
(buckthorn)
pp. 183–184

Ulmus
(elm)
pp. 73–77

Acer
(maple)
pp. 193–201

Celtis
(hackberry)
p. 78

Elaeagnus
(oleaster)
p. 181

9a Flower clusters flat-topped or rounded (cymes, corymbs, umbels) **10**
9b Flower clusters more elongated, clearly longer than wide (panicles, racemes) **13**

10a Flowers bisexual **11**
10b Flowers unisexual, greenish, about 1 cm across, in rounded clusters

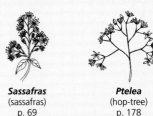

Sassafras
(sassafras)
p. 69

Ptelea
(hop-tree)
p. 178

11a Flowers at least 1 cm across **12**
11b Flowers small (<1 cm), white, in showy, many-branched clusters 5–15 cm across

Viburnum
(viburnum)
pp. 212–214

Sorbus
(mountain-ash)
pp. 157–159

Cornus
(dogwood)
p. 185

12a Flowers white or greenish-white

Tilia
(basswood)
pp. 179–180

Prunus
(cherry, etc.)
pp. 144–152

Crataegus
(hawthorn)
pp. 160–168

Viburnum
(viburnum)
pp. 212–214

12b Flowers pink or purplish

Euonymus
(euonymus)
pp. 187–188

Cercis
(redbud)
p. 171

13a Flower clusters roughly cylindrical, with an unbranched main axis (central stalk)

Robinia
(locust)
p. 174

Gymnocladus
(coffee-tree)
p. 173

Amelanchier
(serviceberry)
pp. 169–170

Gleditsia
(honey-locust)
p. 172

Acer
(maple)
pp. 193–201

Prunus
(cherry, etc.)
pp. 144–152

13b Flower clusters widest near the base, usually branched at least once

Gymnocladus
(coffee-tree)
p. 173

Staphylea
(bladdernut)
p. 189

Toxicodendron
(poison-sumac)
p. 176

Ailanthus
(tree-of-heaven)
p. 177

Rhus
(sumac)
p. 175

Syringa
(lilac)
p. 203

14a Flowers in clusters of 4 or more **15**
14b Flowers single or in clusters of 2–3

Hamamelis
(witch-hazel)
p. 71

Magnolia
(magnolia)
p. 67

Cornus *(flower-like clusters)*
(dogwood)
p. 186

Asimina
(pawpaw)
p. 68

Liriodendron
(tulip-tree)
p. 66

15a Flowers white or pinkish, cupped to star-shaped, about 2–3 cm across with 5 showy petals

Amelanchier
(serviceberry)
pp. 169–170

Malus
(crabapple)
pp. 154–156

Pyrus
(pear)
p. 153

Prunus
(cherry, etc.)
pp. 144–152

Crataegus
(hawthorn)
pp. 160–168

15b Flowers bell-shaped or pea-shaped

Catalpa
(catalpa)
p. 210

Robinia
(locust)
p. 174

Aesculus
(buckeye)
pp. 190–191

1a Cones or fruits with a fleshy (juicy to mealy) outer layer over a stone or several seeds . . . **2**
1b Cones or fruits dry; fruits capsules, nuts or achenes (rarely slightly fleshy) **8**

2a Fruits drupes, berries or fleshy cones; not apple-like **3**
2b Fruits apple-like with a core containing 1 to several seeds

Malus	**Pyrus**	**Amelanchier**
(crabapple)	(pear)	(serviceberry)
pp. 154–156	p. 153	pp. 169–170

Crataegus	**Sorbus**
(hawthorn)	(mountain-ash)
pp. 160–168	pp. 157–159

3a Fruits usually stalked **4**
3b Fruits numerous, stalkless, in dense, head-like clusters (clusters may be stalked)

Morus	**Maclura**
(mulberry)	(Osage-orange)
pp. 80–81	p. 79

4a Fruits small, typically 0.5–1.5 cm long (sometimes larger in domestic cherries) . . **5**
4b Fruits large (2–10 cm long) and juicy

Prunus	**Prunus**	**Asimina**
(peach)	(plum)	(pawpaw)
p. 147	pp. 150–152	p. 68

5a Fruits stalkless, in small, compact clusters of 2–6 (rarely more) at the tips of long stalks

Nyssa	**Cornus**
(tupelo)	(dogwood)
p. 182	p. 186

5b Fruits otherwise **6**

6a Fruits usually in clusters of 3 or more **7**
6b Fruits single or paired (sometimes 3)

Juniperus	**Elaeagnus**	**Celtis**	**Frangula**
(red-cedar)	(oleaster)	(hackberry)	(glossy
p. 64	p. 181	p. 78	buckthorn)
			p. 183

7a Fruit clusters elongated

Rhus	**Toxicodendron**	**Sassafras**	**Prunus**
(sumac)	(poison-sumac)	(sassafras)	(cherry)
p. 175	p. 176	p. 69	pp. 144–146

7b Fruit clusters rounded or flat-topped

Cornus	**Viburnum**
(dogwood)	(viburnum)
p. 185	pp. 212–214

Rhamnus/Frangula	**Prunus**
(buckthorn)	(cherry)
pp. 183–184	pp. 144–146, 148–149

8a Fruits in dense cones or cone-like clusters of firm, overlapping scales or scale-like fruits **9**
8b Fruits not in cone-like clusters **11**

9a Cones or cone-like fruits composed of overlapping scales that cover seeds or seed-like fruits **10**
9b Cones composed of overlapping fruits (samaras or follicles)

Magnolia
(magnolia)
p. 67

Liriodendron
(tulip-tree)
p. 66

10a Cone scales thick, firm and woody

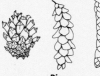 

Pinus
(pine)
pp. 59–63

Alnus
(alder)
pp. 114–116

10b Cone scales relatively thin and bendable

Thuja
(white-cedar)
p. 65

Larix
(larch)
p. 57

Tsuga
(hemlock)
p. 58

Picea
(spruce)
pp. 53–56

Abies
(fir)
p. 52

11a Fruits stalked; single or loosely clustered
. . . . **12**
11b Fruits stalkless or short-stalked; in dense, head-like or cylindrical clusters

Platanus
(sycamore)
p. 70

Carpinus
(blue-beech)
p. 106

Ostrya
(hop-hornbeam)
p. 105

Betula
(birch)
pp. 107–113

Populus
(poplar)
pp. 120–124

Salix
(willow)
pp. 125–138

12a Fruits without wings **13**
12b Fruits winged nutlets (samaras)

Ulmus
(elm)
pp. 73–77

Ptelea
(hop-tree)
p. 178

Ailanthus
(tree-of-heaven)
p. 177

Fraxinus
(ash)
pp. 204–209

Acer
(maple)
pp. 193–201

13a Fruits round to oblong **14**
13b Fruits elongated pods

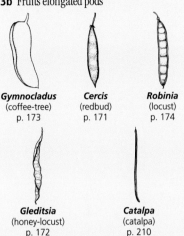

Gymnocladus
(coffee-tree)
p. 173

Cercis
(redbud)
p. 171

Robinia
(locust)
p. 174

Gleditsia
(honey-locust)
p. 172

Catalpa
(catalpa)
p. 210

14a Fruits relatively small nuts or capsules **15**
14b Fruits large (mostly 3–6 cm), round to pear-shaped nuts or capsules containing large, nut-like seeds within an outer husk

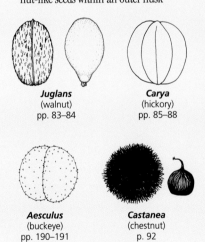

Juglans
(walnut)
pp. 83–84

Carya
(hickory)
pp. 85–88

Aesculus
(buckeye)
pp. 190–191

Castanea
(chestnut)
p. 92

15a Fruits not splitting open when mature (nuts or nut-like capsules)

Tilia
(basswood)
pp. 179–180

Quercus
(oak)
pp. 93–102

15b Fruits splitting open at maturity to release nutlets or seeds

Syringa
(lilac)
p. 203

Hamamelis
(witch-hazel)
p. 71

Euonymus
(euonymus)
pp. 187–188

Fagus
(beech)
p. 91

Staphylea
(bladdernut)
p. 189

1a Leaves evergreen needles or scales **2**
1b Leaves deciduous, absent in winter **3**

2a Leaves small, flat-lying scales

Thuja
(white-cedar)
p. 65

Juniperus
(red-cedar)
p. 64

2b Leaves needle-like

Abies
(fir)
p. 52

Tsuga
(hemlock)
p. 58

Picea
(spruce)
pp. 53–56

Pinus
(pine)
pp. 59–63

3a Branches and bud scars opposite **4**
3b Branches and bud scars alternate **6**

4a Buds covered by 3 or more scales **5**
4b Buds covered by 1 or 2 scales or with 2 naked immature leaves

Salix
(willow)
pp. 125–138

Acer
(maple)
pp. 193–201

Viburnum
(viburnum)
pp. 212–214

Cornus
(dogwood)
p. 186

5a Leaf scars large, often horseshoe-shaped, usually with several vein scars

Fraxinus
(ash)
pp. 204–209

Catalpa
(catalpa)
p. 210

Aesculus
(buckeye)
pp. 190–191

5b Leaf scars small, with 1–3 vein scars

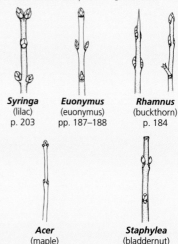

Syringa
(lilac)
p. 203

Euonymus
(euonymus)
pp. 187–188

Rhamnus
(buckthorn)
p. 184

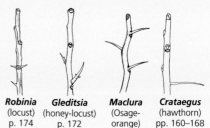

Acer
(maple)
pp. 193–201

Staphylea
(bladdernut)
pp. 189

6a Branches armed with thorns or spine-tipped twigs **7**
6b Branches lacking spines or thorns **8**

7a Branches armed with true thorns

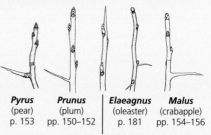

Robinia
(locust)
p. 174

Gleditsia
(honey-locust)
p. 172

Maclura
(Osage-orange)
p. 79

Crataegus
(hawthorn)
pp. 160–168

7b Branches armed with spine-tipped branches or dwarf side-branches

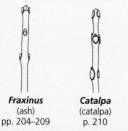

Pyrus
(pear)
p. 153

Prunus
(plum)
pp. 150–152

Elaeagnus
(oleaster)
p. 181

Malus
(crabapple)
pp. 154–156

Rhamnus
(buckthorn)
p. 184

8a Bruised twigs with a noticeable odour **9**
8b Bruised twigs with no noticeable odour ... **10**

9a Bruised twigs or inner bark sweet-smelling

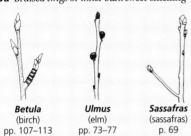

Betula
(birch)
pp. 107–113

Ulmus
(elm)
pp. 73–77

Sassafras
(sassafras)
p. 69

9b Bruised twigs or inner bark foul-smelling

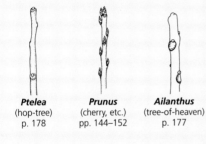

Ptelea
(hop-tree)
p. 178

Prunus
(cherry, etc.)
pp. 144–152

Ailanthus
(tree-of-heaven)
p. 177

10a Pith of twigs solid and uniform, not chambered or banded **11**
10b Pith of twigs chambered or banded

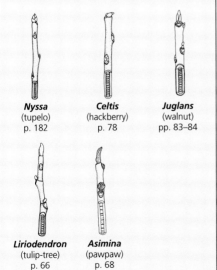

Nyssa
(tupelo)
p. 182

Celtis
(hackberry)
p. 78

Juglans
(walnut)
pp. 83–84

Liriodendron
(tulip-tree)
p. 66

Asimina
(pawpaw)
p. 68

11a Buds protected by scales **12**
11b Buds without scales, so immature leaves exposed

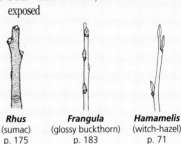

Rhus
(sumac)
p. 175

Frangula
(glossy buckthorn)
p. 183

Hamamelis
(witch-hazel)
p. 71

12a Buds with 1 or 2–3 equal (not overlapping) scales **13**
12b Buds with 3 or more overlapping scales **14**

13a Buds covered by 1 scale

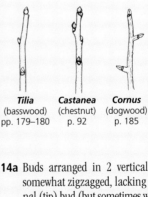

Salix
(willow)
pp. 125–138

Platanus
(sycamore)
p. 70

Magnolia
(magnolia)
p. 67

13b Buds covered by 2–3 scales

Tilia
(basswood)
pp. 179–180

Castanea
(chestnut)
p. 92

Cornus
(dogwood)
p. 185

Alnus
(alder)
pp. 114–116

14a Buds arranged in 2 vertical rows; twigs somewhat zigzagged, lacking a true terminal (tip) bud (but sometimes with a pseudo-terminal bud very near the tip) **15**
14b Buds arranged in 3 or more vertical rows; twigs tipped with a bud **16**

15a Leaf scars containing 4 or more dots (vein scars)

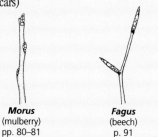

Morus
(mulberry)
pp. 80–81

Fagus
(beech)
p. 91

15b Leaf scars containing 3 dots (vein scars)

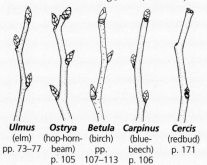

Ulmus
(elm)
pp. 73–77

Ostrya
(hop-horn-beam)
p. 105

Betula
(birch)
pp. 107–113

Carpinus
(blue-beech)
p. 106

Cercis
(redbud)
p. 171

16a Twigs lacking short, dwarf side-branches **17**
16b Twigs with short, dwarf side-branches tipped with leaf, cone or flower buds

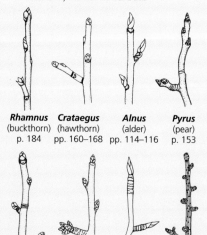

Rhamnus
(buckthorn)
p. 184

Crataegus
(hawthorn)
pp. 160–168

Alnus
(alder)
pp. 114–116

Pyrus
(pear)
p. 153

Malus
(crabapple)
pp. 154–156

Prunus
(cherry, etc.)
pp. 144–152

Populus
(poplar)
pp. 120–124

Larix
(larch)
p. 57

17a Leaf scars containing 3 dots (vein scars)

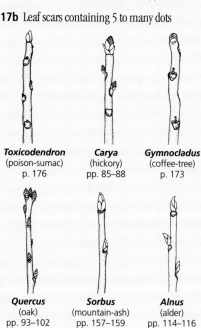

Rhamnus
(buckthorn)
p. 184

Populus
(poplar)
pp. 120–124

Amelanchier
(serviceberry)
pp. 169–170

17b Leaf scars containing 5 to many dots

Toxicodendron
(poison-sumac)
p. 176

Carya
(hickory)
pp. 85–88

Gymnocladus
(coffee-tree)
p. 173

Quercus
(oak)
pp. 93–102

Sorbus
(mountain-ash)
pp. 157–159

Alnus
(alder)
pp. 114–116

THE EASIEST WAY TO IDENTIFY A TREE IS BY USING A KEY. It takes a long time to flip through every page in this guide, and many trees look very similar at first glance. A key provides you with a logical way to evaluate the most important characteristics of a tree and to rapidly narrow your choices.

This guide contains several different keys. All are dichotomous—that is, they present you with pairs of descriptions, only one of which will apply to your specimen. Simply work your way through the key choosing one of the two alternatives and then moving to the next set of choices, as indicated by the number at the end of the line. When the line ends in a name (rather than a number), you have found the name of your tree or the group to which it belongs.

The key below will help you identify the major groups (families and genera) of trees in Ontario. It may appear a bit long and intimidating at first, but remember, you don't have to read every pair of choices. For example, choice **1b** takes you to lead **3, 3b** takes you to lead **14,** and **14b** takes you to lead **22,** over halfway through the key. For large families, you may be directed to other keys further along in the guide. For example, **2b** leads you to the pine family and genus keys on pp. 50–51.

1a Trees not producing true flowers; seeds borne in cones; leaves reduced to needles or scales, usually evergreen **2**
1b Trees producing true (though sometimes very tiny) flowers; leaves broader, not needle-like or scale-like; deciduous **3**

2a Female cones small (<1.3 cm), sometimes berry-like, with whorled or paired scales; leaves usually scale-like, opposite or whorled .... **Cupressaceae, Cypress Family**
    i Cones dry, about 1 cm long, with thin, woody or leathery scales spreading to open at maturity; branchlets flattened, forming horizontal sprays ..... ***Thuja,*** **white-cedar** (p. 65)
    ii Cones berry-like, with fleshy scales fused together at maturity; branches scarcely flattened, if at all .... ***Juniperus,*** **red-cedar** (p. 64)
2b Female cones usually larger, never berry-like; leaves alternate, spirally arranged or bundled .... **Pinaceae, Pine Family** (keys to genera and species, pp. 50–51)

3a Leaves divided into leaflets (compound) **4**
3b Leaves smooth-edged, toothed or lobed, but not divided into leaflets (simple) **14**

4a Fruits winged samaras **5**
4b Fruits not winged samaras **8**

5a Leaves alternate; samaras with the seed near the centre **6**
5b Leaves opposite; samaras with the seed near one end **7**

6a Leaves pinnately divided into 11–41 leaflets; samaras oblong, twisted .... **Simaroubaceae, Quassia Family** (***Ailanthus,*** **tree-of-heaven,** p. 177)
6b Leaves with 3 leaflets (trifoliate); samaras round and flat .... **Rutaceae, Rue or Citrus Family** (***Ptelea,*** **hop-tree,** p. 178)

7a Samaras single .... **Oleaceae, Olive Family** (keys to genera and species, p. 202)
7b Samaras paired .... **Aceraceae, Maple Family** (***Acer,*** **maple,** key to species, p. 192)

8a Fruits thick-husked capsules containing a nut or large, nut-like seed **9**
8b Fruits otherwise **10**

9a Leaves opposite, palmately divided into 5–9 leaflets
.... **Hippocastanaceae, Horsechestnut Family (*Aesculus*, buckeye,** pp. 190–191)
9b Leaves alternate, pinnately divided into 11–23 leaflets
.... **Juglandaceae, Walnut Family** (keys to genera and species, p. 82)

10a Fruits dry capsules or pods **11**
10b Fruits somewhat fleshy pomes or drupes **13**

11a Fruits inflated, thin-walled, 3-pointed pods
.... **Staphyleaceae, Bladdernut Family (*Staphylea*, bladdernut,** p. 189)
11b Fruits elongated, pea-like pods **12**

12a Leaves once-divided .... **Fabaceae, Pea Family (*Robinia*, locust,** p. 174)
12b Leaves twice-divided .... **Caesalpiniaceae, Cassia Family**
  i Branches usually thorny; leaflets up to 1 cm wide; flowers in compact, elongated clusters (racemes) .... **Gleditsia, honey-locust** (p. 172)
  ii Branches without thorns; leaflets 1.5–4 cm wide; flowers in widely branched clusters (panicles) .... **Gymnocladus, coffee-tree** (p. 173)

13a Fruits small pomes (like tiny apples) in rounded to flat-topped clusters (corymbs)
.... **Rosaceae, Rose Family** (keys to genera and species, pp. 139–143)
13b Fruits 1-seeded drupes in conical clusters (panicles) .... **Anacardiaceae, Cashew Family**
  i Leaflets smooth-edged, containing allergenic oils that cause severe skin reactions; fruits smooth, whitish to yellowish berries in loose clusters
.... **Toxicodendron, poison-sumac** (p. 176)
  ii Leaflets toothed, not highly allergenic; fruits fuzzy red berries in dense pyramidal clusters
.... **Rhus, sumac** (p. 175)

14a Leaves and branches paired (opposite) or whorled **15**
14b Leaves and branches single (alternate) **22**

15a Fruits pairs of winged keys; leaves palmately veined and lobed
.... **Aceraceae, Maple Family (*Acer*, maple,** key to species, p. 192)
15b Fruits and leaves otherwise **16**

16a Fruits tiny capsules in dense, elongated clusters (catkins); buds covered by a single scale
.... **Salicaceae, Willow Family (*Salix*, willow,** key to species, pp. 117–118)
16b Fruits and buds not as above **17**

17a Leaves toothed **18**
17b Leaves smooth-edged (not toothed) **20**

18a Fruits 4-lobed capsules
.... **Celastraceae, Staff-tree Family (*Euonymus*, euonymus,** pp. 187–188)
18b Fruits berry-like drupes **19**

19a Flowers and fruits numerous, in broad, widely branched clusters (cymes) at branch tips; flowers 5-parted . . . . **Caprifoliaceae, Honeysuckle Family**
(***Viburnum*, viburnum,** key to species, p. 211)

19b Flowers and fruits few, in small, unbranched clusters (umbels) from leaf axils; flowers 4-parted . . . . . **Rhamnaceae, Buckthorn Family (*Rhamnus*, European buckthorn,** p. 184)

20a Flowers whitish, with separate petals; fruits juicy, berry-like drupes; leaf shape elliptic to oval . . . . **Cornaceae, Dogwood Family (*Cornus*, dogwood,** p. 186)

20b Flowers with bell-shaped corollas of fused petals, in large showy clusters; fruits not berry-like; leaves heart-shaped **21**

21a Flowers large, frilly-edged, somewhat 2-lipped, white with yellow and purple markings; fruits bean-like pods about 30 cm long
. . . . **Bignoniaceae, Trumpet-creeper Family (*Catalpa*, catalpa,** p. 210)

21b Flowers small (about 1 cm), with 4 spreading, purple, blue or white petals; fruits dry, woody capsules 1–1.5 cm long . . . . **Oleaceae, Olive Family (*Syringa*, lilac,** p. 203)

22a Leaves smooth-edged (not toothed) **23**
22b Leaves toothed **33**

23a Flowers large, single, at branch tips, with 6 petals and 3 sepals; fruits large (>7 cm) cones or berries **24**

23b Flowers smaller, usually in clusters of 2 or more; fruits pods, capsules, nuts or berry-like drupes **25**

24a Flowers dull purple; fruits large, sweet-pulpy berries with many large seeds; leaves widest above the middle, not dotted
. . . . **Annonaceae, Custard-apple Family (*Asimina*, pawpaw,** p. 68)

24b Flowers yellowish-green, often with yellow or orange markings; fruits numerous, forming dense, cone-like clusters; leaves with tiny, transparent dots . . . **Magnoliaceae, Magnolia Family**

    i Leaves broad and squarish, usually 4-lobed; fruits dry, winged nutlets (samaras) not splitting open . . . . **_Liriodendron_, tulip-tree** (p. 66)

    ii Leaves oblong to elliptic, never lobed; fruits fleshy pods (follicles), splitting open to release seeds . . . . **_Magnolia_, magnolia** (p. 67)

25a Fruits large (10–14 cm), round, pulpy aggregates of many small fruits; branches thorny, with milky juice . . . . **Moraceae, Mulberry Family (*Maclura*, Osage-orange,** p. 79)

25b Fruits and branches not as above **26**

26a Fruits berry-like drupes, with juicy or mealy flesh enclosing a single, hard stone **27**
26b Fruits dry capsules, pods, nuts or nutlets **31**

27a Leaf surfaces silvery above and below with dense, star-shaped hairs; drupes silvery, mealy . . . . **Elaeagnaceae, Oleaster Family (*Elaeagnus*, oleaster,** p. 181)

27b Leaves and fruits not silvery; drupes dark blue to purplish-black **28**

Key to Families and Genera

28a Flowers 5–8 mm across, yellow, 6-lobed; leaves typically 2–3-lobed; bark, twigs and wood spicy-fragrant.................. **Lauraceae, Laurel Family (*Sassafras*, sassafras,** p. 69)
28b Flowers tiny, greenish to cream, 3–5-lobed, often lacking petals; leaves not lobed; trees not spicy-fragrant **29**

29a Flowers bisexual, borne singly on slender stalks in small clusters from leaf axils; fruits single .... **Rhamnaceae, Buckthorn Family (*Frangula*, glossy buckthorn,** p. 183)
29b Flowers unisexual or bisexual, in dense clusters at the tips of long stalks; fruits usually 2 or more per stalk **30**

30a Flowers bisexual, with 4 stamens and 4 petals; sepals minute; fruits fleshy, red to purplish-black, berry-like drupes .... **Cornaceae, Dogwood Family (*Cornus*, dogwood,** p. 185)
30b Flowers unisexual, with 5 evident sepals and 5–8 minute petals; fruits oily, blue-black, plum-like drupes .... **Nyssaceae, Sourgum Family (*Nyssa*, tupelo,** p. 182)

31a Fruits acorns (1-seeded nuts with the base enclosed in a distinctive cup of overlapping bracts) .... **Fagaceae, Beech Family (*Quercus*, oak,** key to species, pp. 89–90)
31b Fruits otherwise **32**

32a Flowers pea-like; fruits flattened pods (legumes), leaves heart-shaped .... **Caesalpiniaceae, Cassia Family (*Cercis*, redbud,** p. 171)
32b Fruits small, short-stalked capsules in elongated clusters (catkins); leaves linear to ovate .... **Salicaceae, Willow Family** (keys to genera and species, pp. 117–119)

33a Branches spiny or thorny **34**
33b Branches without spines or thorns **35**

34a Flowers tiny, with petals about 1 mm long, borne in tassel-like clusters arising from leaf axils; fruits small, berry-like drupes; leaves often opposite ..... **Rhamnaceae, Buckthorn Family (*Rhamnus*, European buckthorn,** p. 184)
34b Flowers larger (>1 cm), with showy white to pink petals; fruits various; leaves alternate .... **Rosaceae, Rose Family** (keys to genera and species, pp. 139–143)

35a Flowers and fruits in small, flat-topped clusters on slender stalks from the middle of strap-like, membranous bracts; leaves usually unevenly heart-shaped .... **Tiliaceae, Linden Family (*Tilia*, basswood,** pp. 179–180)
35b Fruits, flowers and leaves not as above **36**

36a Flowers tiny, without petals or sepals, unisexual; male flowers numerous, in dense heads or catkins **37**
36b Flowers not in dense heads or catkins **41**

37a Male and female flowers in separate, spherical heads; fruits tiny, club-shaped, 1-seeded nutlets in dry, round heads..... **Platanaceae, Plane-tree Family (*Platanus*, sycamore,** p. 70)
37b Male flowers (and sometimes female also) in elongated clusters (catkins) **38**

38a Fruits tiny, short-stalked capsules in catkins; seeds tipped with tufts of long, silky down; buds covered by 1 scale..... **Salicaceae, Willow Family** (keys to genera and species, pp. 117–119)

38b Fruits otherwise, seeds not tipped with silky hairs; buds not 1-scaled **39**

39a Fruits large, single nuts seated in a scaly cup or in a bristly husk
.... **Fagaceae, Beech Family** (keys to genera and species, pp. 89–90)

39b Fruits small, numerous, in dense clusters **40**

40a Fruits tiny winged nutlets, protected by dry bracts in scaly or woody catkins
.... **Betulaceae, Birch Family** (keys to genera and species, pp. 103–104)

40b Fruits tiny nutlets, each surrounded by juicy, swollen sepals to form blackberry-like clusters
.... **Moraceae, Mulberry Family** (*Morus,* **mulberry,** pp. 80–81)

41a Leaves asymmetrical, with one edge longer than the other at the base **42**

41b Leaves with symmetrical bases **43**

42a Flowers showy, with 4 slender yellow petals, appearing in autumn; fruits woody, 2-seeded capsules; leaves wavy-toothed
.... **Hamamelidaceae, Witch-hazel Family** (*Hamamelis,* **witch-hazel,** p. 71)

42b Flowers inconspicuous, greenish, lacking petals, appearing in spring; fruits round, winged samaras or red to blackish drupes; leaves sharply toothed
.... **Ulmaceae, Elm Family** (keys to genera and species, p. 72)

43a Flowers yellowish-green, <6 mm across, with 4–5 stamens alternating with 4–5 petals; fruits 2–3-stoned, berry-like drupes
.... **Rhamnaceae, Buckthorn Family** (*Rhamnus,* **buckthorn,** p. 184)

43b Flowers usually white or pinkish, larger and showier, with more than 10 stamens; fruits various, but drupes 1-stoned ... **Rosaceae, Rose Family** (keys to genera and species, pp. 139–143)

Sassafras albidum, sassafras

Malus coronaria cultivar, crabapple

Key to Genera in the Pine Family (Pinaceae)

1a Needles in clusters of 2 or more; branches with dwarf shoots **2**
1b Needles single, spirally arranged; branches lacking dwarf shoots **3**

2a Needles drop each autumn (deciduous), numerous, in dense clusters at the tips of stubby dwarf branches . . . . **Larix, larch** (p. 57)
2b Needles evergreen, in bundles of 2–5 along branches . . . . **Pinus, pine** (key to species, below)

3a Needles 4-sided, easily rolled between fingers, spirally arranged like bristles on a bottle brush; twigs rough with persistent woody needle bases; cones hanging
. . . . **Picea, spruce** (key to species, p. 51)
3b Needles flat, with 2 white lines on the lower surface, generally twisted to lie flat in 2 rows along the twig **4**

4a Seed cones erect, gradually shedding their scales while on the tree; leaves attached directly to the branch, leaving a smooth round scar when shed . . . . **Abies, fir** (p. 52)
4b Seed cones hanging, falling with scales intact; leaves attached to elevated woody bases, leaving twigs rough when shed . . . . **Tsuga, hemlock** (p. 58)

Key to the Pines (Genus *Pinus*)

1a Needles soft and slender, in bundles of 5; cone scales thin and flexible, without spiny, thickened tips
. . . . **P. strobus, eastern white pine** (p. 59)
1b Needles firmer, thicker, in bundles of 2–3; cone scales thickened and rather woody **2**

2a Needles in bundles of 3; seed cone scales tipped with a short prickle
. . . . **P. rigida, pitch pine** (p. 63)
2b Needles in bundles of 2; seed cone scales with a small reflexed spine or unarmed **3**

3a Needles 8–16 cm long, straight **4**
3b Needles 2–7 cm long, twisted lengthwise or with pairs spreading **5**

4a Needles stiff, snapping readily when bent in half; seed cones reddish-brown, stalkless when shed; buds chestnut-brown . . . . **P. resinosa, red pine** (p. 60)
4b Needles flexible, not snapping when bent in half; seed cones shiny brown, shed with stalks; buds with whitish resin . . . . **P. nigra, Austrian pine** (p. 61)

5a Needles spirally twisted (both sides visible at once), not noticeably spreading
. . . . **P. sylvestris, Scots pine** (p. 61)
5b Needles only slightly twisted (only 1 side visible), spread in a V **6**

6a Tree native to the boreal forest; needles yellowish-green; seed cones asymmetrical, 2.5–7.5 cm long, usually in pairs . . . . **P. banksiana, jack pine** (p. 62)
6b Tree a small, introduced ornamental, widely planted; needles dark green; seed cones egg-shaped, usually in groups of 3 or more . . . . **P. mugo, mugo pine** (p. 61)

Key to the Spruces (Genus *Picea*)

1a Young twigs and buds hairless (or essentially so) **2**
1b Young twigs and buds with many short, fine hairs **3**

2a Seed cones 3–6 cm long, with smooth-edged scales; branchlets spreading, rarely hanging
. . . . *P. glauca,* **white spruce** (p. 54)
2b Seed cones 10–18 cm long, with irregularly toothed scales; branchlets typically hanging
. . . . *P. abies,* **Norway spruce** (p. 53)

3a Needles bluish-green, with a whitish bloom; seed cones 2–3 cm long, dark purplish, becoming greyish-brown, often persisting for several years; trees slender, columnar to narrowly pyramidal
. . . . *P. mariana,* **black spruce** (p. 55)
3b Needles yellow-green, without a whitish bloom; seed cones 3–5 cm long, purplish-green, becoming brown or reddish-brown, soon shed; trees pyramidal
. . . . *P. rubens,* **red spruce** (p. 56)

Pinus rigida, pitch pine

BALSAM FIR'S regular, conical shape and its fragrant, persistent needles make it a popular Christmas tree. • Balsam fir wood is not commonly used for lumber (occasionally in crates, doors and panelling), but it is an important source of pulp. • The resin, known as Canada balsam, is used in mounting microscope specimens, in making glue and as a fragrance in perfumes, deodorizers, candles and soaps. It was widely used in folk medicine as an antiseptic. • Although this tree lives for about 150 years, it doesn't produce significant amounts of seed until it is about 20–30 years old. Dense, pure fir stands protect steep slopes from erosion and provide food and cover for wildlife. Multitudes of shade-tolerant seedlings often make walking difficult. • This shallow-rooted tree is commonly

toppled by high winds and heavy, wet spring snow. Because of its thin bark, it is easily killed by fire. Balsam fir is susceptible to attacks by eastern spruce budworm *(Choristoneura fumiferana)*, hemlock looper *(Lambdina fiscellaria fiscellaria)*, balsam woolly adelgid *(Adelges piceae)* and butt rot. Controversy continues over the environmental effects of chemical sprays for controlling budworm.

ALSO CALLED: Canada balsam, Canada fir, white fir

FRENCH NAMES: Sapin baumier, sapin blanc, sapin rouge

SIZE AND SHAPE: Coniferous trees 10–25 m tall, narrowly cone-shaped; **crowns spire-like; roots shallow.**

TRUNKS: Straight, 50–70 cm in diameter; young bark thin, smooth, with **blister-like pockets of aromatic resin;** mature bark brownish, irregularly scaly; wood soft, light, somewhat brittle.

BRANCHES: Stout, spreading; **twigs slender, smooth,** yellow-green to greyish, hairy; buds dark orange-green, lustrous, **broadly egg-shaped,** 3–6 mm long, usually resinous.

LEAVES: Dark shiny green, **flat evergreen needles,** with **2 white bands on the lower surface;** 1.5–2.5 cm long on lower branches (1–1.2 cm on upper), aromatic, blunt or notched, stalkless; spirally attached but twisted into 2 rows on one plane; leaf scars flat and round; needles drop after 4–5 years.

CONES: Male and female cones on same tree; male cones yellow, 4 mm long; female cones **dark purple when young, erect, barrel-shaped,** 4–10 cm long, often resinous; seeds purple to brown, 3–6 mm long with a shiny, light brown wing 1–1.5 cm long, abundant; female cones usually mature in first September; both scales and seeds are shed, leaving erect cores (axes) on branches for several years.

HABITAT: Low, swampy ground to well-drained hillsides; needs moist soil and air.

THIS SPRUCE has 2 forms: the 'brush' form, with bunched shoots typical of spruce trees; and the 'comb' form, with sparser, upcurved branches from which smaller side branches hang in lines (like teeth on a comb). • Norway spruce is one of the most important timber trees in central and northern Europe. The timber, known as 'whitewood' or 'deal,' is used in roofing, in house interiors and as a source of pulp. In Britain, Norway spruce is the traditional Christmas tree, and in Germany, turpentine is extracted from the trunks for use in tanning. • Norway spruce is widely planted as an ornamental tree and windbreak in temperate North America. It has also been cultivated here for Christmas tree purposes and is used in many reforestation projects in eastern Canada and the northeastern U.S. The trees are hardy enough to survive in regions north of Lake Superior, but they are often stunted by winter frosts near their northern limit. • Plant breeders have developed more than 100 cultivars of Norway spruce, in many shapes and sizes, but only a few are commonly cultivated.

ALSO CALLED: Common spruce • *P. excelsa*

FRENCH NAMES: Épicéa commun, épinette de Norvège, pesse, sapin de Norvège, sapin rouge

SIZE AND SHAPE: Coniferous trees up to 40 m tall (to 65 m in Europe); crowns cone-shaped.

TRUNKS: Tall, up to 130 cm in diameter; young bark reddish-brown, smooth to shredding; mature bark dark purplish-brown with small, rounded scales.

BRANCHES: Drooping; twigs hairless, creamy green to light orange-brown, rough with small peg-like, leaf-bearing bumps; buds pale to reddish-brown, cone-shaped, blunt, not resinous.

LEAVES: Dark green, 4-sided evergreen needles, 1.2–2.5 cm long, sharp-pointed; spirally arranged but curved upwards and forwards; shed after several years.

CONES: Male and female cones on same tree; male cones small, yellow; female cones greyish- or reddish-brown when mature, **cylindrical, tapered at the tip, 10–18 cm long,** hanging near branch tips; scales thin, flat, tapered to a slightly toothed tip; seeds small, winged, 2 behind each scale; female cones drop in first autumn to winter.

HABITAT: Varied, but prefers shaded or partially shaded sites with deep, rich, moist soils.

DISTRIBUTION: Introduced from northern and central Europe and Asia; grows wild near parent stands in southern Ontario.

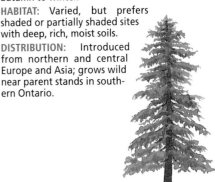

53

White Spruce *Picea glauca*

Pine Family

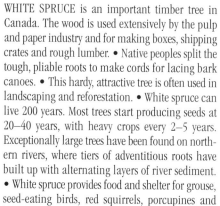

WHITE SPRUCE is an important timber tree in Canada. The wood is used extensively by the pulp and paper industry and for making boxes, shipping crates and rough lumber. • Native peoples split the tough, pliable roots to make cords for lacing bark canoes. • This hardy, attractive tree is often used in landscaping and reforestation. • White spruce can live 200 years. Most trees start producing seeds at 20–40 years, with heavy crops every 2–5 years. Exceptionally large trees have been found on northern rivers, where tiers of adventitious roots have built up with alternating layers of river sediment. • White spruce provides food and shelter for grouse, seed-eating birds, red squirrels, porcupines and black bears. Red squirrels nip off the cones and young shoots. Porcupines often deform spruce trunks when they eat the bark. Black bears can also

damage trees when they strip off the outer bark to get at the sweet inner bark. • White spruce needles often drop prematurely as a result of infection by rust diseases. Eastern spruce budworm (*Choristoneura fumiferana*) and spruce sawflies (various species) are also serious pests. • White spruce is the provincial tree of Manitoba.

ALSO CALLED: Black Hills spruce, cat spruce, skunk spruce, pasture spruce, Canadian spruce, single spruce

FRENCH NAMES: Épinette blanche, épicéa glauque, épinette grise, épinette du Canada

SIZE AND SHAPE: Coniferous trees up to 25 m tall; crowns narrowly (northern) to broadly (southern) cone-shaped; roots shallow.

TRUNKS: Tall, up to 60 cm in diameter; mature bark dark grey, with thin, scaly plates; **newly exposed bark pinkish;** wood light, soft and straight-grained.

BRANCHES: Bushy, spreading to drooping, up-curved at the tips; **twigs stout, pale greenish-grey to orange-brown, hairless** (seedling twigs may be hairy), with many small, peg-like, leaf-bearing bumps; buds blunt, 6 mm long, with tight, ragged, hairless scales.

LEAVES: Straight, stiff, **4-sided** evergreen needles; **needles green, often with a greyish bloom,** white-lined on all sides, 1.5–2.2 cm long, aromatic; spirally arranged but curved upward and crowded on the upper side; shed after several years.

CONES: Male and female cones on same tree; male cones yellow, 1.5–2 cm long; female cones pale brown when mature, **3–6 cm long, cylindrical, resilient,** stalkless, hanging near branch tips; **scales thin, smooth-edged, close-fitting;** seeds pale brown, 2–4 mm long with a wing 4–8 mm long, 2 behind each scale; female cones mature in one season, shed seeds over winter and then drop.

HABITAT: Wide range of soils and climates but prefers rich, moist soil.

BLACK SPRUCE is a small tree used for pulp and fuel. • This spruce lives up to 200 years. Healthy trees are prolific seed producers from about 10 years of age, with good crops every other year. Fire stimulates cones to open and shed seeds onto newly exposed soil. • When lower branches touch the ground, they often develop roots and send up shoots. This process (layering) produces small clumps around parent trees. In habitats where seed success is limited (e.g., cold, wet, acidic sites), layering is often the main means of regeneration. • Red squirrels nip the tips off cone-bearing branches to gather the cones and eat the seeds. This pruning can result in a dense mass of branches in the upper crown with a bare stretch of trunk immediately underneath. • This shallow-rooted tree is susceptible to damage from high winds, flooding and fire. Black spruce buds open 1–2 weeks later than those of white spruce, so black spruce is less likely to be damaged by late spring frosts. • Black spruce and red spruce (p. 56) often produce hybrids with intermediate characteristics.

ALSO CALLED: Bog spruce, swamp spruce, water spruce • *P. nigra, Abies mariana*

FRENCH NAMES: Épinette noire, épicéa marial, épinette bâtarde, épinette des marais, épinette des tourbières, épinette de savane

SIZE AND SHAPE: Coniferous trees, **columnar** and 5–20 m tall on poorly drained sites, **cone-shaped** and up to 30 m tall on upland sites; **crowns dense;** roots usually shallow.

TRUNKS: Straight, 15–30 cm in diameter; mature bark dark greyish-brown with thin, irregular scales; **newly exposed bark olive- or yellowish-green;** wood yellowish-white, soft, light.

BRANCHES: Short, spreading to drooping, upturned at tips; **twigs dull orange- to yellowish-brown,** with peg-like, leaf-bearing bumps; **new twigs minutely reddish-hairy; buds grey-brown, hairy, blunt,** 3–5 mm long, with **slender-pointed scales** projecting beyond tips.

LEAVES: Stiff, **straight, 4-sided,** evergreen needles; **needles greyish-green** with a whitish bloom, **8–15 mm long,** short-stalked; spirally arranged, curved up and forward; persist several years.

CONES: Male and female cones on same tree; male cones small, numerous; female cones dull greyish- to **purplish-brown, rigid, 2–3 cm long,** hanging on **curved, short, scaly stalks** near branch tips; **scales thin, stiff, brittle,** close-fitting and firmly attached; seeds 2 mm long with a 2–4 mm wing, 2 per scale; female cones mature in first September, shed seeds over many (up to 30) years or quickly after fires.

HABITAT: Well-drained, moist flatlands in the north, to cool, damp sites (e.g., bogs) farther south.

Columnar form   Cone-shaped form

RED SPRUCE wood is very similar to that of white spruce, and it is usually sold as white spruce or simply 'spruce.' Red spruce lumber has been used in construction and in the production of stringed instruments. • This spruce is relatively long-lived, becoming 300–400 years old. It usually begins to produce cones after about 15 years, with reliable seed production at 20–25 years of age and large seed crops every 2–11 years. Light is an important environmental factor. Growth is slow in dense shade and moderately fast in full sun. • Both white-tailed deer and rabbits browse young twigs in winter. Squirrels and seed-eating birds such as the white-winged crossbill eat the seeds in autumn. • This shallow-rooted tree is susceptible to windfall. It also falls prey to eastern spruce beetle *(Dendroctonus rufipennis)*, eastern spruce budworm *(Choristoneura fumiferana)*, at least six species of rust and two types of needle-cast fungi. • Red spruce often hybridizes with its close relative, black spruce (p. 55). The hybrids share characteristics of both parents, so they are often difficult to identify. • Red spruce is the provincial tree of Nova Scotia.

ALSO CALLED: Eastern spruce, yellow spruce, he-balsam • *P. rubra, P. australis*

FRENCH NAME: Épinette rouge

SIZE AND SHAPE: Coniferous trees 20–25 m tall, broadly cone-shaped.

TRUNKS: Straight, 60 cm in diameter, lower 1/3–2/3 often without branches; young bark light reddish-brown, shredded; mature bark reddish-black, thinly scaled; newly exposed bark (under scales) dull light yellow or reddish-brown; wood light-coloured, lightweight, soft and straight-grained.

BRANCHES: Relatively long, horizontal to sloping, with upturned tips; twigs shiny, rough, with peg-like, leaf-bearing bumps; **new twigs with tiny, reddish hairs;** buds chestnut-brown, shiny, with hairy, slender-pointed scales extending beyond the tips.

LEAVES: Shiny, **yellow-green, 4-sided, curved** evergreen needles 1–1.6 cm long, pointing upwards and forwards; usually drop after several years.

CONES: Male and female cones on same tree; male cones yellowish-green, 1.2–1.4 cm long; female cones brown or reddish-brown and dry when mature, 3–5 cm long, oblong, hanging at branch tips; **scales stiff,** easily detached, **smooth- or slightly rough-edged;** seeds dark brown, 2 mm long with a 3–5 mm wing, 2 per scale; female cones mature in autumn, shed most seeds the same year.

HABITAT: Wetlands to dry, rocky woods; prefers well-drained, acid soils.

LARCH WOOD is not valued for lumber but has been used occasionally in rough construction and as poles, piers and railway ties. • Tannin-rich tamarack bark was used traditionally for tanning leather. • This relatively short-lived tree usually survives about 150 years, with peak seed crops at 50–75 years of age. In cold, nutrient-poor environments, tamarack often becomes stunted and produces small needles and narrow-scaled cones. • In early fall, red squirrels strip off the cones and eat the seeds. Chipmunks, mice and red crossbills also gather the seeds. White-tailed deer browse on young shoots, and porcupines often kill tamarack trees by stripping off the outer bark to feed on the sweeter inner bark. • Tamarack is relatively free of serious infection by fungal diseases but its foliage is sometimes damaged severely by larch sawfly *(Pristiphora erichsonii).* • The **European larch** *(L. decidua* or *L. europaea)* is often planted in eastern North America as an ornamental or for forestry purposes, and it occasionally escapes cultivation near parent stands. It is readily distinguished by its large (2–3.5 cm long) cones, which have more than 30 finely hairy scales.

Photo, bottom left: *L. decidua*

ALSO CALLED: American larch, hackmatack, eastern larch, Alaska larch

FRENCH NAME: Mélèze laricin

SIZE AND SHAPE: Coniferous trees up to 25 m tall, roughly cone-shaped, irregular with age.

TRUNKS: Usually straight, 40 cm in diameter; young bark grey, smooth, thin; mature bark light reddish-brown, with narrow, peeling scales; **newly exposed bark reddish-purple;** wood heavy, strong.

BRANCHES: Of 2 types: long, **slender, spreading branches** with scattered leaves, often gracefully curved; and **stubby, dwarf side-branches** elongating slowly over many years; buds brown to dark red, hairless or ringed by hairs.

LEAVES: Light bluish-green, **soft, slender, deciduous needles,** 2–5 cm long; tightly spiralled in clusters of 15–60 at tips of stubby side shoots; **yellow** when shed each autumn.

CONES: Male and female cones on same tree; male cones small, yellow; **female cones yellow-green or reddish when young, pale brown when mature, 1–2 cm long,** on short, curved stalks at tips of leafless, stubby side-branches; **scales 10–20, stiff, hairless, longer than wide;** seeds light brown, 3 mm long with a 6 mm wing; female cones mature in mid-August, soon shed seeds, often persist through the year.

HABITAT: Usually cold, wet sites such as bogs and muskeg, but grows best on moist, well-drained upland sites.

EASTERN HEMLOCK wood tends to separate along radial lines and between annual rings, making it brittle and easily split. However, the knots are very hard and can dull saw blades and deflect nails. The poor-quality lumber is sometimes used in construction. When burned as firewood, eastern hemlock tends to 'pop,' sending sparks flying. • Hemlock bark was once gathered commercially for leather tanning, leaving behind many bare, decaying logs. • This tree adapts to different soils and responds to pruning, so it is planted as an ornamental and in windbreaks. Fallen twigs and leaves increase soil acidity, discouraging competition from other plants. • Eastern hemlock can live up to 600 years, and some trees reach almost 1000 years. Young trees produce seed after 20–40 years, with heavy crops every 3–4 years. • Hemlocks provide dense cover and food for white-tailed deer, snowshoe hares, porcupines, ruffed grouse and wild turkeys. After deep snowfalls, white-tailed deer take shelter in hemlock stands, heavily browsing the lower branches. In years when cones are plentiful, songbirds such as black-capped chickadees, pine siskins and crossbills descend en masse to feast on the oil-rich seeds.

ALSO CALLED: Canada hemlock, hemlock spruce
FRENCH NAME: Pruche du Canada
SIZE AND SHAPE: Coniferous trees up to 30 m tall, densely conical when young, irregular with age, **tipped with a nodding leader**.
TRUNKS: Straight, up to 1 m in diameter; young bark reddish-brown, scaly; mature bark dark brown, furrowed, broadly ridged; **inner bark bright reddish-purple;** wood light orange-yellow to reddish-brown, lightweight.

BRANCHES: Slender, flexible, **irregular, spreading, with drooping tips;** forming **flat, horizontal sprays;** twigs hairy, with tiny, leaf-bearing bumps; buds brownish, hairy, 2 mm long.
LEAVES: Flat, flexible, evergreen needles, dark yellowish-green and grooved above, with 2 whitish bands within green margins beneath; 1–2 cm long, blunt or notched, edged with tiny teeth; spirally attached but twisted into **2 rows on one plane.**
CONES: Male and female cones on same tree, near branch tips; male cones yellowish, round; female cones light brown and dry when mature, **1.2–2 cm long,** hanging on slender, hairy, 2–3 mm stalks; scales few, thin, the **exposed part of middle scales wider than long,** smooth-edged or faintly toothed; seeds light brown, 1–2 mm long with a 6–8 mm wing; female cones shed seeds from autumn to early winter but persist 1 year.
HABITAT: Cool, moist, shady, protected sites.

THIS STATELY SOFT PINE is Ontario's provincial tree and one of eastern North America's most commercially valuable trees. Before the arrival of Europeans, white pine stands in eastern North America contained an estimated 900 billion board feet (about 2 billion m³) of lumber, but most were cut in the 1700s–1800s. The tall, straight trunks made excellent ship masts, so some stands were reserved for the Royal Navy. • The wood is moderately strong and easily worked, with uniform texture and low shrinkage. It has been used in construction, interior and exterior finishing, furniture, cabinets and carvings. • This attractive, fast-growing tree is widely used in landscaping and reforestation projects. • Eastern white pine trees live about 200 years and produce seed regularly after 20–30 years. Seed production fluctuates, with good crops every 3–5 years and little or no production in between. Seedlings can persist in the understorey up to 20 years. The bark resists fire well, and after forest fires, surviving trees readily shed their seed over freshly exposed ground. • White pine blister rust *(Cronartium ribicola)* and white pine weevil *(Pissodes strobi)* have killed many white pine trees.

ALSO CALLED: Northern white pine, Weymouth pine, soft pine

FRENCH NAME: Pin blanc

SIZE AND SHAPE: Coniferous trees up to 30 m tall; crowns conical when young, becoming irregular (often lopsided) with age.

TRUNKS: Tall, straight, up to 1 m in diameter; young bark greyish-green, thin, smooth; mature bark dark greyish-green, 2–5 cm thick, with broad ridges of purple-tinged scales; wood pale brown, soft, lightweight, straight-grained.

BRANCHES: Stout, irregular, horizontal to ascending; twigs flexible, green and hairy (first year) to orange-brown and hairless (second year); buds slender, up to 1.5 cm long, reddish-brown, with overlapping scales.

LEAVES: Light **bluish-green, soft, slender, straight, flexible** evergreen needles; **needles 5–15 cm long,** 3-sided, finely toothed; **bundled in 5s** and sheathed with membranous scales at the base; drop after 1–4 years.

CONES: Male and female cones on same tree; male cones yellow, small, clustered at the base of this year's growth; female cones light brown and woody when mature, **cylindrical,** often curved, **8–20 cm long,** hanging on 2 cm long stalks; scales 50–80, exposed portions thin, rounded, lacking prickles; seeds mottled reddish-brown, 5–8 mm long with a 1.5–2 cm wing, 2 per scale; female cones mature in 2–3 years, drop soon after shedding seeds.

HABITAT: Dry rocky ridges to sphagnum bogs; does best on cool, humid sites with well-drained soil.

RED PINE is an important timber and pulp tree. The moderately hard wood readily absorbs preservatives, making it useful for structural beams, bridges, piles and railway ties. • Red pine has relatively little genetic variation, so it has a fairly consistent form and growth rate. It is often used in reforestation projects, tree plantations, parks and windbreaks. • This tree lives about 200 years. It is slow growing at first, but once established it can shoot up at 30 cm per year. Most red pine trees produce seed consistently at 15–25 years of age, with good crops every 3–7 years. • Red pine requires sunny sites, and it grows well on open sites with thin, infertile soils, where its deep roots help it withstand strong winds. Natural stands usually establish when fire removes competing plants and insect pests, leaving an open seedbed for the wind-borne seeds. • Many songbirds, especially red crossbills, pine grosbeaks and pine siskins, eat red pine seeds. Red squirrels harvest the ripening cones from the trees, and chipmunks, mice and voles gather seeds on the ground.

ALSO CALLED: Norway pine
FRENCH NAME: Pin rouge
SIZE AND SHAPE: Coniferous trees up to 25 m tall; crowns conical when young, rounded and irregular with age.
TRUNKS: Tall, straight, 75 cm in diameter; young bark reddish to pinkish-brown, scaly; mature bark with broad, scaly plates, 2.5–4 cm thick; wood pale to reddish-brown, lightweight, straight-grained.

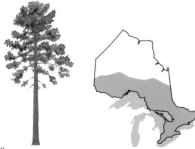

BRANCHES: Spreading or drooping (lower) to upcurved (upper); twigs stout, ridged; buds red-brown, 1.5–2 cm long, with white-fringed scales.
LEAVES: Shiny, dark green, evergreen needles; **needles straight, 10–16 cm long,** brittle (snap easily), finely sharp-toothed; **bundled in 2s** with persistent membranous sheaths; crowded towards branch tips; drop in 4–5 years.
CONES: Male and female cones on same tree; male cones small, yellow, clustered at the base of new shoots; female cones light chestnut-brown, woody, 4–7 cm long, stalkless, hanging at upper branch tips; **scales only slightly thickened, concave,** tipped with a **spineless** bump; seeds mottled chestnut-brown, 5–7 mm long with a 1.5–1.8 cm wing, 2 per scale; female cones mature in 2–3 years, shed seeds in autumn, usually drop that year.
HABITAT: Dry, sandy or rocky areas; grows best in dry to moderately wet areas with light, slightly acidic, sandy loam.

SCOTS PINE is the world's most widely distributed pine and was one of the first trees introduced to North America. Its great variability reflects genetic and habitat differences as well as damage from diseases and pests. In Europe, Scots pine is commonly tall and straight trunked with high-quality wood. In North America, however, trees usually have irregular trunks and poor-quality wood, in large part owing to poor seed selection when the species was first introduced. Because of this poor quality, Scots pine was often abandoned in favour of other species for lumber, shelterbelts and erosion control. • This fast-growing, blue-green, densely conical, sweet-smelling tree has good needle retention and makes an excellent Christmas tree. • Other introduced pines occasionally escape cultivation. **Austrian Pine *(P. nigra)* and mugo pine *(P. mugo)*** are 2-needle pines with straight (not spirally twisted), dark green (not blue-green) needles. Austrian pine is a tall (to 30 m) tree with long (8–16 cm), flexible (not easily snapped) needles. Mugo pine is a shrub or small tree with short (3–6 cm) needles spread in a V. Both of these pines are widely planted as ornamentals.

ALSO CALLED: Scotch pine

FRENCH NAME: Pin sylvestre

SIZE AND SHAPE: Coniferous trees up to 30 m tall; crowns cone-shaped when young, becoming rounded and irregular with age.

TRUNKS: Short and crooked with large branches, rarely straight and branch-free; **young bark orange-red, papery,** peeling in strips; mature bark greyish-brown to **orange-brown,** in irregular, loose plates; inner bark brownish-red.

BRANCHES: Irregular, spreading; twigs greenish- to greyish-brown, hairless, ridged; buds red-brown, sharp-tipped, 6–12 mm long, with some loose-tipped lower scales.

LEAVES: Slender, **stiff, spirally twisted, dark blue-green** evergreen needles; **needles 4–8 cm long,** sharp-pointed, finely toothed; **bundled in 2s** with persistent, 5–8 mm long, membranous sheaths.

CONES: Male and female cones on same tree; male cones small, yellow, clustered at the base of new shoots; female cones usually in 2s or 3s, woody, yellowish- to purplish-brown, 2.5–7 cm long, often asymmetrical and **bent backwards on the branch; scales flattened, tipped with a (usually) spineless bump;** seeds dark brown, 2–4 mm long, the 1–1.5 cm wing soon lost, 2 per scale; female cones mature in second autumn, shed seeds over winter and spring, often long-persistent.

HABITAT: Second-growth woodlands and pine plantations.

DISTRIBUTION: Introduced from Europe; grows wild in Ontario north to Iroquois Falls.

Jack Pine *Pinus banksiana*

Pine Family

JACK PINE wood provides mine timbers, railway ties, poles, pilings, lumber and wood fibre for pulp and paper. • This slow-growing, relatively short-lived tree lives about 150 years. Mature cones remain closed on the tree for many years, until heat from fire, or from sunlight on hot days, melts the resin that seals the scales shut, thereby allowing the cones to open. Fire produces a favourable seedbed, free of competing plants and disease. However, repeated burns at intervals of less than 15 years will destroy the seed supply. • White-tailed deer browse on new growth; snowshoe hares eat seedlings; porcupines often eat the bark. Intensive browsing can deform trees, particularly young trees. Red squirrels, chipmunks, white-footed mice and songbirds such as goldfinches, grackles and robins eat large quantities of fallen seeds. • The globally endangered songbird Kirtland's warbler, also called the jack pine warbler, requires large (more than 30 ha), pure stands of small (less than 6 m tall) jack pine trees in order to nest. It once may have bred commonly in Ontario but is now a rare visitor.

ALSO CALLED: Black pine, scrub pine, Banksian pine, grey pine, Hudson Bay pine • *P. divaricata*

FRENCH NAMES: Pin gris, pin cyprés

SIZE AND SHAPE: Small coniferous trees up to 20 m tall; crowns cone-shaped, open.

TRUNKS: Straight, up to 30 cm in diameter; young bark reddish- to greyish-brown, thin, flaky; mature bark dark brown, 1–2.5 cm thick, with irregular, narrow, rounded ridges; wood heavy, close-grained.

BRANCHES: Spreading to ascending, often arched; twigs yellowish-green to purplish-brown, slender, flexible, ridged; buds cinnamon-brown, resinous, up to 1.5 cm long.

LEAVES: Stout, stiff, yellowish-green, evergreen needles; 2–4 cm long, straight or slightly twisted, sharp-pointed, finely toothed; **bundled in 2s** with spreading tips and sheathed bases; drop after 2–3 years.

CONES: Male and female cones on same tree; male cones yellow, 8–10 mm long, clustered at the base of new shoots; female cones yellowish-brown when mature, shiny, woody, usually **asymmetrical**, 2.5–7.5 cm long, **erect** or nearly so, mostly in 2s–3s near branch tips; scales 80, glued shut with resin, their tips thick, **smooth or with a tiny spine;** seeds dark, 3 mm long with a pale, 8–10 mm wing, 2 per scale; female cones mature in 2–3 years but most remain closed for many years or until fire.

HABITAT: Dry, infertile, acidic, often sandy or rocky soils.

PITCH PINE wood resists decay, so colonists used it in shipbuilding. Later, it was used to manufacture charcoal (for iron-ore smelting), turpentine and rough lumber. • This hardy tree has been used to reforest bare, sandy soil and 'worn-out' land. It takes about 5 years to establish but then grows rapidly on very poor soils. • Pitch pine can live 200 years and survive fires that would eliminate other trees. In fact, it depends on fire for success. Large natural stands establish only after fire has removed competing plants and diseases. Many cones remain closed on trees for decades but open and shed seeds immediately after a fire. Mature trees also recover quickly from fires, using dormant buds in their bark. These buds sprout quickly when the tree's needles are killed, producing new shoots and needles almost immediately. On seedlings and small trees, hidden buds often lie protected in crooks near the ground. • In Ontario, pitch pine is in decline because of excessive porcupine browsing and limited reproduction (poor seed set, germination and recruitment) as a result of wildfire suppression.

FRENCH NAME: Pin rigide

SIZE AND SHAPE: Coniferous trees 15–20 m tall; crowns rounded, irregular (open-grown) to regular (forest-grown).

TRUNKS: Short, twisted (open-grown) to tall, straight (forest-grown), up to 30 cm in diameter; young bark reddish-brown; mature bark dark grey, with loose, irregular plates; wood pale reddish-brown, soft, coarse-grained.

BRANCHES: Irregular, numerous, gnarled (open-grown), sometimes **stubby, clustered and cone-bearing** (cones appear to grow from trunks); twigs stout, hairless, ridged; buds chestnut-brown, resinous, about 1.5 cm long, with loose, fringed scales.

LEAVES: **Stiff**, shiny, **yellowish-green** evergreen needles; **needles 7–12 cm long,** blunt, 3-sided, twisted, minutely sharp-toothed; **bundled in 3s** (usually) with membranous sheaths; grow from **trunks, branches and twig tips;** persist 2–3 years.

CONES: Male and female cones on same tree; male cones yellow, 1.5–2 cm long, clustered below new shoots; female cones light brown, **woody, 5–9 cm long,** clustered near branch tips; **scales flat** with thick, ridged tips bearing a **curved, 1–3 mm spine;** seeds dark, 4–5 mm long with a 1.5–2 cm wing; female cones mature in 2–3 years, open irregularly (some immediately, others only after fire), persist many years.

HABITAT: Dry, rocky or sandy sites; restricted to the Thousand Islands and adjacent mainland.

EASTERN RED-CEDAR was once the main wood used for making wooden pencils, but depletion of large trees led to the use of incense-cedar *(Calocedrus decurrens)* instead. • The beautiful reddish wood resists decay, is easily worked and takes a fine finish. It has been used for interior trim, sills and posts. Its aromatic oils repel insects such as moths, so cedar chests have traditionally been used for storing woollens. Cedar oil (distilled from the wood) has been used as perfume. • This conifer is the most widespread and drought resistant in eastern North America. Breeders have developed many cultivars for use in landscaping. • Eastern red-cedar lives about 200–350 years. Mature females produce some seed every year but bear large crops every 3 years or so. • Many birds use eastern red-cedar for food and cover. Game birds such as quail, grouse, pheasant and wild turkey as well as many songbirds feed on the 'berries.' Seed-eating birds (especially cedar waxwings) readily disperse the seeds, so that trees often grow in isolated places along bird migration routes. • The name 'red-cedar' is also used for the western tree *Thuja plicata.*

ALSO CALLED: Red-cedar juniper

FRENCH NAMES: Cèdre rouge, genévrier de Virginie

SIZE AND SHAPE: Small coniferous trees up to 10 m tall; crowns conical to almost cylindrical, irregular with age, highly variable.

TRUNKS: Irregular, often buttressed at base, up to 20 cm in diameter, branched to near base; bark light reddish-brown, 3–6 mm thick, in long, narrow strips; wood reddish, aromatic,

moderately heavy and hard, brittle, weak, fine-grained.

BRANCHES: Spreading to ascending; twigs light green to reddish-brown, slender, 4-sided.

LEAVES: Evergreen, dark bluish-green (yellowish-brown in winter), of **2 types:** on mature branches, **flat-lying scales** 2 mm long, convex, **in overlapping pairs;** and on young branches, **sharp needles** 5–7 mm long, spreading to erect; both leaf types sometimes on one branch.

CONES: Male and female cones usually on **separate trees;** male cones yellowish, 2.5–3 mm long; **female cones berry-like, deep blue with a whitish bloom** when mature, 3–6 mm across, firm, resinous, aromatic, not splitting open, short-stalked at twig tips; scales thick, fleshy, eventually fused; seeds 1–2 per 'berry,' light brown, grooved, pitted, 2–4 mm long; 'berries' (seed cones) **ripen in first autumn.**

HABITAT: Dry, rocky or sandy sites and abandoned fields.

ALTHOUGH CEDAR WOOD is known for its resistance to rot, the trunks of living trees are often hollow from heart-rot. Cedar wood is commonly used for construction in and near water—in cedar-strip canoes, boats, fence posts, shingles and dock posts. The wood also splits easily and has provided rails for many split-rail fences. • This attractive, versatile species provides dense growth in foundation plantings, hedges and windbreaks on both wet and dry sites. Many cultivars are available.
• Some stunted eastern white-cedar trees on limestone cliffs of the Niagara Escarpment are over 700 years old. Eastern white-cedar has maximum cone production at 75–150 years of age, with large crops every 3–5 years. • Red squirrels eat cedar buds in spring and later store cone-laden branches in winter caches. The plentiful seeds are an important food for pine siskins, goldfinches, redpolls and other winter finches. Cedar trees provide cover and shelter for white-tailed deer, who also favour the tender branch tips as winter food. • Native peoples used eastern white-cedar to prevent scurvy and taught this practice to French settlers, giving rise to the name arborvitae, or 'tree of life.'

ALSO CALLED: Eastern arborvitae, northern white-cedar, eastern thuja, swamp-cedar, tree-of-life, white arborvitae

FRENCH NAMES: Cèdre de l'est, arborvitae, balai, thuya occidental, thuya du Canada, cèdre blanc, thuya de l'est

SIZE AND SHAPE: Coniferous trees 15 m tall; crowns steeple-shaped, compact and 'neatly trimmed' (open-grown) to irregular (forest).

TRUNKS: Often buttressed, knobby and/or curved, up to 30 cm in diameter; mature bark grey, 6–15 mm thick, shredding in narrow, flat strips; wood pale yellowish-brown, fragrant, lightweight, soft.

BRANCHES: Short, wide-spreading, gradually upturned; twigs many, soft, **forming flat, fan-shaped sprays;** buds tiny, protected by leaves.

LEAVES: Dull yellowish-green (sometimes bronze in winter), **scale-like,** evergreen; leaves near branch tips **2–4 mm long, gland-dotted,** overlapping, **opposite, in 4 longitudinal rows** with side leaves folded and upper/lower leaves flattened; leaves on older branches lance-shaped, 4–5 mm long, glandless.

CONES: Male and female cones on same tree; male cones yellowish, 1–2 mm long; female cones dry, pale red-brown, 7–12 mm long, upright at branch tips; **scales in 4–6 overlapping pairs,** middle ones producing 2–3 seeds; seeds light brown, 2–3 mm long, with 2 narrow wings about 1/2 as long as the body; female cones produced in April–May, release seeds that autumn, drop over several months.

HABITAT: Swampy ground to dry limestone outcrops; prefers humid habitats with high snowfall and calcium-rich soils.

THE TULIP-TREE is a valuable hardwood timber tree in the U.S. The easily worked wood has been used in interior finishing, cabinet making, construction and pulp and paper, and for making furniture, musical instruments and plywood. • Native peoples used the tall, straight trunks to make large canoes, some capable of carrying 20 people or more, and used the sharp-tasting roots to treat rheumatism and fevers. • This large, fast-growing, attractive tree is occasionally used in landscaping in areas beyond its normal range, but it needs plenty of open space to flourish. • Tulip-tree lives about 150 years and usually begins producing flowers and seed when it is 15–20 years old. • Bees gather considerable amounts of nectar from the large flowers. Quail, finches, cardinals, rabbits, red squirrels, grey squirrels, mice and deer eat the abundant seeds. White-tailed deer and rabbits browse on saplings and young trees. • This massive hardwood is sometimes called 'Apollo of the woods.' Its flowers resemble those of tulips, hence the common name 'tulip-tree' and the scientific name *Liriodendron,* from the Greek *leirion,* 'lily,' and *dendron,* 'tree.' The specific epithet, *tulipifera,* means 'tulip-bearing.'

ALSO CALLED: Tulip-poplar, yellow-poplar, tulip-magnolia, whitewood

FRENCH NAMES: Tulipier de Amérique, tulipier de Virginie, bois jaune, tulipier à tulipes

SIZE AND SHAPE: Trees up to 35 m tall.

TRUNKS: Tall, straight, to 1 m in diameter, ²/₃ or more branch-free; mature bark ash-grey to brown, with intersecting, rounded ridges; wood pale yellow, fine-grained, lightweight.

BRANCHES: Stout; twigs brittle; buds dark red, **flat, duckbill-shaped, with 2 scales** meeting at the edges, **1.2–1.4 cm long at twig tips** (smaller below), powdery.

LEAVES: Alternate, simple, deciduous; blades bright green above and paler beneath, **7–12 cm long, with squared, notched tips** and 2–3-lobed sides; stalks often longer than blades; stipules large (in spring), leaving a thin scar encircling the twig; leaves yellow in autumn.

FLOWERS: Showy, tulip-shaped, 4–5 cm wide, single at branch tips, bisexual; petals 6, **pale greenish-yellow with orange bases,** erect, each 4–6 cm long and 2–3 cm wide; sepals 3, large, green; stamens many, flattened; carpels pale yellow, numerous, in a 'cone' at the flower's centre; flowering in May–June (after the leaves expand).

FRUITS: Dry, **green to straw-coloured,** long-winged nutlets (samaras), 3–5 cm long, overlapping in **cone-like clusters 5–7 cm long;** fruits drop in autumn, leaving erect central stalks at branch tips.

HABITAT: Prefers deep, rich, moist but well-drained soils.

CUCUMBER-TREE is the only magnolia native to Canada. It is extremely rare in Ontario and is threatened with extirpation throughout its Canadian range. • Magnolia wood is fairly durable and has been used to make boxes, crates, cabinets, inexpensive furniture and panelling. Otherwise, cucumber-tree has little economic importance. Its yellow-green blooms are relatively inconspicuous, and although showier cultivars have been developed, they are planted only occasionally. The relatively hardy roots provide stocks for grafting fragile exotic magnolias that would otherwise die in winter. Most common ornamentals, including **saucer magnolia *(Magnolia* x *soulangiana)*** and **star magnolia *(M. stellata)*,** come from Asia. • Cucumber-tree is the largest, hardiest and most widespread magnolia in North America. This shade-intolerant, fast-growing tree can live 125–150 years but may not flower until it is 25–30 years old. Once mature, cucumber-trees produce seeds each year, with good crops every 3–5 years. • Many birds and rodents eat magnolia seeds. • *Magnolia* commemorates Pierre Magnol (1638–1715), director of the botanical garden in Montpellier, France. The common name reflects the resemblance of the green fruit clusters to cucumbers.

Photo, bottom right: *M. stellata*

ALSO CALLED: Cucumber magnolia, pointed-leaved magnolia

FRENCH NAMES: Magnolia acuminé, magnolier acuminé, magnolia à feuilles acuminées

SIZE AND SHAPE: Trees to 25 m tall, broadly cone-shaped.

TRUNKS: Straight, to 75 cm in diameter; mature bark dark grey-brown, with narrow ridges, **aromatic;** wood pale, lightweight, close-grained.

BRANCHES: Spreading or drooping to ascending; twigs brittle, hairless, **aromatic; buds dark red, 1-scaled, silvery-hairy,** 1.5–2 cm long at twig tips (smaller below).

LEAVES: Alternate, simple, deciduous; blades shiny dark green above, paler and finely hairy beneath, **smooth-edged, prominently veined,** abruptly **pointed, 10–25 cm long;** stalks flattened, 2.2–4 cm long; stipule scars encircling twigs; leaf scars horseshoe-shaped, 5–9-dotted; leaves yellow in autumn.

FLOWERS: Greenish-yellow, cupped, **5–8 cm long, odourless, single at branch tips,** bisexual; petals 6, erect, 3–8 cm long and 1.8–3 cm wide; sepals 3, petal-like, bending backwards; stamens many, flattened; carpels pale yellow, spirally attached in a cone-like structure at the flower centre; flowering in May (as leaves expand).

FRUITS: Leathery, fleshy pods (follicles), **shiny dark red,** in **erect, cone-like clusters 5–8 cm long;** seeds 1–2 per follicle, shiny, reddish-orange, 9–11 mm long; follicles open in late summer and seeds hang on white threads.

HABITAT: Moist to wet, protected sites with deep, rich soils.

67

PAWPAW IS RARE in Ontario and in Canada, where its scattered populations have been depleted by deforestation. • Native peoples gathered the fleshy, edible fruits, but pawpaws are seldom eaten today. The flavour varies greatly from site to site, deteriorating gradually from south to north. It has been likened to that of bananas, pineapples, apples, custard, cream and even eau-de-cologne and turpentine. Pawpaws with orange flesh are said to be more flavourful than yellow-fleshed varieties. • Early settlers used the ripe pulp for making yellow dye. • This small tree is occasionally planted for its attractive form, large leaves, unusual (though fetid) flowers and juicy fruits. Pawpaw thrives in low, wet sites where other shrubs would fail. It often forms dense colonies from suckers and is easily propagated from root cuttings. • Ripe pawpaw fruits can be hard to find, because many animals, including raccoons, opossums, squirrels, bears (historically) and wild turkeys, enjoy their sweet, juicy flesh. • The generic name, *Asimina,* was taken from a Native name for pawpaw, *assimin.* The specific epithet, *triloba,* is easy to translate; it means '3-lobed' and refers to the flower parts, which are grouped in 3s.

ALSO CALLED: Common pawpaw, false banana, pawpaw custard-apple, tall pawpaw

FRENCH NAMES: Asiminier trilobé, corossol, faux-bananier

SIZE AND SHAPE: Large shrubs or small trees 3–8 m tall; crowns broad.

TRUNKS: Single, 10–20 cm in diameter; mature bark thin, with warty bumps; wood pale yellow, often red- or brown-streaked, lightweight.

BRANCHES: Straight, spreading; twigs rusty-hairy when young, slender, zigzagged; pith banded (in long-section); **buds reddish-hairy,** lacking scales, flattened, 2–4 mm long.

LEAVES: Alternate, simple, deciduous; **blades 15–30 cm long, hanging near branch tips,** green above and paler with reddish-brown veins beneath, smelly when crushed, **widest towards tips, tapered to bases,** with **prominent veins looped to adjacent veins at their tips; stalks 5–10 mm long,** grooved; leaf scars crescent-shaped around a bud.

FLOWERS: Pale greenish-yellow to **reddish-purple or maroon,** fetid-smelling, **3–4 cm across,** broadly bell-shaped, single or in small clusters, bisexual; petals 6 (3 large, 3 small), veiny; sepals 3; flowering in May (before or as leaves expand).

FRUITS: Large berries **4–15 cm long, yellowish to brownish** with soft, **yellow to orange flesh** when ripe; fragrant, **cylindrical to pear-shaped,** hanging along year-old twigs; seeds dark brown, **flattened, bean-like,** 1.5–2.5 cm long, several in 1–2 rows; mature in October.

HABITAT: Floodplains and woodland sites with damp sandy or clayey soils.

THE LIGHT, BRITTLE WOOD of sassafras has no commercial value, but the bark produces an orange dye and the roots yield aromatic 'oil of sassafras,' which has been used as a fragrance in soaps and perfumes. • Sassafras bark was traditionally used to make a fragrant, invigorating tea and to flavour root beer. It was also added to some patent medicines. Sassafras roots were once believed to have great healing powers, but these claims proved false. **Caution:** Dried sassafras bark (available in health-food and gourmet stores) should be used with extreme caution, if at all. It contains safrole, a carcinogenic compound banned for use in foods in the U.S. and Canada. • This small, moderately fast-growing tree can flower after only 10 years, with good seed crops every 2–3 years. Sassafras often forms dense colonies by sending up new shoots (suckers) from underground runners. Such vegetative reproduction, as well as seed dispersal (usually by birds), allows sassafras to quickly colonize disturbed habitats such as abandoned fields. • Wild turkeys, bobwhite, squirrels, black bears (historically) and foxes occasionally feed on the fruits of sassafras.

ALSO CALLED: White sassafras, cinnamon-wood, greenstick, mitten-tree

FRENCH NAMES: Sassafras officinal, sassafrax, saxifrax, laurier-sassafras

SIZE AND SHAPE: Large shrubs or small to medium trees 5–15 m tall.

TRUNKS: Branched from near base, **zigzagged, slender,** up to 30 cm in diameter; bark fragrant, **dark brown with corky ridges;** wood fragrant, orange-brown to yellow, soft, light, coarse-grained, weak.

BRANCHES: Crooked, **wide-spreading with upturned tips,** corky-ridged; twigs glossy purplish or light green, brittle, **often with side-shoots longer than branch tips;** buds greenish, plump, several-scaled, 1–1.5 cm long at twig tips (smaller below).

LEAVES: Alternate, simple, deciduous, fragrant; blades bright green, **ovate or broadly 2- or 3-lobed** (all 3 shapes usually present), **10–25 cm long,** 5–10 cm wide; **leaves yellow to red in autumn.**

FLOWERS: Greenish-yellow, 5–8 mm across, inconspicuous; unisexual with male and female flowers usually on separate trees, in **loose, stalked clusters** at the base of new shoots; tepals 6; flowers appear in late May (with leaves).

FRUITS: Dark blue, berry-like drupes, 1–1.5 cm across, each sitting in a bright red cup at the tip of a club-shaped, red, 3.5–4 cm long stalk; seeds single, large, brown stones; fruits ripen July–August.

HABITAT: Dry, open, sandy sites; occasionally shady areas with loamy soil.

AMERICAN SYCAMORE wood has been used for cabinet making, furniture, boxes, interior trim and butcher's chopping blocks. Early French settlers hollowed out large sycamore trunks to make barges capable of carrying several tons of freight. • American sycamore lives up to 250 years. This fast-growing tree is among the largest in the eastern deciduous forest; it can reach 20–25 m in height by 20 years of age, and may eventually exceed 35 m. Trunks can reach 4.6 m in diameter. • The small, stiffly hairy seeds are carried to new sites by wind and water. American sycamore is moderately shade-tolerant, but the seeds require light to germinate. • Seed-eating birds seldom feed on sycamore seeds, but some small rodents gather them. • American sycamore is sometimes planted as an ornamental shade tree, often outside its natural range. However, the **London plane** (***Platanus* x *acerifolia*,** most likely a hybrid of *P. occidentalis* and *P. orientalis*) is more widely used in cities because it tolerates pollution and can grow with limited root space. The London plane is distinguished by its more deeply lobed leaves and by its paired flower and fruit clusters.

ALSO CALLED: Buttonwood, buttonball-tree, American plane-tree

FRENCH NAMES: Platane occidental, boule de boutons, platane d'occident

SIZE AND SHAPE: Trees up to 35 m tall; **crowns irregular, with massive, crooked branches.**

TRUNKS: Straight, 60–120 cm in diameter; **bark mottled,** reddish-brown, **jigsaw-like scales flaking off to expose pale inner bark;** wood light brown, hard, coarse-grained, weak.

BRANCHES: Stout, spreading; twigs slender, zigzagged; buds shiny reddish-brown, **6–10 mm** long, **1-scaled, none at twig tips,** covered by leaf-stalk bases.

LEAVES: Alternate, simple, deciduous; **blades 10–20 cm across, bright green** above and paler beneath, hairless (except lower veins), maple leaf–like, **shallowly 3–5-lobed,** coarsely and irregularly toothed; stipules prominent in spring, stipule scars encircling twigs; leaf scars narrow, encircling buds; **leaves orange to orange-brown** in autumn.

FLOWERS: Tiny, in dense heads; unisexual with male and female flower clusters on **separate branchlets of same tree;** male flowers yellowish-green, in 7–10 mm 'balls' along second-year twigs; female flowers reddish, in 1–1.4 cm 'balls' near older twig tips; appear in spring (with leaves).

FRUITS: Yellowish, seed-like achenes about 1 cm long, brownish-hairy, club-shaped, in **solitary 2–3.5 cm 'balls' on slender 8–16 cm stalks;** mature by early fall and break apart slowly, some remaining through winter.

HABITAT: Low, wet areas with rich soil, usually on floodplains.

THESE TRUNKS are too small to provide lumber, but evenly forked witch-hazel branches have been used as divining rods for locating underground water and minerals. • Witch-hazel oil (extracted from leaves, twigs and bark) is said to have astringent and sedative properties and to stop bleeding. This volatile oil has been used in liniments, medicines, eye-washes, after-shave lotions and salves for soothing insect bites, burns and poison ivy rashes.

• This slow-growing shrub is sometimes used in landscaping because of its showy, fragrant flowers and interesting, persistent fruits. This witch-hazel is the only Canadian tree or shrub to bloom in autumn.

• The name 'witch-hazel,' suggesting magical powers, probably originated with the divining powers attributed to the branches. The 'hazel' in the name refers to the similarities between witch-hazel and the true hazels of the genus *Corylus*. 'Snapping-hazel' alludes to the sound the capsules make when they shoot seeds up to 12 m from the parent shrub. 'Spotted-alder' and 'striped-alder' indicate that the bark resembles that of alders (pp. 114–116).

ALSO CALLED: Snapping-hazel, spotted-alder, striped-alder, winterbloom • *H. macrophylla*

FRENCH NAMES: Café du diable, hamamélis de Virginie

SIZE AND SHAPE: Shrubby trees or large, spreading shrubs 4–8 m tall; crowns broad, rounded.

TRUNKS: Usually 2 or more, crooked, 10–15 cm in diameter; bark light brown or greyish, often mottled, thin, with horizontal pores (lenticels); inner bark reddish-purple; wood light brown, hard, heavy.

BRANCHES: Slender; twigs zigzagged; buds flattened, stalked, curved, with **dense reddish- to yellowish-brown hairs, lacking scales,** 1–1.4 cm long at twig tips (smaller below).

LEAVES: Simple, alternate, deciduous; blades 6–15 cm long, dark green above and paler beneath, hairless (except lower veins), **asymmetrical at base, scalloped,** sometimes coarsely toothed, with 5–7 **straight, parallel, ascending veins per side;** leaves yellow in autumn.

FLOWERS: Fragrant, small but showy, **clustered in 3s along twigs,** bisexual; **petals 4, bright yellow, twisted, ribbon-like,** 1.5–2 cm long; sepals 4, orange-brown, hairy; appear September–October (as or after the leaves fall).

FRUITS: **Short, thick, 2-beaked capsules** 1–1.6 cm long, light brown and **woody** when mature; seeds 2 per capsule, black, shiny, 7–10 mm long; capsules mature next summer, shoot seeds from capsule tips, empty **capsules often persist** several years.

HABITAT: Moist, shady sites with deep, rich soil, to open woodlands with dry, sandy soil.

Key to Genera in the Elm Family (Ulmaceae)

1a Leaf blades single-toothed, with 3 main veins at the base; fruits berry-like drupes with thin flesh
. . . . ***Celtis*, hackberry** (p. 78)
1b Leaf blades usually double-toothed, with many conspicuous pinnate veins; fruits dry, thin, broadly winged samaras . . . . ***Ulmus*, elm** (key to species, below)

Key to the Elms (Genus *Ulmus*)

1a Leaves small (2–7 cm long), often single-toothed, with mostly symmetrical bases **2**
1b Leaves larger (usually over 7 cm long), double-toothed, with asymmetrical bases **3**

2a Flowers and fruits produced in autumn; bark platy and relatively smooth
. . . . ***U. parvifolia*, Chinese elm** (p. 76)
2b Flowers and fruits produced in spring; bark rough and deeply fissured with rectangular plates
. . . . ***U. pumila*, Siberian elm** (p. 76)

3a Samaras fringed with hairs; leaves somewhat smooth on the upper surface, mostly with more than 15 pairs of veins. **4**
3b Samaras not fringed with hairs; leaves very rough on the upper surface, mostly with 15 or fewer pairs of veins **5**

4a Flowers/fruits in elongated, branched clusters; samara wings hairy
. . . . ***U. thomasii*, rock elm** (p. 77)
4b Flowers/fruits in tassel-like clusters; samara wings hairless (except for the fringe along the edges)
. . . . ***U. americana*, American elm** (p. 73)

5a Leaves mostly with 12 pairs of side-veins; samaras hairless, 1–1.5 cm wide, with the notch at the tip extending almost to the seedcase . . . . ***U. procera*, English elm** (p. 76)
5b Leaves mostly with 15 pairs of side-veins; samaras either hairy or larger **6**

6a Leaves 8–16 cm long, hairless along the edges, often 2-lobed near the tip and with the larger basal lobe curled over the stalk; samaras hairless, 2–2.5 cm long
. . . . ***U. glabra*, wych elm** (p. 75)
6b Leaves 15–20 cm long, fringed with fine hairs, neither lobed near the tip nor with a basal lobe curled over the stalk; samaras 1–1.5 cm long, with hairy seedcases
. . . . ***U. rubra*, slippery elm** (p. 74)

Ulmus americana, American elm

Ulmus glabra, wych elm

ELM WOOD is tough and flexible and keeps well in water, so it has been used to make wharves, boat frames, wheel hubs and spokes, hockey sticks, tool handles, furniture and panelling. Because it is relatively odourless, the wood was used to make crates and barrels for cheeses, fruits and vegetables. Elm wood is seldom used for firewood because it is difficult to split. • This graceful tree was common in parks and along roads and fence lines until Dutch elm disease essentially eliminated the species in southern Ontario. This plague, caused by the fungi *Ophiostoma ulmi* and *O. novo-ulmi,* arrived in Canada in 1944 in infected wooden crates. Within 15 years, 600,000 to 700,000 elms had died. The fungal spores are carried from tree to tree by small beetles *(Scolytus scolytus* and *Hylurgopinus rufipes),* which tunnel under the bark to breed. The fungus blocks the flow of water in the trunk, killing the tree within a few years. • Many methods have been tested to control Dutch elm disease, but all have proven either ineffective or too expensive and labour intensive. Attempts to breed disease-resistant trees have had some success, and clones of these trees are available for landscaping.

ALSO CALLED: White elm, grey elm, soft elm, swamp elm, water elm

FRENCH NAMES: Orme blanc, orme d'Amérique

SIZE AND SHAPE: Stately trees 18–24 m tall; fan-, umbrella- or **vase-shaped.**

TRUNKS: Typically forked below crown and buttressed at base, 60–80 cm in diameter; bark greyish, with coarse, oblique ridges of **alternating corky layers of thin, pale scales and thicker, dark scales;** wood pale yellowish-brown, hard, heavy, strong.

BRANCHES: Gracefully arched, often weeping; twigs zigzagged, sometimes corky-winged; **buds 6–9-scaled,** reddish-brown, slightly hairy, **lying flat in 2 rows,** absent at twig tips.

LEAVES: Alternate, simple, deciduous, **in 2 vertical rows;** blades 10–15 cm long, **thick,** usually **slightly rough** above, **oval,** abruptly **pointed,** with **rounded, asymmetrical bases;** veins 30–40, **prominent, straight,** ending in sharp teeth, **0–3 veins with forks;** leaves yellow in autumn.

FLOWERS: Small, hanging in **tassel-like clusters** along year-old twigs, bisexual; petals absent; sepals tiny, 6–9; anthers red; pistil single, tiny; flowers appear in early spring **(before the leaves).**

FRUITS: Dry, oval, flat-winged nutlets (samaras) 8–10 mm long, with a **membranous wing around a seedcase, deeply notched at the tip, hairy along edges only,** hanging on slender stalks **in clusters;** drop by late spring (before the leaves expand fully).

HABITAT: Generally moist bottomlands and protected slopes.

Slippery Elm *Ulmus rubra*

SLIPPERY ELM wood is sometimes sold as American elm but is considered inferior. It has been used to make furniture, panelling, boxes and crates. • Some tribes used slippery elm bark to cover canoe shells, when birch bark was unavailable. Early adventurers chewed the slippery inner bark to relieve thirst. The inner bark was also commonly used in traditional medicine; it was boiled, dried and then ground into a powder, which was used in teas for treating fevers, sore throats and various urinary-tract problems. Poultices of the fresh inner bark were sometimes applied to inflammations. • This moderately fast-growing species has a lifespan of about 125 years. Young trees usually start to flower at 15–20 years and produce good seed crops every 2–4 years. • Slippery elm seeds provide food for finches and grouse, as well as chipmunks, squirrels and other small rodents. White-tailed deer and rabbits sometimes browse the twigs. • This

elm is less susceptible to Dutch elm disease than the more common American elm, but some slippery elms trees still die each year from infection. • The specific epithet, *rubra*, means 'red' and describes the reddish-brown bark and buds.

ALSO CALLED: Red elm, budded elm, moose elm, slippery-barked elm, soft elm, sweet elm • *U. fulva*

FRENCH NAMES: Orme rouge, orme roux, orme gras

SIZE AND SHAPE: Trees 15–25 m tall; somewhat umbrella-shaped.

TRUNKS: Straight, forked below the crown, 30–60 cm in diameter; bark reddish-brown, 1.8–2.5 cm thick, with irregular ridges of **uniformly brown, corky layers**; inner bark fragrant, slimy; wood reddish-brown, hard, heavy.

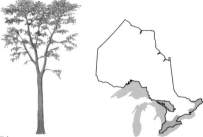

BRANCHES: Gradually spreading to arched; **twigs hairy, not corky,** often zigzagged; **buds dark brown, rusty-hairy, blunt,** 5–7 mm long, **in 2 rows,** absent at twig tips.

LEAVES: Alternate, simple, deciduous; blades 15–20 cm long, **fragrant, thick,** dark green and **very rough** above, paler beneath, **hairy on both sides,** abruptly **long-pointed,** with sharp double teeth and **rounded, asymmetrical bases;** veins prominent, **straight, forked; leaf stalks 6–9 mm long;** leaves yellow in autumn.

FLOWERS: Small, short-stalked, forming **dense, tassel-like clusters** on year-old twigs, bisexual; petals absent; sepals tiny, 6–9; anthers dark red; pistil single; flowering in spring **(before the leaves expand).**

FRUITS: Dry, flat, green, winged nutlets (samaras) 1–1.5 cm long, with a **membranous wing surrounding each seedcase, rusty-hairy on seedcases only, shallowly notched** at tips, in **tight clusters;** drop by late spring (before the leaves expand fully).

HABITAT: Low hills and river flats (usually) to rocky ridges; often on calcium-rich soils.

THIS LARGE, SPREADING TREE was introduced in colonial times and is now widely planted across eastern North America. The hard, heavy wood resists splitting and wetting. • 'Wych' (pronounced 'witch') comes from an Old English word meaning 'weak,' referring to this tree's branches. The specific epithet, *glabra,* means 'smooth' and refers to the bark, which is smooth even on quite large branches and trunks. The leaves, on the other hand, are relatively harsh and hairy. • Wych elm is very similar to English elm (p. 76), and some taxonomists believe that these two trees belong to the same species. English elm is distinguished by its smaller (1–1.5 cm) fruits, which have notches that extend almost to the seedcases, and seedcases that lie more than halfway from the base of the fruit. Also, English elm has leaves with only 10–12 veins per side (rather than 15) and smaller basal lobes that don't conceal the stalk; the flowers have shorter (1 mm) stalks; and the twigs are often corky-winged. • Wych elm is also similar to slippery elm (p. 74), but slippery elm has smaller (1 cm vs. 2–2.5 cm), hairy fruits and larger (15–20 cm vs. 8–16 cm) leaves, with hairy (not smooth) edges, pointed (not 3-lobed) tips and rounded, asymmetrical bases that do not conceal the leaf stalk.

ALSO CALLED: Scotch elm • *U. campestris*
FRENCH NAME: Orme de montagne
SIZE AND SHAPE: Trees up to 40 m tall; crowns broad, oval.
TRUNKS: Straight; bark grey, relatively smooth (for an elm), eventually brownish-grey with fissures and rectangular plates; wood hard, heavy.
BRANCHES: Spreading; twigs reddish-brown, **hairy,** often zigzagged; **buds hairy, triangular, blunt,** 5–7 mm long, arranged in **2 rows.**
LEAVES: Alternate, simple, deciduous; **blades thick,** 8–16 cm long, deep green and **very rough above,** paler and **hairy beneath, often with a lobe to each side of the pointed tip,** bases rounded and **strongly asymmetrical with one side curled over the stalk,** edged with **hairless, sharp, double teeth;** veins prominent, **straight; stalks short, almost concealed.**

FLOWERS: Small, borne on 2–3 mm stalks, in **dense, 1 cm long, tassel-like clusters** on year-old twigs, bisexual; petals absent; sepals tiny; stamens 3–5; flowering in March **(before the leaves expand).**
FRUITS: Greenish to pale brown, **hairless,** dry, flat, winged nutlets (samaras) **2–2.5 cm long,** with a **broad, membranous wing** around a seedcase, notched at tips, in **tassel-like clusters;** drop in July.
HABITAT: Moist sites along roadsides and forest edges.
DISTRIBUTION: Introduced from Europe and western Asia; sometimes grows wild in Ontario.

ENGLISH ELM was once the dominant hedgerow and landscaping tree in the English countryside, but populations were devastated by Dutch elm disease. • The classification of English elm is unclear. Some taxonomists think it may be a hybrid. Trees reproduce vegetatively from root suckers and rarely if ever set viable seed. All English elm trees may be descended from 1 or 2 trees brought to England during the Iron Age. Many localized forms are found in different parts of Britain. • Another introduced species, **Siberian elm** or *orme de Sibérie* (*U. pumila*), is our province's only wild-growing elm with small (2–7 cm), single-toothed, almost symmetrical leaves. These hardy trees are capable of surviving extreme cold and long summer droughts. Siberian elm was introduced from eastern Asia in the 1860s and now grows wild in southern Ontario. • Siberian elm is sometimes erroneously called **Chinese elm,** a name for another Asian species (*U. parvifolia*). These 2 species have similar leaves, but Chinese elm produces its flowers and fruits in autumn (not spring), and it has relatively smooth (not furrowed), platy bark. Chinese elm is occasionally planted in southern Ontario.

Photo, bottom left: *U. pumila*

ALSO CALLED: *U. campestris*

FRENCH NAME: Orme champêtre

SIZE AND SHAPE: Trees to 20 m tall; crowns rounded; roots often freely suckering.

TRUNKS: Straight, often with sprouts; bark dark brown to grey, rough, deeply fissured around small, rectangular plates; wood hard, heavy, resistant to wetting and splitting.

BRANCHES: Few, large; twigs slender, hairy, **often corky-ridged;** buds small, **dark brown, mostly hairless, in 2 rows.**

LEAVES: Alternate, simple, deciduous; **blades dark green and rough above,** finely **hairy beneath,** 5–9 cm long, **broadly elliptic, asymmetrical,** edged with **sharp double teeth;** veins prominent, **straight, 10–12** per side, often forked; **stalks short,** downy; leaves yellow when shed, sometimes persisting into early winter.

FLOWERS: Dark reddish, 3 mm wide, on 1 mm stalks, forming **tassel-like clusters** on year-old twigs, bisexual; petals absent; sepals tiny; stamens 3–5; flowering in early spring **(before the leaves expand).**

FRUITS: Greenish, **hairless,** winged nutlets (samaras), in **dense, tassel-like clusters; nutlets 1–1.5 cm across,** with a **broad, membranous wing** tipped with a **notch almost reaching the seedcase;** seedcases above mid-fruit; nutlets drop in May.

HABITAT: Moist, open sites such as roadsides, forest edges, thickets and clearings.

DISTRIBUTION: Introduced from England and western Europe; occasionally grows wild in southern Ontario.

ROCK ELM has the heaviest, toughest wood of any elm. In the 1800s, it was exported to England for use in shipbuilding. It was also used for automobile chassis and ploughs before steel became widely used. In North America, rock elm has been used for construction and in furniture, piano frames, tool handles and hockey sticks. Unfortunately, this strong, hard wood is no longer readily available. • This moderately fast-growing tree lives about 125 years. It begins to flower after 20–25 years and produces good seed crops every 2–3 years. Regeneration in the wild is slow. Seedlings can tolerate some shade, but they need full sunlight to grow quickly. Saplings may persevere for several decades in the forest understorey, waiting to fill new openings in the canopy. • Rock elm seeds provide food for many birds, including pheasants, grouse and wood ducks. Beavers and muskrats sometimes eat the bark, and white-tailed deer along with squirrels, chipmunks and other small mammals feed on the twigs, buds and seeds. • Like other elms, rock elm is vulnerable to Dutch elm disease.

ALSO CALLED: Cork elm, winged elm
• *U. racemosa*

FRENCH NAMES: Orme liège, orme à grappes, orme de Thomas

SIZE AND SHAPE: Rough, shaggy-looking trees 15–25 m tall; crowns narrow, rounded.

TRUNKS: Straight, undivided, 60–75 cm in diameter; bark shaggy, with thick ridges of **alternating corky layers of thin, pale scales and thicker, dark scales;** wood light brown, fine-grained, hard, heavy, strong.

BRANCHES: Almost horizontal, often gnarled and drooping, **corky-ridged;** twigs developing 2–4 corky ridges in first year; **buds chestnut-brown, sharp-pointed, pointing outwards in 2 rows,** 5–7 mm long, with fringed scales.

LEAVES: Alternate, simple, deciduous; blades 5–10 cm long, **thick, shiny dark green** above, paler and somewhat hairy beneath, abruptly **pointed, with rounded, asymmetrical bases;** veins about 40, **rarely forked,** ending in sharp, **incurved teeth; stalks 5–7 mm long;** leaves turn bright yellow in autumn.

FLOWERS: Reddish, small, borne on year-old twigs, bisexual; petals absent; sepals tiny, 7–8; flowers in small **clusters with short central stalks;** flowering in early spring **(before the leaves expand).**

FRUITS: Dry, flat, **hairy, indistinctly winged** nutlets (samaras) 1–1.5 cm long, **tapered to both ends, shallowly notched** at the tip, **hanging in elongated clusters;** drop by late spring (before the leaves expand fully).

HABITAT: Varied, ranging from till to rock outcrops; often on heavy clay soils.

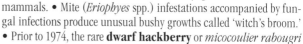

Common Hackberry *Celtis occidentalis* Elm Family

HACKBERRY WOOD has an attractive grain, but it is weak and has little commercial value. Settlers in Illinois used it to produce a substance for treating jaundice. • This hardy, drought-resistant tree is used in landscaping in some areas; it is easily transplanted and readily sends up suckers after cutting or burning. • Common hackberry can live 150–200 years. The tiny, wind-pollinated flowers produce good crops of fruit most years. • The small, sweet-tasting 'berries' are edible but are not widely used by people. Instead, they are usually eaten by game birds and small mammals. • Mite (*Eriophyes* spp.) infestations accompanied by fungal infections produce unusual bushy growths called 'witch's broom.' • Prior to 1974, the rare **dwarf hackberry** or *micocoulier rabougri* **(*C. tenuifolia*)** was commonly considered a variety of common hackberry. Dwarf hackberry is now distinguished by its smaller, brownish-orange fruit and smaller, broader, almost symmetrical leaves. Also, the leaves on its flowering shoots lack teeth. A 'species of special concern' in Canada according to COSEWIC (2000), dwarf hackberry grows on sand dunes and limestone plains in southwestern Ontario.

ALSO CALLED: Northern hackberry, western hackberry, bastard-elm, nettle-tree, sugarberry, Georgia hackberry • *C. georgiana*

FRENCH NAMES: Micocoulier occidental, bois inconnu, bois connu, micocoulier de Virginie, micocoulier d'Amérique

SIZE AND SHAPE: Shrubs or small trees 1–5 m (occasionally 10–15 m) tall; crowns broad.

TRUNKS: Short, forked, 20–50 cm in diameter; bark 2.5–3.5 cm thick, with **wart-like bumps** on irregular **corky ridges;** wood brown, heavy, coarse-textured, hard, weak.

BRANCHES: Ascending to spreading, often with drooping tips; twigs slender, finely hairy; pith

banded with cavities (visible in long-section); buds 6–8 mm long, 5–6-scaled, pointed, flattened, **in 2 rows** (absent at twig tips).

LEAVES: Alternate, simple, deciduous; blades 6–9 cm long, **deep bluish-green and usually rough above,** paler and hairy on veins beneath, papery, **asymmetrical at bases,** tapered at tips, **15–40 coarse, sharp teeth per side;** yellow in autumn.

FLOWERS: Small, greenish; unisexual with male and female flowers on the same tree; petals absent; sepals 4–5; male flowers 4–5 stamened, clustered below new shoots; female flowers with 1 pistil, 1–3 in new leaf axils; flowering April–May (as leaves expand).

FRUITS: Reddish-purple, 6–8 mm, **dry, berry-like drupes** hanging on slender stalks; seeds single, in brown, pitted (dimpled) stones; fruits mature September–October, often persist through winter.

HABITAT: Rocky hills and sand dunes to bottomlands on varied soils; often associated with limestone and floodplains.

MAP: Pale green, *C. occidentalis;* dark green, *C. occidentalis/C. tenuifolia* overlap.

THE TOUGH, DURABLE WOOD of the Osage-orange has little commercial value because the trunks are small. The wood does, however, make excellent fuel, and the Osage people used it for making bows. The roots and bark have been used to produce a yellow dye for colouring baskets, cloth and leather. The bark is also rich in tannins and has been used in tanning leather. The strong-smelling fruits can be used as cockroach repellent.

• This attractive, shade-intolerant tree thrives in a broad range of environments, often surviving stressful conditions. It was once widely planted as an ornamental and in windbreaks and hedgerows in eastern North America, including warmer parts of southern Ontario. • Once established, Osage-orange spreads readily from sprouting roots. Unfortunately, cleaning up the heavy, fleshy fruits can be a messy chore each year. The juicy fruits resemble green oranges, but they are not edible. The tree's sap may cause skin reactions. • Despite the fruits, this tree is of little importance to wildlife. Squirrels and foxes may occasionally tear apart the messy fruits to eat the seeds. • The specific epithet, *pomifera*, means 'apple-bearing' and refers to the large, apple-shaped fruits.

ALSO CALLED: Hedge-apple, bodark, bowwood
FRENCH NAMES: Oranger des Osages, bois d'arc
SIZE AND SHAPE: Small, **thorny** trees up to 12 m tall, with **milky sap;** crowns irregular, rounded.
TRUNKS: Small, soon branched; bark orange-brown, irregularly ridged; **wood bright orange,** heavy, hard.
BRANCHES: Stout; twigs green to light orange-brown, zigzagged, slender, armed with **stout thorns; buds tiny,** dark brown, partly embedded in twigs, none at branch tips.
LEAVES: Alternate, simple, deciduous; blades 7–12 cm long, 5–7 cm wide, **shiny dark green** above and paler beneath, slender-pointed; stalks slender, 3.5–5 cm long; yellow in autumn.
FLOWERS: Tiny, in **dense, round clusters** on slender stalks; unisexual with male and female flowers on separate trees; male flower clusters 2.5–3.8 cm across; female clusters 1.8–2.5 cm across; appear in early summer.
FRUITS: Large, green, dimpled, fleshy or pulpy aggregates of many small fruits, 10–14 cm across, containing milky juice; seeds small, flattened, embedded in fleshy fruit; mature by autumn.
HABITAT: Lowland sites; grows best on rich, deep soils but tolerates a wide range of soils.

DISTRIBUTION: Introduced from south-central U.S.; grows wild in southern Ontario.

THE LEAVES of white mulberry are the main source of food for silkworms in eastern Asia. The milky juice is rich in rubber-like compounds said to add tenacity to the silk fibres spun by the worms. The silk industry has been especially important in China, and in that country, white mulberry has been cultivated for thousands of years. In order to accommodate the silkworms, the trees are repeatedly pruned back to the trunk (pollarded), in order to stimulate a dense head of leafy shoots. • Mulberry shrubs were first brought to North America along with silkworms, in an attempt to establish a western silk industry. This ambitious undertaking soon failed, but since then, these hardy trees have thrived and spread across eastern and southern North America. • White mulberry grows well in urban centres, and it is often used for landscaping. An attractive cultivar with drooping branches, 'Pendula,' is especially popular as an ornamental. • The Chinese and Japanese use white mulberry wood for decorative carving. In North America this wood has also been used to make fences and boats. • *Morus* is derived from the Greek name for mulberry, *morea*. The specific epithet, *alba*, means 'white' and refers to the whitish fruits.

FRENCH NAME: Mûrier blanc

SIZE AND SHAPE: Small trees up to 15 m tall; crowns widely spreading.

TRUNKS: Short, 30–90 cm in diameter; mature bark pale greyish to yellowish-brown, furrowed.

BRANCHES: Spreading; twigs slender, light brown, with **milky sap;** buds plump, red-brown, in 2 rows along twigs.

LEAVES: Alternate, simple, deciduous; blades light green, **lustrous, essentially hairless,** unlobed to variously lobed, widest below the middle, curved to a broad, blunt, wedge-shaped tip; yellow in autumn.

FLOWERS: Tiny, green; unisexual with male and female flowers in separate clusters on same tree (usually) or on separate trees; male clusters loose and elongated; female clusters short, dense and cylindrical; appear in early spring.

FRUITS: White, reddish or purplish to blackish, rounded, blackberry-like; clusters (multiple fruits) **1–2 cm long,** composed of tiny seed-like fruits (achenes) each surrounded by a small, juicy segment; mature June–July.

HABITAT: Open, disturbed sites, along fences and near the edges of forests.

DISTRIBUTION: Introduced from eastern Asia; grows wild in much of southern Ontario north to Georgian Bay.

RED MULBERRY is endangered in Ontario and in Canada, and it is the only mulberry native to this country. Unfortunately, red mulberry frequently hybridizes with its European cousin, white mulberry (p. 80), and this genetic alteration is probably its single greatest threat. Hybrids are often difficult to identify. • Mulberry wood is very durable, so it has been used to make fence posts and barrels. • The sweet, juicy fruits are best fresh (though some people find them seedy), but they can also be baked in pies and cakes. • **Caution:** Some people develop skin reactions from contact with mulberry leaves and branches. Green mulberry fruits cause stomach upset. • Many birds and small mammals (e.g., raccoons, squirrels) feed on mulberries and help to disperse the seeds. • This attractive, fast-growing species could be planted as an ornamental or fruit tree, but it requires sufficient space to accommodate its spreading branches. Female trees attract many birds and small mammals to parks and yards, but their abundant crops of fruit can stain lawns purple and may be messy to clean up. Sometimes mulberries are planted to lure birds away from other fruit. • The specific epithet, *rubra*, means 'red.'

FRENCH NAMES: Mûrier rouge, mûrier rouge d'Amérique, mûrier sauvage

SIZE AND SHAPE: Small trees up to 10 m tall, larger (up to 20 m) in forests; crowns broad and rounded.

TRUNKS: Short, 10–20 cm in diameter; mature bark dark **reddish-brown,** with **long, flaky strips;** wood soft, weak.

BRANCHES: Spreading, stout; twigs green to grey-brown or reddish-brown, with **milky sap;** buds plump, 5–7 mm long, in 2 rows along twigs; none at branch tips.

LEAVES: Alternate, simple, deciduous; blades thin, **dull yellowish-green and sandpapery above, soft-hairy beneath, unlobed to broadly 2–5-lobed,** 7–13 cm long, **tapered** to a long-pointed tip, notched and 3-veined at the **asymmetrical base,** sharply toothed; yellow in autumn.

FLOWERS: Tiny, green; unisexual with male and female flowers in separate clusters on separate trees, on same tree or mixed in same cluster (occasionally); male clusters loose and elongated; female clusters short and dense; appear in spring (before or with leaves).

FRUITS: Red to dark purple or almost black, **cylindrical,** blackberry-like; clusters (multiple fruits) **2–3 cm long,** composed of tiny seed-like fruits (achenes) each surrounded by a small, juicy segment; mature late June–July.

HABITAT: Moist sites on floodplains and in valleys; prefers deep, rich soil.

Key to Genera in the Walnut Family (Juglandaceae)

1a Leaflets usually 5–9, with the tip leaflet largest; branch pith uniform, lacking horizontal partitions (in long-section); fruit husks usually splitting into 4 parts
.... ***Carya*, hickory** (key to species, below)

1b Leaflets usually at least 11, those near midleaf largest; branch pith with horizontal partitions (visible in long-section); fruit husks not splitting open
.... ***Juglans*, walnut** (key to species, below)

Key to the Hickories (Genus *Carya*)

1a Bud scales 2–4, paired, not overlapping; leaflets usually 9; fruit husks prominently keeled along the sutures .... ***C. cordiformis*, bitternut hickory** (p. 88)

1b Bud scales up to 12, overlapping; leaflets usually 5–7; fruit husks lacking prominent keels ... **2**

2a Branch-tip buds 1.2–2.5 cm long; fruits large (often >3.5 cm long), with 3–12 mm thick husks soon splitting almost to the base to reveal a 4–6-sided nut **3**

2b Branch-tip buds rarely more than 1 cm long; fruits smaller (mostly <3.5 cm) with thin (<4 mm thick) husks.. **4**

3a Leaflets 5 (rarely 7), fringed with hairs when young, essentially hairless beneath when mature but the teeth often tipped with tiny tufts of hair; fruits 3–5 cm across, single or paired
.... ***C. ovata*, shagbark hickory** (p. 86)

3b Leaflets 7 or 9, with permanently hairy lower surfaces; fruits 5–7 cm across, in small clusters
.... ***C. laciniosa*, shellbark hickory** (p. 85)

4a Leaf blades and stalks hairless or blades hairy beneath, along the veins; leaflets 5 (rarely 7); twigs reddish-brown, hairless; mature bark close (not shaggy); fruit husks shiny dark brown, sometimes slowly splitting open along 1–2 lines (if at all)......... ***C. glabra*, pignut hickory** (p. 87)

4b Leaves and twigs scurfy with yellowish scales; leaflets usually 7; mature bark often shaggy in small plates; fruit husks pale dull brown, promptly splitting in 4
.... ***C. ovalis*, red hickory** (p. 87)

Key to the Walnuts (Genus *Juglans*)

1a Leaves with 5–9 smooth-edged leaflets; introduced tree, occasionally escaped from cultivation
.... ***J. regia*, English walnut** (p. 84)

1b Leaves with 11–22 finely toothed leaflets; native trees **2**

2a Leaf stalks, young twigs and fruits sticky-downy; fruits oblong-egg-shaped and somewhat pointed; twig pith chocolate-brown .... ***J. cinerea*, butternut** (p. 83)

2b Leaf stalks, young twigs and fruits finely short-hairy or slightly downy, but scarcely sticky; fruits almost spherical; twig pith tan to cream-coloured .... ***J. nigra*, black walnut** (p. 84)

BUTTERNUT NUTS are difficult to shell, and resins in the husks stain hands and clothing, but the sweet, oily kernels are delicious. They are eaten like walnuts—either alone (plain, salted, hickory-smoked) or added to candies, cakes, pies and muffins. Some tribes boiled butternut kernels and skimmed off the oil to use like butter. The remaining kernels were dried and ground into a rich meal for adding to cornmeal mush. • The nut husks and root bark produce an orange or yellow dye. Butternut bark and nut husks were used (without a mordant) to dye uniforms for foot soldiers during the American Civil War. The leaves, with an alum mordant, produce a brown to bronze dye. • The outer bark was once used in medicinal teas for treating toothaches and dysentery, and dried inner bark was taken to purge the system. • This fast-growing, relatively short-lived tree can survive about 80 years. The leaves, bark and nuts contain toxins that inhibit the growth of other plants. • Butternut is disappearing rapidly, as trees succumb to a lethal blight introduced from Europe. Infected trees will develop black, oozing cankers and soon die.

ALSO CALLED: White walnut, lemon walnut, oilnut

FRENCH NAMES: Noyer cendré, arbre à noix longues, noyer à beurre, noyer gris, noix longues, noyer tendre

SIZE AND SHAPE: Trees 12–25 m tall; crowns irregular, open; roots deep.

TRUNKS: Soon forked, 30–75 cm in diameter; mature bark rough with flat-topped, intersecting ridges; wood light brown to reddish-brown, light, soft.

BRANCHES: Few, ascending; twigs orange-yellow, hairy, **sticky;** buds hairy, mainly small, but **large (1.2–1.8 cm), pale yellow at twig tips**.

LEAVES: Alternate, deciduous, **30–60 cm long, aromatic,** sticky when young; compound, **pinnately divided into 11–17 leaflets** that are yellowish-green and rough above, paler and **thickly hairy beneath,** finely toothed, almost stalkless, 5–12 cm long, the **3 tip leaflets equal-sized,** gradually smaller downwards; **leaf scars prominent, with 3 vein scars, downy-hairy across the flat top.**

FLOWERS: Tiny, green; unisexual with male and female flowers on same tree; male flowers hanging in catkins 6–14 cm long; female flowers 4–7 in erect catkins; appear in spring (with the leaves).

FRUITS: **Lemon-shaped, green nuts,** 1 to few together, 4–6 cm long, with firm, sticky, hairy husks over oblong, hard, **irregularly jagged-ridged shells;** oily seed kernel inside shell has 2 irregular lobes (cotyledons); nuts mature and drop in autumn.

HABITAT: Dry, rocky sites to moist, rich sites; usually with maples.

BLACK WALNUT is North America's most highly prized hardwood. Standing trees have fetched $5000 at auction. The lustrous, rich chocolate-brown wood has a beautiful grain, stains and polishes well, is easily worked and doesn't shrink or warp. It is used for rifle butts and stocks, high-quality furniture, veneers and boats. • Most of Canada's original black walnut stands have been cut, but reforestation programs continue in southern Ontario and Quebec. This slow-growing nut tree is also planted as an ornamental. • The sweet, oily kernels can be used like domestic walnuts and butternuts. They are difficult to shell, but cultivars with larger, thinner-walled nuts are being developed. • Walnut husks are rich in tannins and toxins. Ground husks have provided insecticides, fish poison and black dye. • The toxin juglone is exuded from the roots and leached from decaying leaves, preventing other broad-leaved plants (including walnut seedlings) from taking root and providing competition. • The majestic **English walnut (*J. regia*)**, introduced from Europe and Asia, may occasionally escape from cultivation. It is readily distinguished by its leaves, with 5–9 hairless, smooth-edged leaflets, and by its large, easily shelled nuts—the commercially available walnuts.

ALSO CALLED: American walnut, American black walnut, eastern black walnut

FRENCH NAMES: Noyer noir, noyer noir d'Amerique

SIZE AND SHAPE: Trees 20–30 m tall; crowns open, rounded; roots deep, spreading.

TRUNKS: Straight, 60–120 cm in diameter; mature bark almost black, with rounded, intersecting ridges; wood dark brown (heartwood) to almost white (sapwood), hard, heavy, strong, decay-resistant, straight-grained.

BRANCHES: Few, large, ascending; twigs orange-brown, **faintly hairy, not sticky;** buds small, pale grey-brown, slightly hairy, largest (8–10 mm) at twig tips.

LEAVES: Alternate, deciduous, **20–60 cm long, aromatic;** compound, **pinnately divided into 14–23 leaflets** that are yellowish-green, smooth above, **faintly hairy below,** finely toothed, short-stalked, 5–9 cm long, middle leaflets largest, **tip leaflet small or absent; leaf scars heart-shaped, not hairy;** leaves turn yellow in autumn.

FLOWERS: Green, tiny; unisexual with male and female flowers on same tree; male flowers in hanging catkins 5–10 cm long; female flowers in erect clusters of 1–4; appear in spring (with the leaves).

FRUITS: Round, yellow-green to brown, aromatic nuts 4–6 cm across, with a hard, **irregularly smooth-ridged shell** in a firm, slightly hairy husk, hanging in clusters of 1–3; oily seed kernel inside shell has 2 irregular lobes (cotyledons); nuts mature and drop in autumn.

HABITAT: Deep, well-drained, fertile lowlands.

SHELLBARK HICKORY is rare in Canada, but the tough, strong wood makes excellent tool handles, ladders, baskets and fuel. • This tree produces our largest hickory nuts, with good crops every 1–3 years. The sweet, edible kernels are encased in thick, hard shells within thick, woody husks, so some effort is required to extract them. However, like pecans, they are delicious raw or in baked goods. • The thick green husks were sometimes ground and used as a fish poison. • Foxes, black bears (historically), deer, hares, rabbits, raccoons, muskrats, squirrels and chipmunks all seek out these nuts. Even ducks, wild turkeys and quail occasionally eat hickory nuts. The nuts are dispersed by animals and by flowing water. They can remain viable for several years. • The specific epithet, *laciniosa,* is derived from the Latin *lacinia,* 'cut in shreds,' in reference to the shaggy bark. The name 'hickory' may have come from the Native name *pocohicora* or *pauchohiceora.* • Hickories are highly variable, and identification can be difficult. Shellbark hickory resembles shagbark hickory (p. 86), but shellbark hickory is a larger tree with larger leaves, buds, twigs and nuts.

ALSO CALLED: Big shellbark hickory, shellback hickory, kingnut hickory, big shagbark hickory, bigleaf, bottom shellbark

FRENCH NAMES: Caryer lacinié, caryer à écore lacinée

SIZE AND SHAPE: Trees 20–30 m tall; crowns narrow, open.

TRUNKS: Straight, 60–100 cm in diameter; mature bark grey, in long, shaggy strips; wood dark brown, hard, strong.

BRANCHES: Short; twigs stout, **orange-brown** (usually); **pith solid;** buds dark brown, **2–2.5 cm long at twig tips.**

LEAVES: Alternate, deciduous, 25–50 cm long, **aromatic;** compound, **pinnately divided into 7 (sometimes 9, rarely 5) leaflets** that are dark yellowish-green above, paler and soft-hairy below, finely toothed, edges hairless or with non-tufted hairs, **leaflets largest at leaf tips, much smaller downwards;** leaf scars conspicuous, raised; leaves drop in autumn, often losing leaflets before main stalk.

FLOWERS: Tiny, green; unisexual with male and female flowers on same tree; male flowers yellow-green, in long, hanging catkins; female flowers in erect clusters of 2–5; flowers appear in spring (with the leaves).

FRUITS: Round, greenish-brown, aromatic nuts 4–7 cm across, usually 1–2 hanging, with a thick, hard, **flattened, 4-ridged shell** within a woody, 6–12 mm thick **husk that splits into 4;** seed kernel inside shell has 2 large, irregular lobes (cotyledons); nuts drop in autumn.

HABITAT: Moist to wet sites, usually on floodplains.

OF ALL OUR NATIVE HICKORIES, shagbark hickory has the best quality wood and is the most important source of edible hickory nuts. The sweet, walnut-like kernels can be eaten alone or used in recipes. • Shagbark hickory nuts were a staple food for many tribes. The kernels were ground and boiled in water to produce a milky, oil-rich liquid that was used in cornbread and cornmeal mush. The sweet-tasting sap was boiled down to make syrup. Isolated stands near Georgian Bay and Lake Huron may have originated from nuts carried there by Native peoples. • The strong, resilient wood has been used to make wheel spokes, tool handles, ploughing instruments and machine parts. It also makes excellent fuel. A cord produces almost as much heat as a ton of anthracite coal. Shagbark hickory wood is used for smoking meat (ham, bacon) and for producing high-quality charcoal. • The inner bark produces a yellow dye, which was patented in the 18th century, but more intense yellows were also available so there was limited demand. • The nuts are an important food source for squirrels.

ALSO CALLED: Upland hickory, scalybark hickory

FRENCH NAMES: Caryer ovale, noyer blanc, arbre à noix piquées, caryer à fruits doux, caryer à noix douce, noyer écailleux, noyer tendre

SIZE AND SHAPE: Trees 19–25 m tall; roots deep.

TRUNKS: Straight, 30–60 cm in diameter; **mature bark dark grey, shaggy,** with long, peeling plates; wood hard, heavy, fine-grained.

BRANCHES: Short; twigs stout, shiny, **solid;** buds greenish-brown, **1.2–1.8 cm long at twig tips,** **upper scales hairy,** loosely overlapping, lower 2–4 scales paired, with abutting edges.

LEAVES: Alternate, deciduous, 15–30 cm long, **aromatic;** compound, **pinnately divided into 5 leaflets** (occasionally 7) that are yellowish-green above, paler and **almost hairless beneath,** fine-toothed, **fringed with 2–3 tufts per tooth** (especially when young), essentially stalkless, 8–18 cm long, **largest at leaf tip;** leaf scars conspicuous, raised.

FLOWERS: Tiny, green; unisexual with male and female flowers on same tree; male flowers in hanging catkins 5–13 cm long; female flowers in small, erect clusters; flowering in spring (as the leaves expand).

FRUITS: **Round, greenish- to dark reddish-brown, aromatic nuts, 3–5 cm across,** with a **thin, hard, 4-angled shell** within a thick, **woody husk that splits in 4 to the base;** seed kernel inside shell has 2 large, irregular lobes (cotyledons); nuts single or paired, drop in autumn.

HABITAT: Rich, moist sites, mixed with other broad-leaved trees.

PIGNUT HICKORY is rare in Canada. It is also highly variable, and its relationship to **red hickory** *(C. ovalis,* also called *C. ovalis* var. *odorata)* is unclear. Some taxonomists do not consider red hickory sufficiently distinct to be treated as a separate species; they treat it as *C. glabra* var. *odorata.* Of those who recognize two species, some say red hickory occurs in Ontario and others report that it grows only in the eastern U.S. Pignut hickory and red hickory are distinguished, respectively, on the basis of their twigs (smooth reddish-brown vs. yellowish-scurfy); leaflets (usually 5 vs. usually 7); bark (close and shallowly ridged vs. often shaggy with peeling plates); nut kernels (astringent vs. sweet); nut shells (slightly or not at all compressed and not angled vs. compressed and strongly angled above); and fruit husks (dark shiny brown and splitting slowly or not at all vs. dull, warty light-brown and promptly splitting to the base). • The tough, heavy wood makes excellent tool handles, broom handles and sporting implements (tennis rackets, lacrosse sticks). • The bitter, inedible nutmeats are probably best left to pigs and wild animals.

ALSO CALLED: Sweet pignut hickory, false shagbark hickory, black hickory, broom hickory, smoothbark hickory • *C. leiodermis*

FRENCH NAMES: Caryer glabre, carya glabre, caryer à cochon, caryer des pourceaux, noyer à cochon, noyer à noix de cochon

SIZE AND SHAPE: Trees 15–20 m tall; crowns narrow, irregular; roots deep.

TRUNKS: Straight, 30–100 cm in diameter; young bark thin, grey, with pale **crisscross markings;** mature bark rough with **rounded ridges;** wood hard, strong.

BRANCHES: Short, crooked; twigs shiny reddish-brown to grey, often long-ridged; **pith solid;** buds light brown, **6–9 mm long at twig tips,** upper scales hairy and overlapping, lower 2–4 scales paired and soon shed.

LEAVES: Alternate, deciduous, 15–30 cm long, **aromatic;** compound, **pinnately divided into 5–7 leaflets** that are dark yellow-green above, paler and hairless below (except main veins), **finely sharp-toothed, largest at the tip.**

FLOWERS: Tiny, green; unisexual with male and female flowers on same tree; male flowers in long, hanging catkins; female flowers in small, erect clusters; flowering in spring (as the leaves expand).

FRUITS: Pear-shaped, yellowish-brown to dark brown, aromatic nuts 2–3 cm (rarely 5 cm) long, with a hard, **slightly flattened, smooth to 4-lobed shell** within a thin, 4-ridged husk that **splits in 4;** seed kernel inside shell has 2 large, irregular lobes (cotyledons); nuts hang in small clusters, drop in autumn.

HABITAT: Open, well-drained woodlands.

MAP: Pale green, *C. glabra;* pink, *C. ovalis;* dark green, overlap.

ALTHOUGH THIS TREE is Canada's most abundant hickory, reserves are small and commercial hickory comes from the U.S. • Bitternut hickory is Canada's only native pecan hickory. 'Pecan hickories' differ from 'true hickories' in their distinctive buds (without overlapping scales); thin, 4-ridged fruit husks; and larger number of leaflets. The sulphur yellow buds of bitternut hickory are easily identified year-round. • The wood is brittle (compared to that of other hickories) but amazingly shock-resistant. It has been used in wooden wheels, tool handles, sporting goods, panelling and furniture. As fuel, it burns intensely, leaving little ash. Bitternut hickory is favoured for smoking ham, bacon and other meats because it imparts a distinctive flavour. • Bitternut hickory kernels are relatively easy to extract from their thin husks and shells, but they are also extremely bitter. Even squirrels eat them only as a last resort. • *Carya* comes from the Greek *karuon,* an ancient name for a close relative, the walnut. Walnuts and hickories are distinguished, respectively, by the pith of their twigs (chambered vs. solid), their fruit husks (remaining whole vs. splitting into 4) and their wood (light to dark brown vs. white to reddish-brown).

ALSO CALLED: Swamp hickory

FRENCH NAMES: Caryer cordiforme, noyer dur, arbre à noix amères, carya amer, caryer amer

SIZE AND SHAPE: Trees 15–25 m tall; crowns short, rounded.

TRUNKS: Straight, 30–50 cm in diameter; young bark smooth, with pale, vertical lines; mature bark with flat, shallow, greyish ridges; wood hard, heavy, close-grained.

BRANCHES: Ascending to spreading; twigs shiny greenish- to greyish-brown and slender; pith solid; buds sulphur-yellow to bright orange-yellow, flattened, 1–1.8 cm long at twig tips, with 2–4 large, abutting scales.

LEAVES: Alternate, deciduous, 15–30 cm long, aromatic; compound, pinnately divided into 7–11 (usually 9, rarely 5) leaflets that are dark shiny green above, paler, hairy and dotted with glands below, slightly curved, toothed, 10–15 cm long, uppermost largest.

FLOWERS: Tiny, green; unisexual with male and female flowers on same tree; male flowers in 7–10 cm, hanging catkins; female flowers erect, usually 1–2; flowering in spring (as the leaves expand).

FRUITS: Round, greenish-brown, aromatic nuts, sharp-tipped, 2–3.5 cm long, with smooth, thin shells enclosed in thin, yellow-felted, 4-ridged husks that split in 4 to the middle; reddish-brown seed kernel inside shell has 2 large, irregular lobes (cotyledons); nuts hang singly or in pairs, drop in autumn.

HABITAT: Sheltered, rich, moist woods from swamps to drier hillsides.

Key to the Beech Family (Fagaceae)

1a Fruit a single nut seated in a cup of firm, overlapping scales (acorn); leaves usually lobed; leaf veins not extending beyond the lobe/tooth tips .... ***Quercus,* oak** (key to species, below)

1b Fruit with 1–4 (rarely 5) nuts enclosed in a prickly, bur-like covering that splits open along as many lines as there are nuts; leaves coarsely toothed; leaf veins various **2**

2a Nuts sharply triangular, usually 2 in burs 2–3 cm wide; leaves oblong-ovate, shallowly toothed, with veins not extending beyond the teeth; bark smooth, pale grey..... ***Fagus,* beech** (p. 91)

2b Nuts flattened on 1 or 2 sides, 2–4 in burs 5–8 cm wide; leaves coarsely sharp-toothed, with veins extending beyond the tips of the teeth; bark rough, greyish-brown
.... ***Castanea,* chestnut** (p. 92)

Key to the Oaks (Genus *Quercus*)

1a Leaves with sharp, bristle-tipped lobes; acorns maturing in the second year, woolly on the inner surface of the shell **2**

1b Leaves with rounded to slightly pointed lobes or teeth; acorns maturing in the first year, hairless on the inner surface of the shell **8**

2a Leaves with star-shaped hairs beneath and often along the upper midvein; acorn cups downy on the inner surface and sometimes fringed; winter buds various **3**

2b Leaves essentially hairless (sometimes with tufts in vein axils); acorn cups hairless or with a few hairs around the scar, never fringed; winter buds hairless or with fringed scales **4**

3a Leaves small (5–10 cm long) with broadly triangular lobes; star-shaped hairs minute, barely visible with a 10x lens; buds smooth reddish-brown
.... ***Q. ilicifolia,* bear oak** (p. 99)

3b Leaves larger (10–20 cm) with parallel-sided lobes; star-shaped hairs loose, conspicuous, clearly visible with a 10x lens; winter buds densely whitish-hairy
.... ***Q. velutina,* black oak** (p. 99)

4a Length of the largest leaf lobes (on leaves growing in full sun) equal to or slightly greater than the width of the middle part of the leaf (between opposing notches)
.... ***Q. rubra,* red oak** (p. 100)

4b Largest leaf lobes much (up to 3 times) longer than the width of the middle part of the leaf **5**

Quercus velutina, black oak

5a Acorns large and round (1.5–3 cm across); buds pale greyish-brown, hairless
.... ***Q. shumardii,* Shumard oak** (p. 102)
5b Acorns smaller (9–18 mm long).. **6**

6a Acorns round, 9–13 mm across, with saucer-like cups covering ¹/₄–¹/₃ of the nut
.... ***Q. palustris,* pin oak** (p. 101)
6b Acorns ellipsoid-cylindrical, 1–2 cm long, with deeper cups covering ¹/₃–¹/₂ of the nut **7**

7a Leaf stalks >1 mm wide; acorns tipped with rings; acorn cups 1.5–2 cm wide
.... ***Q. coccinea,* scarlet oak** (p. 101)
7b Leaf stalks <1 mm wide; acorns lacking rings at their tips; acorn cups 1–1.5 cm wide
.... ***Q. ellipsoidalis,* northern pin oak** (p. 102)

8a Leaves coarsely toothed, with 3–14 teeth per side, indented less than ¹/₃ of the way to the midrib;
lower leaf surfaces densely covered with whitish, star-shaped hairs **9**
8b Leaves with 1–5 distinct lobes per side, indented more than ¹/₃ of the way to the midrib; lower leaf
surfaces various **11**

9a Acorns single or paired on long (2–10 cm) stalks; cup scales swollen, with pointed, recurved tips
.... ***Q. bicolor,* swamp white oak** (p. 96)
9b Acorn stalks absent or shorter than the leaf stalks; cup scales only slightly swollen and lacking
recurved tips.. **10**

10a Leaves small (usually 4–10 cm long) with 4–9 main veins per side; shrubby, rarely reaching the
size of a small tree .... ***Q. prinoides,* dwarf chinquapin oak** (p. 98)
10b Leaves larger (about 10–18 cm long) with 8–15 main veins per side; tall shrub or a medium-tall
tree............................... ***Q. muehlenbergii,* chinquapin oak** (p. 97)

11a Lower leaf surfaces hairy... **12**
11b Lower leaf surfaces hairless.. **13**

12a Leaves shallowly and irregularly lobed; acorns on long (2–10 cm) stalks; twigs usually hairless
.... ***Q. bicolor,* swamp white oak** (p. 96)
12b Leaves deeply notched below the middle and broadly lobed at the tip; acorns on shorter (<2 cm)
stalks; bristles on cup scales forming a distinctive fringe around the nut; first-year twigs hairy
.... ***Q. macrocarpa,* bur oak** (p. 95)

13a Leaves small (5–12 cm long), dark green, with 2 small, ear-shaped basal lobes; acorns large
(1.5–4 cm long) on long (3–8 cm) stalks; occasional garden escape
.... ***Q. robur,* English oak** (p. 94)
13b Leaves larger (10–22 cm long), shiny green, without small, ear-shaped basal lobes; acorns
smaller (1.2–2 cm long) on shorter (<2 cm) stalks; native tree
.... ***Q. alba,* white oak** (p. 93)

BEECH WOOD has been used for spindles, rungs, inexpensive furniture, handles, utensils, containers, flooring, plywood, railway ties, barrels and casks. Because of its elastic qualities, it was once used to make all-wood clothespins. • Beech nuts are best after the first frosts. They make a tasty trail nibble but should be eaten in moderation because large amounts can cause intestinal inflammation. Dried, roasted, ground beech nuts make a traditional coffee substitute that was mixed with coffee, milk or chocolate and sweetened with honey. Early settlers gathered many beech nuts to extract the oil, which is similar to olive oil and was used as both food and lamp oil. • Beech nuts are eagerly sought by many birds and mammals, which then disperse the seeds. These fat-rich nuts are an important food for muskrats, squirrels, chipmunks, black bears and birds such as grouse, wood ducks and wild turkeys. • The canker caused by the fungus *Nectria coccinea* can kill beech trees, especially those weakened by beech scale, an introduced, sucking insect (*Cryptococcus fagisuga*). Porcupines also kill beech trees by girdling their trunks.

ALSO CALLED: Red beech

FRENCH NAMES: Hêtre à grandes feuilles, hêtre américain, hêtre rouge

SIZE AND SHAPE: Trees 18–25 m tall; crowns rounded; roots wide-spreading.

TRUNKS: Often sinuous, 60–100 cm in diameter; **mature bark silvery-grey, thin, smooth,** sometimes with dark markings; wood reddish-brown, heavy, hard, tough, but not durable.

BRANCHES: Smooth; twigs shiny light brown, slender, slightly zigzagged; buds reddish-brown to greyish-brown, **slender, 1.5–2.5 cm long,** pointing outwards, in 2 vertical rows.

LEAVES: Alternate, simple, deciduous; blades 5–15 cm long, dark bluish-green above and paler below, leathery, narrowly oval, with **9–14 straight, parallel veins per side, each ending in a coarse tooth;** leaf scars small, semicircular; leaves drop in autumn, occasionally persisting on lower branches or saplings.

FLOWERS: Tiny, yellowish-green; unisexual with male and female flowers on the same tree; male flowers clustered in dense, 2.2–2.8 cm heads hanging on slender stalks; female flowers erect, in small clusters of 2–4; flowering in spring (as the leaves expand).

FRUITS: Small **burs, with pairs of sharply 3-angled, 1.8–2.2 cm long, smooth-shelled nuts** enclosed in a prickly, greenish- to reddish-brown husk that splits in 2–4; seeds single kernels inside each nut; burs split open in late summer to autumn.

HABITAT: Moist, well-drained slopes and bottomlands.

91

CANADA'S ONLY NATIVE CHESTNUT was once common in hardwood forests, but chestnut blight *(Endothia parasitica),* introduced from Asia in 1904, eliminated 99% of the chestnut trees in North America by 1937. The chestnut blight fungus spreads by wind-carried spores and causes uncontrolled bark growth. It commonly infects Eurasian chestnuts, but the New World species have almost no resistance. A few trees persist by sprouting from stumps, but shoots usually succumb to the blight before they reach 10 m in height. Very few produce seed before dying. A less virulent strain of the fungus was introduced to compete with the deadly blight, but with limited success. • American chestnut was an important commercial tree in the 19th century, valued for its durable wood and its large, sweet, edible nutmeats. • Settlers boiled the leaves to make a jelly for treating burns and sweaty feet. A tea of the bark was gargled to soothe inflamed tonsils, and it was swallowed (with honey) to cure whooping cough. • A relatively blight-resistant horticultural species, **Chinese chestnut *(C. mollissima,*** also called *C. bungeana* and *C. formosana),* has been introduced from Korea and China. It resembles American chestnut, but its leaves are woolly-hairy beneath.

ALSO CALLED: Sweet chestnut

FRENCH NAMES: Châtaignier d'Amérique, châtaignier denté

SIZE AND SHAPE: Trees 3–10 m tall (up to 35 m before the blight), from sprouting stumps.

TRUNKS: Straight, up to 15 cm in diameter (up to 100 cm before the blight); young bark dark brown, smooth; mature bark with broad, flat-topped ridges; wood reddish-brown, straight-grained, hard, resistant to decay.

BRANCHES: Stout; twigs shiny reddish-brown, stout; **pith star-shaped** (in cross-section); buds greenish-brown, hairless, egg-shaped, 5–8 mm long, 2–3-scaled.

LEAVES: Alternate, simple, deciduous; blades yellowish-green, smooth, **narrowly oblong, 15–28 cm long; veins straight, parallel, 15–20 per side, ending in coarse, bristle-tipped teeth.**

FLOWERS: Tiny, **creamy-white,** fragrant; unisexual with male and female flowers on same tree; male flowers in 12–20 cm long, **semi-erect catkins;** female flowers **1–3 at the base of some male catkins;** flowering in June–July (immediately after the leaves expand).

FRUITS: Large burs **(chestnuts)** 5–8 cm across, with 1–3 (rarely 4–5), brownish, pointed, smooth-shelled nuts enclosed in a **greenish- to reddish-brown, prickly husk that splits in 4;** seeds single kernels inside nuts; chestnuts mature in autumn, drop after first frost.

HABITAT: Many different site types, but usually coarse, acidic, well-drained soils.

Quercus alba **White Oak**

WHITE OAK is one of our most important hardwoods. The strong, durable wood is amazingly elastic. Before the widespread use of steel, oak was the mainstay of ship-building and was also used in automobile and airplane frames and in ploughs. White oak wood is still used for cabinets, floors, panelling, veneer, plywood, support timbers, caskets, pianos and organs. Oak wood is famous for its use in watertight barrels, which give aged whisky and wine a special colour and flavour. • Boiled bark tea was once used for treating diarrhea, intestinal inflammation and bleeding gums. Such medicinal uses are not advised, because the concentrated tannins may be **toxic** and carcinogenic. • White oak acorns were an important source of food for many tribes. The edible, somewhat sweet kernels can be eaten raw, but traditionally they were usually dried, ground into meal and made into cakes or used to thicken soups. Acorns were also roasted in coals or boiled, then peeled and eaten as a vegetable or snack, often with suet. • Dark-roasted, ground kernels are said to make an excellent, caffeine-free coffee substitute. Acorn flour adds an interesting flavour to breads, muffins and cakes.

Bottom photo: immature acorns (not fully elongated)

ALSO CALLED: Northern white oak, stave oak

FRENCH NAMES: Chêne blanc, chêne de Québec

SIZE AND SHAPE: Trees 15–35 m tall; crowns broad, full; roots deep, spreading.

TRUNKS: Straight, 60–120 cm in diameter; **mature bark pale grey**, often red-tinged, **coarsely flaky;** wood light brown, hard, heavy, water-impermeable, decay-resistant.

BRANCHES: Wide-spreading; twigs greenish to reddish to **smooth** ash-grey; **pith 5-pointed** (in cross-section); buds reddish-brown, 3–5 mm long, with **broad scales;** buds at twig tips clustered, side-buds spreading.

LEAVES: Alternate, simple, deciduous; blades 10–22 cm long, bright green above and paler beneath, firm, **hairless when mature, deeply pinnately lobed; lobes rounded, 5–9;** leaves sometimes reddish-purple in autumn, and a few may persist through winter.

FLOWERS: Tiny; unisexual with male and female flowers on same tree; male flowers many, in hanging catkins; female flowers usually 2–4; flowering in spring (as leaves expand).

FRUITS: Elongated nuts **(acorns)** 1.2–2 cm long, single or paired, with leathery shells; tips rounded with a small, abrupt point, lower 1/4 **seated in a cup of overlapping, knobby scales;** seeds single **white kernels;** acorns remain in cup, mature in first autumn.

HABITAT: Many habitats, from deep, rich, well-drained soils to rock outcrops and limestone pavements.

THIS MAJESTIC TREE was introduced to North America in colonial times. In our province, it is hardy as far north as Georgian Bay and Ottawa. • When oak forests covered much of England, this tree was an important timber species. English war ships were constructed from sturdy English oak beams. No forester dared to fell a crooked tree before maturity, because its twisted knees and elbows were so valuable for shipbuilding. Railway carriages were made of oak, and in earlier days oak panelling adorned the walls of castles, churches and Parliament. King Arthur's Round Table was made of a single slice from an enormous oak bole. • This slow-growing tree can survive for centuries. The largest English oaks have decayed centres but are estimated at 1000–2000 years old. The famous Fairlop Oak in Hainault Forest, England, had a trunk 3.5 m in diameter, with spreading boughs covering an area 30 m wide. • The edible acorns were very important to English farmers as a pig feed and were also eaten by peasants during famines. Flavour was improved by drying, so kernels were often ground into a nourishing, though difficult to digest, flour.

ALSO CALLED: Pedunculate oak

FRENCH NAME: Chêne pédonculé

SIZE AND SHAPE: Trees 25 m tall (35 m with age); crowns broad, full, often irregular.

TRUNKS: Straight, sturdy, 60–90 cm in diameter; **mature bark dark grey,** deeply furrowed; wood light brown, hard, heavy, water-impermeable, decay-resistant.

BRANCHES: Wide-spreading; twigs greenish-brown and slightly powdery; **pith 5-pointed** (in cross-section); buds 7–9 mm long, blunt, with **broad scales,** buds at twig tips clustered.

LEAVES: Alternate, simple, deciduous; blades 5–12 cm long, dark green above and paler bluish-green beneath, firm, **pinnately lobed, notched at the base with 2 small, ear-like lobes; lobes rounded, 6–14; stalks short or absent**.

FLOWERS: Tiny; unisexual with male and female flowers on same tree; male flowers in hanging catkins; female flowers 2–5, clustered at leaf bases; flowering in May (as leaves expand).

FRUITS: Elongated nuts **(acorns)** 1.5–2.5 cm long, **in clusters of 2–5 on 3–8 cm long stalks,** with leathery shells; tips rounded with a small, abrupt point; **lower $1/4$–$1/3$ seated in a cup of knobby scales;** seeds single **white kernels;** acorns remain in cup, mature in first autumn.

HABITAT: Moist roadsides and forest edges.

DISTRIBUTION: Introduced from Europe; escapes cultivation in southern Ontario.

CANADA'S 12 OAK SPECIES can be divided into 3 main groups: 1) White oaks (bur oak, white oak, Garry oak) with deep, rounded leaf lobes, sweet, edible acorns that ripen in 1 season and scaly bark; 2) Chestnut oaks (swamp white oak, chinquapin oak, dwarf chinquapin oak) with shallowly lobed to coarsely toothed leaves, sweet acorns that ripen in 1 season and scaly bark; 3) Red or black oaks (red oak, black oak, bear oak, pin oak, northern pin oak, Shumard oak) with deep, pointed leaf lobes, bitter acorns that ripen in 2 years and non-scaly bark. • Bur oak is Canada's most common and widespread white oak. With its thick bark and deep roots, it is fire and drought resistant enough to grow in grasslands. In wetter areas, bur oak often hybridizes with swamp white oak (p. 96). • Bur oak wood, acorns, bark and leaves are similar to those of white oak (p. 93) and have been used in the same ways, with the same limitations. • This attractive tree is often planted in parks, gardens and boulevards as a shade-giving ornamental. It tolerates air pollution in urban centres, but its deep taproots make it difficult to transplant.

ALSO CALLED: Mossycup oak, blue oak, mossy oak, over-cup oak, scrubby oak

FRENCH NAMES: Chêne à gros fruits, chêne à gros glands

SIZE AND SHAPE: Trees 12–18 m tall; crowns broad, full; roots deep.

TRUNKS: Straight, 60–80 cm in diameter; mature bark grey, often reddish-tinged, with thick, irregular, scaly ridges; wood hard, heavy, water-impermeable, decay-resistant.

BRANCHES: Spreading to ascending; twigs hairy, **often corky-ridged; pith 5-pointed** (in cross-section); **buds hairy,** 3–6 mm long, **flat-lying,** broad-scaled with a few **loose, slender basal scales.**

LEAVES: Alternate, simple, deciduous; blades shiny green above, paler and **hairy beneath,** firm, 10–25 cm long, **pinnately lobed; lobes rounded,** with 2–4 (sometimes 6–8) small lobes below a broad, coarse-toothed upper lobe; leaves drop in autumn, some may persist through winter.

FLOWERS: Tiny; unisexual with male and female flowers on same tree; male flowers yellowish-green, numerous, in hanging catkins; female flowers reddish, in clusters of 1–5; flowering in spring (as leaves expand).

FRUITS: Round nuts **(acorns)** 2–3 cm long, usually single; tips rounded with a small, abrupt point, the **lower $^1/_2$–$^3/_4$ or more in a conspicuously fringed cup of overlapping, knobby, pointed scales;** seeds single **white kernels;** acorns remain in cup, mature in first autumn.

HABITAT: Deep, rich bottomlands to rocky uplands, mixed with other trees.

SWAMP WHITE OAK is uncommon in Canada, where it has both small populations and a limited range. In Quebec, where it is endangered, the Marcel-Raymond Ecological Reserve on the Richelieu River preserves swamp white oak habitat. • Swamp white oak wood is similar to, and sometimes sold as, white oak wood, but the swamp type is knottier and of poorer quality. Still, it has been used in barrels, furniture, cabinets, interior finishing, veneers and construction. • The sweet, edible acorns can be used like those of white oak for food. • This tree can live 300 years or more, but its shallow roots and relatively thin, scaly bark makes it susceptible to fire damage. Swamp white oak usually begins to flower at about 25–30 years of age, and it produces large acorn crops every 3–5 years. • The generic name, *Quercus,* means 'tree above all others' and was the traditional Latin name for oak. It may have been derived from the Celtic *quer cuez,* meaning 'fine tree.' The specific epithet, *bicolor,* means 'two-coloured' and refers to the contrasting shiny green and fuzzy white upper and lower leaf surfaces. • This oak often crosses with bur oak (p. 95) to produce hybrids **(*Quercus* x *schuettei*)** with intermediate characteristics.

ALSO CALLED: Blue oak, swamp oak

FRENCH NAMES: Chêne bicolore, chêne bleu

SIZE AND SHAPE: Trees 12–20 m tall; crowns broad, irregular, **untidy below;** roots shallow.

TRUNKS: Straight, 60–90 cm in diameter; young bark reddish-brown, scaly, peeling; mature bark greyish-brown, flat-ridged; wood light brown, hard, heavy, close-grained, water-impermeable, decay-resistant.

BRANCHES: Short, **with small, crooked, hanging**

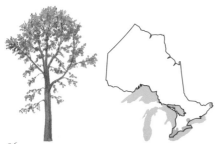

branchlets; twigs stout; **pith 5-pointed** (in cross-section); buds reddish-brown, 2–4 mm long, tip bud in a cluster.

LEAVES: Alternate, simple, deciduous; blades 12–20 cm long, **shiny dark green above, pale and white-hairy beneath,** firm, widest above the middle, **shallowly pinnately lobed,** with 4–6 main veins per side, each ending in a rounded lobe/tooth; leaves drop in autumn, some may persist.

FLOWERS: Tiny; unisexual with male and female flowers on same tree; male flowers in hanging, 7.5–10 cm long catkins; female flowers in clusters of 1–5; flowering in spring (as the leaves expand).

FRUITS: Round nuts **(acorns)** 2–3 cm long, **1–2 on 2–10 cm long stalks,** with a leathery shell; tips rounded with a small point, $1/4–1/2$ of the base in a cup of thick, overlapping scales with outcurved tips; seeds single white kernels; acorns mature in first autumn.

HABITAT: Rich floodplains and along the edges of swamps.

CHINQUAPIN OAK wood is sometimes sold as white oak. Although strong and durable, it has little commercial value, largely because of limited supplies. It has been used for construction, railway ties, split-rail fences and fuel. • The sweet, edible acorns are milder than those of most other oaks. They can be eaten fresh from the tree or prepared like white oak acorns. • This tree is sometimes planted as an ornamental. • **Chestnut oak** or *chêne châtaignier* (**Q. prinus** or *Q. montana*) is a species of the eastern United States that may be confused with chinquapin oak. Chestnut oak is distinguished by its sparsely hairy lower leaf surfaces and its rounded (not bristle-tipped) leaf teeth. Also, its acorns are slightly larger, with cups 2–2.5 cm wide rather than 1–1.5 cm wide. Chestnut oak was believed to grow in Canada, but reexamination of specimens revealed misidentified chinquapin oak. • The name 'chinquapin' is a Native word for the American chestnut tree (p. 92). The yellowish-green young leaves of chinquapin oak and its similarity to chestnut oak have given rise to another common name, 'yellow chestnut oak.'

ALSO CALLED: Chinkapin oak, yellow oak, yellow chestnut oak, rock oak

FRENCH NAMES: Chêne jaune, chêne chincapin, chêne de Mühlenberg, chêne à chinquapin

SIZE AND SHAPE: Trees 12–15 m tall (to 30 m in forests); crowns narrow, rounded.

TRUNKS: Straight, 30–60 cm in diameter, **swollen at the base; mature bark pale greyish, thin-scaled, flaky;** wood brown, hard, heavy, close-grained, decay-resistant.

BRANCHES: Short; twigs green to greyish-brown or orange-brown, stiff, slender; **pith 5-pointed** (in cross-section); buds pale reddish-brown, hairless, 4–6 mm long, buds at twig tips clustered.

LEAVES: Alternate, simple, deciduous; **blades 10–18 cm long,** glossy yellowish-green to deep green above, densely hairy with star-shaped hairs beneath, firm, **with 8–15 straight, parallel veins per side ending in large, pointed** (sometimes slightly rounded), **minutely bristle-tipped teeth;** leaves drop in autumn, some may persist.

FLOWERS: Tiny; unisexual with both male and female flowers on same tree; male flowers in hanging, 7.5–10 cm long catkins; female flowers in clusters of 1–5; flowering May–June (as the leaves expand).

FRUITS: Slightly elongated, leathery-shelled nuts **(acorns)** 1.2–2.5 cm long, single or paired; tips rounded with a small, abrupt point, **lower $1/3$–$1/2$ in a cup of hairy, overlapping, slightly thickened scales;** seeds single white kernels; acorns mature in first autumn.

HABITAT: Dry sites such as sand dunes and rocky (especially limestone) ridges.

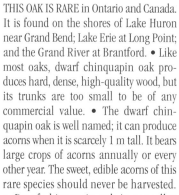

THIS OAK IS RARE in Ontario and Canada. It is found on the shores of Lake Huron near Grand Bend; Lake Erie at Long Point; and the Grand River at Brantford. • Like most oaks, dwarf chinquapin oak produces hard, dense, high-quality wood, but its trunks are too small to be of any commercial value. • The dwarf chinquapin oak is well named; it can produce acorns when it is scarcely 1 m tall. It bears large crops of acorns annually or every other year. The sweet, edible acorns of this rare species should never be harvested. • Dwarf chinquapin oak is a smaller, shrubbier version of chinquapin oak (p. 97). It also differs from its larger cousin in its smaller leaves (mostly 4–10 cm long rather than 10–18 cm long), with fewer (4–9 rather than 10–15) veins and teeth per side. These 2 species often hybridize, making identification even more difficult. • Dwarf chinquapin oak, chinquapin oak, chestnut oak (p. 97) and swamp white oak (p. 96) are all classified as 'chestnut oaks.' Trees in this group have toothed to shallowly lobed leaves, unlike the deeply lobed leaves usually associated with oaks.

ALSO CALLED: Dwarf chestnut oak

FRENCH NAME: Chêne nain

SIZE AND SHAPE: Small trees (occasionally) or spreading shrubs (usually), **1–4 m tall,** often forming colonies; crowns broad, rounded.

TRUNKS: Short, usually clumped; **mature bark pale brown, thin-scaled, flaky;** wood hard, heavy, close-grained, decay-resistant.

BRANCHES: Spreading; twigs reddish-brown to pale grey, smooth, slender, brittle; **pith 5-pointed** (in cross-section); tip bud in a cluster of buds.

LEAVES: Alternate, simple, deciduous; **blades 4–10 cm (sometimes to 15 cm) long,** shiny bright yellowish-green above, densely hairy with white star-shaped hairs beneath, firm, with **3–9 (usually 6) straight, parallel veins per side ending in large, relatively blunt, dark-tipped teeth;** leaves drop in autumn, some may persist.

FLOWERS: Tiny; unisexual with male and female flowers on same tree; male flowers in hanging catkins up to 2.5 cm long; female flowers 1 to few per cluster; flowering in May (as the leaves expand).

FRUITS: Slightly elongated, leathery-shelled nuts **(acorns)** 1–2.5 cm long, single or in 2s or 3s; tips rounded with a small, abrupt point, lower $^1/_3$–$^1/_2$ in a cup of hairy, overlapping, slightly thickened scales; seeds single white kernels; acorns mature in first autumn.

HABITAT: Dry, rocky or sandy slopes, especially limestone outcrops and sand dunes.

BLACK OAK'S tannin-rich inner bark contains the yellow pigment quercitron, which became a popular dye in Europe and was sold commercially until the late 1940s. • White-tailed deer, small mammals, wild turkeys, jays and grouse all eat the bitter acorns and help to disperse the seeds. • This highly variable oak hybridizes with red oak (p. 100) and with northern pin oak (p. 102), further complicating identification. Generally, black oak is identified by its 6–10 mm, woolly, 4-angled buds (vs. 3–5 mm, hairless or ciliate, egg-shaped buds); by the loose, fringing (vs. compact, non-fringing) scales of its acorn cups; and by its bright yellow-orange (vs. reddish) inner bark. • In 1994, **bear oak *(Q. ilicifolia),*** also called scrub oak, was discovered in Ontario in Lennox and Addington counties. An earlier (1800s) report at Grand Bend has not been confirmed in recent years. Bear oak is a small tree or tall shrub (seldom over 5 m tall) with small (5–10 cm long) leaves cut into broadly triangular lobes. The leaf undersides have a felt-like covering of minute, greyish, star-shaped hairs (barely visible with a 10x lens).

ALSO CALLED: Yellow-barked oak, yellow oak, quercitron oak

FRENCH NAMES: Chêne noir, chêne des teinturiers, chêne quercitron, chêne velouté

SIZE AND SHAPE: Trees 15–20 m tall; crowns open, irregular; roots deep, spreading.

TRUNKS: Straight, 30–100 cm in diameter; **mature bark dark greyish-brown to blackish, deeply cracked into squares; inner bark yellow to yellowish-orange;** wood light brown, hard, heavy.

BRANCHES: Horizontal to ascending; twigs stout, **dark reddish-brown, becoming hairless; pith 5-pointed** (in cross-section); **buds grey- to white-woolly, 4-angled, pointed, 6–10 mm long.**

LEAVES: Alternate, simple, deciduous; blades 10–20 cm long, **dark glossy green above, dull yellowish-brown beneath with star-shaped hairs on veins and in the vein axils, deeply pinnately lobed; lobes 5–7, parallel-sided,** perpendicular to main axis; teeth few, coarse, bristle-tipped; **notches U-shaped.**

FLOWERS: Tiny; unisexual with male and female flowers on same tree; male flowers in hanging, 10–15 cm catkins; female flowers in small clusters; flowering in spring (as the leaves expand).

FRUITS: Round, leathery-shelled nuts **(acorns) 1.2–2 cm long,** single or paired, **lower 1/3–1/2 in a dull brown cup of thin, loose, overlapping scales;** tips with a small, abrupt point; seeds single yellow kernels; acorns mature in second autumn; both large (second-year) and small (first-year) acorns usually present.

HABITAT: Often in pure stands on dry, well-drained sites with sandy to heavy soils.

MAP: Pale green, *Q. velutina;* pink, *Q. ilicifolia.*

RED OAK wood is prized for its durability and beautiful grain, but it is susceptible to decay under moist conditions because it is very porous. If you dip a piece in soapy water, remove it and blow on one end, bubbles will form at the other end. Red oak has been used to make furniture, interior trim, hardwood floors and veneers. It makes excellent barrels, but these can be used for storing only dry goods. • The bitter acorns can be eaten in small quantities only. Eating raw acorns has poisoned cattle. Some Native tribes soaked red oak acorn kernels in flowing water for several days to draw out the **toxic** tannins. Alternatively, the kernels were buried over winter or were boiled in water with wood ash (lye) to improve their edibility. • Red oak is an attractive shade tree that transplants readily, grows quickly and resists most pests and diseases. Introduced to Europe in 1724, it now grows wild in European forests. • Small mammals such as raccoons and squirrels, as well as white-tailed deer, black bears, wild turkeys and blue jays, eat red oak acorns. Deer also browse on the young twigs in winter.

ALSO CALLED: northern red oak, grey oak • *Q. borealis*

FRENCH NAMES: Chêne rouge, chêne boréal

SIZE AND SHAPE: Trees 18–25 m tall; crowns round; roots deep, spreading.

TRUNKS: Straight, 30–90 cm in diameter; young bark smooth, slate grey; mature bark with long, low, pale grey ridges, eventually checkered; inner bark pinkish-red; wood pinkish to reddish-brown, hard, heavy, coarse-grained.

BRANCHES: Stout; **twigs reddish-brown and hairless; pith 5-pointed** (in cross-section);

buds shiny reddish-brown, mostly hairless, pointed, 6–8 mm long.

LEAVES: Alternate, simple, deciduous; **blades 10–20 cm long, deeply pinnately lobed** to shallowly lobed on lower branches or simply toothed on young trees, dull yellowish-green above and paler beneath, vein axils often hairy-tufted; **lobes 7–11, roughly triangular;** teeth few, coarse, tipped with bristles; notches rounded, V-shaped; leaves red in autumn.

FLOWERS: Tiny; unisexual with male and female flowers on same tree; male flowers in hanging, 10–13 cm catkins; female flowers in small clusters; flowering in spring (as leaves expand).

FRUITS: **Round,** leathery-shelled nuts **(acorns) 1.2–2.8 cm long,** single or paired, **lower 1/4–1/3 in saucer-shaped cup of thin, hairless, reddish-brown scales;** tips rounded with a small, abrupt point; seeds single yellow kernels; **acorns mature in second autumn;** both large (second-year) and small (first-year) acorns generally present.

HABITAT: Varied, but prefers dry, sunny slopes.

NATURAL STANDS of pin oak are rare in Canada, but this attractive, symmetrical tree provides checkered shade in many parks and gardens. Pin oak is shallow-rooted and easily transplanted, and it will tolerate urban conditions in areas well outside its natural range. Because of taxonomic confusion, trees sold as pin oak may be northern pin oak (p. 102) or **scarlet oak *(Q. coccinea).*** Scarlet oak is a horticultural species from the eastern U.S. distinguished by thick (>1 mm) leaf stalks and by concentric rings at the tips of large (1.5–2 cm wide) acorns. • The knotty, poor-quality wood is sometimes sold as red oak for construction, fence posts and firewood. • This fast-growing tree is among the first oaks to bloom each spring. It can live for 100–200 years. • White-tailed deer, small mammals, wild turkeys and waterfowl eat the bitter acorns. • Large round galls called 'oak apples' appear on the leaves of some oaks, caused by a substance certain insects release when they lay eggs in the leaves. • 'Pin oak' refers to the stiff, persistent, 'pin-like' branchlets that often project from trunks of larger trees.

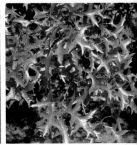

ALSO CALLED: Swamp oak, Spanish oak, water oak

FRENCH NAMES: Chêne des marais, chêne palustre, chêne à épingles

SIZE AND SHAPE: Trees 15–20 m tall; crowns compact, pyramidal.

TRUNKS: Straight, 30–60 cm in diameter; mature bark greyish-brown, **smooth or with small, inconspicuous ridges;** inner bark reddish; wood light brown, hard, heavy.

BRANCHES: Slightly drooping (lower) to ascending (upper); twigs reddish-brown, slender, hairless; **pith 5-pointed** (in cross-section); buds chestnut-brown, 2–4 mm long, essentially hairless.

LEAVES: Alternate, simple, deciduous; blades 7–15 cm long, **shiny dark green above,** paler beneath with hair tufts in main vein axils, **deeply pinnately lobed; lobes 5–7,** each 3 times as long as the width between opposite notches, **wide-spreading, upper sides perpendicular to the midvein;** teeth few, coarse, each with bristle at tip; notches widely U-shaped; leaves bright red in autumn.

FLOWERS: Tiny; unisexual with male and female flowers on same tree; male flowers numerous, in hanging, 5–7.5 cm, hairy catkins; female flowers in clusters of 1–4; flowering in early spring (as the leaves expand).

FRUITS: Round, leathery-shelled nuts **(acorns) 9–13 mm long,** 1–3 together, **lower ¼ in a finely hairy, reddish-brown, saucer-shaped cup of thin, pointed scales;** tips rounded with a small, abrupt point; seeds single yellow kernels; acorns mature and separate from cup in second autumn.

HABITAT: Moist, poorly drained sites such as wetlands and streamsides.

NORTHERN PIN OAK resembles pin oak but prefers upland sites. Also, it has slightly elongated acorns with deep cups (rather than round acorns with saucer-shaped cups). It often hybridizes with black oak (p. 99) and could be confused with that species, but northern pin oak has smaller leaves, pale yellow (not bright yellow) inner bark, and persistent 'pin-like' branchlets on its trunks and larger branches (absent on black oak). • **Shumard oak** or *chêne de Shumard (Q. shumardii)* is a larger tree (20–40 m tall) that has larger (10–20 cm long) leaves with 7–11 relatively broad lobes. Its large (1.5–3 cm), round acorns have tam-shaped cups that enclose ¹/₃ of the nut. Shumard oak has been confused with black oak (p. 99) and red oak (p. 100), or placed among the hybrids of those species. It is distinguished by its more deeply indented leaves and its preference for moist, clayey soils (rather than sandy sites). • Both northern pin oak and Shumard oak are rare in Canada. Northern pin oak was removed from the Canadian flora in 1978 but has since been reinstated. Shumard oak was added to the Canadian flora in 1977.

Photo, bottom left: *Q. shumardii*

ALSO CALLED: Hills oak, jack oak, upland pin oak

FRENCH NAMES: Chêne ellipsoïdal, chêne des marais du Nord, chêne Jack

SIZE AND SHAPE: Trees 15–20 m tall; crowns cylindrical, rounded.

TRUNKS: Straight, 30–60 cm in diameter; mature bark dark greyish-brown, with **shallow, narrow ridges;** inner bark light yellow; wood pale brown, hard, heavy.

BRANCHES: Stout, spreading to ascending; twigs bright reddish-brown and hairy when young, soon greyish-brown and hairless; **pith**

5-pointed (in cross-section); buds shiny reddish-brown, 4–6 mm long.

LEAVES: Alternate, simple, deciduous; **blades 7–13 cm long, bright shiny green above,** paler with hairy-tufted vein axils beneath, **deeply pinnately lobed; lobes 5–7,** each 3 times as long as the width between opposite notches, **wide-spreading, upper lobes perpendicular to the midvein;** teeth few, bristle-tipped; notches widely U-shaped; leaves bright red in autumn.

FLOWERS: Tiny; unisexual with male and female flowers on same tree; male flowers in hanging, 3.5–5 cm long catkins; female flowers in clusters of 1–3; flowering in spring (as the leaves expand).

FRUITS: Ellipsoidal to almost round, leathery-shelled nuts **(acorns) 1.2–1.8 cm long,** single or paired, **lower ¹/₄–¹/₂ in cup of finely hairy, light brown, thin scales;** tips abruptly small-pointed; seeds single yellow kernels; acorns mature in second autumn.

HABITAT: Dry, sandy or rocky soil in upland sites; occasionally near water.

MAP: Pale green, *Q. ellipsoidalis;* pink, *Q. shumardii;* dark green, overlap.

Key to Genera in the Birch Family (Betulaceae)

1a Nutlets in persistent, woody, cone-like catkins; pith 3-sided (in cross-section)
.... ***Alnus*, alder** (key to species, below)
1b Nutlets not borne in woody 'cones'; pith round or oval (in cross-section) **2**

2a Twigs and leaves often dotted with glands; nutlets tiny, winged, numerous, protected by small, 3-lobed scales in compact, elongating catkins .... ***Betula*, birch** (key to species, p. 104)
2b Twigs and leaves not gland-dotted; nutlets wingless **3**

3a Bark smooth, pale or bluish-grey, over muscle-like ridges; leaf veins not forked; nutlets borne at the bases of leafy, 2–3-lobed bracts in loose, elongated catkins .... ***Carpinus*, blue-beech** (p. 106)
3b Bark shaggy, light brown, with rough lengthwise strips; leaf veins forked; nutlets enclosed in inflated bladders in compact catkins .... ***Ostrya*, hop-hornbeam** (p. 105)

Key to the Alders (Genus *Alnus*)

1a Branch-tip buds stalkless, covered by 3–5 unequal, overlapping scales; woody seed catkins equal to their stalks in length; nutlets broadly winged .... ***A. viridis*, green alder** (p. 114)
1b Branch-tip buds evidently stalked, covered by 2–3 equal scales; woody seed catkins longer than their stalks; nutlets narrowly winged or merely margined............................ **2**

2a Seed catkins 1.5–2.5 cm long, very sticky, in clusters of 2–5; leaves widest at or above midleaf, usually with 5–6 veins per side .... ***A. glutinosa*, European alder** (p. 116)
2b Seed catkins 1.3–1.6 cm long, not sticky, in clusters of 3–10; leaves widest below midleaf, usually with 9–12 veins per side .... ***A. incana* ssp. *rugosa*, speckled alder** (p. 115)

Alnus viridis, green alder   *Betula papyrifera*, paper birch   **103**

Key to the Birches (Genus *Betula*)

1a Twigs and bark with the smell and flavour of wintergreen; leaves of flowering branches with at least 8 pairs of prominent veins **2**

1b Twigs and bark neither smelling nor tasting like wintergreen; leaves on flowering branches with 7 or fewer pairs of main veins **3**

2a Seed catkins with hairless scales 6–12 mm long; bark reddish-brown to purplish-black when young, greyish-brown with age . . . . *B. lenta*, **sweet birch** (p. 108)

2b Seed catkins with hairy scales 5–7 mm long; bark shiny reddish-brown when young, dull yellow to bronze and usually peeling with age . . . . *B. alleghaniensis*, **yellow birch** (p. 107)

3a Leaves broadly triangular, with a squared base and long, slender-pointed tip . . . . *B. populifolia*, **grey birch** (p. 109)

3b Leaves not as above **4**

4a Leaves dotted with conspicuous resin glands **5**

4b Leaves not conspicuously gland-dotted **7**

5a Mature bark orange-brown to grey, neither white nor peeling; nutlet wings about as wide as the seed-bearing body; branchlets with reddish resin glands . . . . *B. occidentalis*, **water birch** (p. 112)

5b Mature bark white (sometimes tinged with pink or yellow), often peeling in sheets; nutlet wings usually wider than the seed-bearing body; twigs various **6**

6a Leaves small (2–7 cm long), with 4–6 veins per side, squared to broadly wedge-shaped at the base; a western species, found from Alaska to western Ontario . . . . *B. neoalaskana*, **Alaska birch** (p. 111)

6b Leaves larger (6–12 cm long), with 7–9 veins per side, notched at the base; an eastern species, not reaching the Manitoba border . . . . *B. cordifolia*, **heart-leaved birch** (p. 110)

7a Branches ascending; mature bark peeling in sheets; leaves 5–10 cm long, hairy beneath (at least in vein axils when young); widespread native tree . . . . *B. papyrifera*, **paper birch** (p. 110)

7b Branches slender and drooping; mature bark peeling in long strands; leaves 3–7 cm long, hairless beneath; introduced tree, escaped from cultivation . . . . *B. pendula*, **European white birch** (p. 113)

THIS SHORT-LIVED TREE is too small to be of any commercial importance, but it produces the densest, hardest, most resilient wood in Canada. Hop-hornbeam wood makes excellent tool handles, mallets, sleigh runners and other items requiring hard, resilient wood. Although it is also a very good fuel, it is almost impossible to split. The trunks have been used occasionally to make fence posts. • This attractive tall shrub or small tree, with its unusual fruit clusters, is cultivated as an ornamental in European parks and gardens. • The inconspicuous spring flowers are wind-pollinated. • White-tailed deer browse on hop-hornbeam twigs. The seeds, buds and catkins provide food for squirrels, grouse and various songbirds. • The generic name, *Ostrya,* is derived from the Greek *ostrua* or *ostuoes,* the name for a tree with very hard wood. The specific epithet, *virginiana,* means 'of Virginia.' The name 'ironwood' refers to the hard wood, but this name has also been applied to blue-beech (p. 106) and to various other trees in other parts of the world. The fruit clusters resemble those of hops, hence the common name 'hop-hornbeam.'

ALSO CALLED: Eastern hop-hornbeam, ironwood, American hop-hornbeam, leverwood, deerwood, rough-barked ironwood

FRENCH NAMES: Ostryer de Virginie, bois dur, bois de fer, bois à levier

SIZE AND SHAPE: Trees 7–12 m tall; crowns wide-spreading.

TRUNKS: Straight, 13–25 cm in diameter; mature bark greyish-brown, **shaggy, with narrow, peeling strips** loose at both ends; wood light brown, fine-grained, very hard, tough and heavy.

BRANCHES: Long, slender; twigs pale green, finely hairy, becoming dark reddish-brown and hairless; buds greenish-brown, slightly hairy, 3–4 mm long, **pointing outwards.**

LEAVES: Alternate, simple, deciduous; 6–13 cm long, arranged **in 2 rows,** largest at twig tips; blades dark **yellowish-green,** soft, **sharp-toothed,** tapered to a sharp point, with **straight veins forked near leaf edges;** leaves dull yellow in autumn.

FLOWERS: Tiny; unisexual with male and female flowers on same tree; male flowers in dense, cylindrical, hanging catkins 1.5–5 cm long; female flowers in small, loose, elongated catkins 5–8 mm long; flowering in spring (as the leaves expand).

FRUITS: Hop-like, **hanging, 3–5 cm clusters of greenish to brownish, flattened-ovoid, 1–2 cm long, papery, inflated sacs,** each containing 1 nutlet; **seeds single, inside flattened nutlets 5–8 mm long;** fruits mature in autumn, drop in winter.

HABITAT: Well-drained, shady sites.

THIS SMALL TREE is not commercially very important, but it has exceptionally dense, strong wood. Blue-beech wood is so hard that it is used to make levers, hammer handles and wedges for wood-splitting. It does not split or crack, so pioneers used it for making bowls and plates. Despite its toughness, blue-beech wood rots quickly when left in contact with soil. • This attractive, shade-tolerant species, with its scarlet to golden fall leaves, makes an excellent ornamental. Unfortunately, it is seldom used in landscaping. • Because of its smooth, blue-grey bark, blue-beech is often confused with the true beeches of the genus *Fagus* (e.g., American beech, p. 91). Beech trees have very smooth trunks without muscle-like ridges, and their leaves are not double-toothed. • Birds and small rodents such as squirrels eat the buds, flower clusters and seeds, but browsing mammals seldom touch the twigs. In some regions, selective browsing has created understories almost entirely of blue-beech and other unpalatable species, severely limiting the replacement of overstorey trees. • *Carpinus* comes from the Celtic *car*, 'wood,' and *pen* or *pin*, 'head,' referring to the use of the wood in yokes.

ALSO CALLED: American hornbeam, muscle-wood, ironwood, muscle-beech, smooth-barked ironwood, water-beech

FRENCH NAMES: Charme de Caroline, bois dur, bois de fer, charme bleu, charme d'Amérique

SIZE AND SHAPE: Small trees 4–9 m tall; crowns low, rounded, bushy.

TRUNKS: Usually short and crooked, 10–25 cm in diameter, **with muscle-like ridges; mature bark slate grey, thin, smooth;** wood heavy, hard, strong.

BRANCHES: Few, short, irregular; twigs slender, zigzagged, forming **flat sprays,** greenish and hairy to reddish-brown or grey and hairless; buds 2–4 mm long, reddish-brown with pale scale edges, **pressed against the twig in 2 rows.**

LEAVES: Alternate, simple, deciduous, arranged **in 2 rows,** largest at twig tips; **blades 5–10 cm long, bluish-green above, yellowish-green beneath,** firm, **doubly sharp-toothed,** tapered to a sharp point, with **straight veins only slightly forked** (if at all); leaves red to golden in autumn.

FLOWERS: Tiny; unisexual with male and female flowers on same tree; male flowers in dense, cylindrical, hanging catkins 2.5–4 cm long; female flowers in loose catkins 1–1.5 cm long; flowering in spring (as the leaves expand).

FRUITS: Ribbed nutlets 6–9 mm long, single in axils of green, 3-lobed, 2–3 cm long, leaf-like bracts that hang in 10–15 cm long clusters; seeds 1 per nutlet; nutlets mature in autumn.

HABITAT: Rich, moist, shady sites, often near water.

YELLOW BIRCH is Ontario's largest birch, and it is an important source of hardwood lumber. The hard, golden to reddish-brown wood can be stained and buffed to a high polish. It has been used to make furniture, hardwood floors, doors, panelling, veneer, plywood, tool handles, snow-shoe frames, sledges and railway ties. In the 1700s, yellow birch was preferred over oak for building submerged parts of ships. Yellow birch wood is too dense to float, so it is seldom used for pulp. • The aromatic twigs and leaves make excellent tea. Trees can also be tapped in spring, and the sap can be boiled down to make syrup or fermented to make beer. • Yellow birch can live 150–300 years. Seedling roots cannot penetrate thick blankets of decaying leaves, but seeds often germinate on rotting logs. Young trees soon send roots down to the ground, and when the logs disintegrate, trees are left standing on 'stilts.' • Never tear bark from living trees; you could scar or even kill the tree. • Young paper birches (p. 110) are very similar to yellow birches, but they have no wintergreen fragrance or flavour.

ALSO CALLED: Swamp birch, curly birch, gold birch, hard birch, Newfoundland-oak, red birch, silver birch, tall birch • *B. lutea*

FRENCH NAMES: Bouleau jaune, bouleau des Alleghanys, bouleau frisé, bouleau merisier, merisier blanc, merisier jaune, merisier ondé

SIZE AND SHAPE: Trees 15–25 m tall; crowns rounded.

TRUNKS: Straight, 60–100 cm in diameter; young bark shiny reddish-brown, with prominent horizontal pores (lenticels); mature bark yellowish to bronze, tightly curling in papery shreds, not peeling easily, eventually platy; wood hard, often wavy-grained.

BRANCHES: Large, spreading to drooping; twigs with a moderate wintergreen fragrance and flavour, slender, with dwarf shoots near the base; buds brown, mostly hairy, flat-lying, 5–7-scaled at twig tips, 3-scaled below; scales 2-toned.

LEAVES: Alternate, simple, deciduous; blades 6–13 cm long, deep yellowish-green above and paler beneath, with 9–11 straight veins per side each ending in a large tooth with 2–3 smaller intervening teeth; leaves yellow in autumn.

FLOWERS: Tiny; unisexual with male and female flowers on same tree; male flowers in hanging catkins 2–8 cm long; female flowers in erect, cone-like catkins 1.5–2 cm long; flowers form by autumn, mature next spring (before the leaves expand).

FRUITS: Small, flat, 2-winged nutlets in the axils of 3-lobed, hairy, 5–7 mm long scales, borne in erect, cone-like, 2–3 cm long catkins; seeds 1 per nutlet; nutlets mature in autumn, gradually drop over winter.

HABITAT: Rich, moist, often shady sites.

ALTHOUGH SWEET BIRCH is widespread in the eastern U.S., it is rare in Canada. There are only about 50 mature sweet birch trees in Ontario, all located near the shore of Lake Ontario at Port Dalhousie. The late addition of this species to the Canadian flora in 1967 resulted in part from confusion with yellow birch (p. 107). • Sweet birch is an important hardwood in the U.S. Its wood, which oxidizes to a deep red, has been passed off as mahogany. Of Canada's birches, sweet birch has the densest wood. One cubic metre of air-dried wood weighs 656 kg. • The bruised bark, twigs, buds and leaves all taste and smell like wintergreen *(Gaultheria procumbens)*. Pioneers harvested stands of young trees to extract oil-of-wintergreen for flavouring candy, gum, mouthwash, toothpaste and foul-tasting medicines. The bark of both yellow birch and sweet birch has been used as a commercial source of this oil. Today, oil-of-wintergreen is extracted from wintergreen or is synthesized. • This relatively fast-growing tree reaches full size at 80–100 years of age. It produces fruit after about 40 years, with large crops every year or two.

ALSO CALLED: Cherry birch, black birch, mountain-mahogany

FRENCH NAME: Bouleau flexible

SIZE AND SHAPE: Small trees **rarely to 20 m tall;** crowns rounded.

TRUNKS: Straight, 30–100 cm in diameter; **young bark shiny deep mahogany-red to blackish, thin,** with **prominent, horizontal pores** (lenticels); **mature bark greyish, tightly curling in papery shreds,** not peeling easily, eventually platy; wood hard, often wavy-grained.

BRANCHES: Large, spreading to drooping; twigs with a **strong wintergreen fragrance and flavour, slender,** with **basal dwarf shoots;** buds brown, **mostly hairless, pointing outwards,** 5–7-scaled at twig tips, 3-scaled below; **scales 2-toned.**

LEAVES: Alternate, simple, deciduous; blades 6–10 cm long, deep green above and paler beneath, with **9–11 straight veins** per side, each **ending in a large tooth with 2–3 smaller intervening teeth;** leaves yellow in autumn.

FLOWERS: Tiny; unisexual with male and female flowers on same tree; male flowers in hanging catkins 7–10 cm long; female flowers in erect, cone-like catkins 1.5–2 cm long; flowers form by autumn, mature next spring (before the leaves expand).

FRUITS: Flat, 2-winged nutlets in axils of 3-lobed, **hairless, 6–12 mm long scales,** borne in **erect, cone-like, 2–3 cm long catkins;** seeds 1 per nutlet; nutlets mature in autumn, drop over winter.

HABITAT: Moist woods.

GREY BIRCH wood is sometimes used for firewood and for turning (i.e., for producing spindles, handles and other such items). • This small tree is occasionally planted as an ornamental. It is also sometimes grown in plantations as a nurse tree (to protect seedlings from heat and desiccation), but it soon interferes with young crop trees and must be cut. • Grey birch lives about 50 years. A pioneer tree, it tolerates shade and thrives on dry, almost sterile soils. It can multiply rapidly to cover fields, burned areas and clear-cut sites. Human activity often provides suitable habitat, and grey birch has been expanding west and north from its home range in the Maritimes. • White-tailed deer eat the twigs and buds in early spring. Ruffed grouse and small mammals eat the seeds, buds and young catkins. Many songbirds also feed on the seeds. • Grey birch trees usually have triangular black patches below each branch caused by the fungus *Pseudospropes longipilus*, which grows on excretions from the bark. • The name *populifolia* means 'with poplar-like leaves.' Like the leaves of trembling aspen (p. 122), grey birch leaves tremble in the slightest breeze.

ALSO CALLED: Wire birch, fire birch, old field birch, swamp birch, white birch

FRENCH NAMES: Bouleau gris, bouleau à feuilles de peuplier, bouleau rouge

SIZE AND SHAPE: Small trees 4–12 m tall; crowns narrow, open and irregular.

TRUNKS: Often clumped and leaning, 10–15 cm in diameter; young bark dark reddish-brown, **thin, smooth,** with **horizontal pores (lenticels); mature bark chalky-white, peeling with difficulty in small plates;** wood light reddish-brown, light and soft.

BRANCHES: Often S-shaped with age; twigs dotted with warty resin glands, **slender, lacking wintergreen fragrance;** buds pale greyish-brown, often hairy, **gummy,** 3-scaled.

LEAVES: Alternate, simple, deciduous; blades 4–7 cm long, shiny, rough and dark green above, smooth and paler beneath, with **6–9 straight veins** per side **ending in large teeth edged with smaller teeth, triangular,** square-based, **slender-tipped;** leaves turn yellow in autumn.

FLOWERS: Tiny; unisexual with male and female flowers on same tree; male flowers in single (usually), hanging, 6–10 cm catkins; female flowers in semi-erect, 1.5–3 cm catkins; flowers form by autumn, mature next spring (before the leaves expand).

FRUITS: Small, flat, 2-winged nutlets, 2.2–3 mm wide, in the axils of **hairy, 3-lobed scales;** seeds 1 per nutlet; nutlets mature in autumn, drop into early winter.

HABITAT: Wet to mesic, sandy or gravelly soils, often in disturbed areas such as old fields.

Paper Birch *Betula papyrifera*

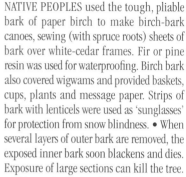

NATIVE PEOPLES used the tough, pliable bark of paper birch to make birch-bark canoes, sewing (with spruce roots) sheets of bark over white-cedar frames. Fir or pine resin was used for waterproofing. Birch bark also covered wigwams and provided baskets, cups, plants and message paper. Strips of bark with lenticels were used as 'sunglasses' for protection from snow blindness. • When several layers of outer bark are removed, the exposed inner bark soon blackens and dies. Exposure of large sections can kill the tree. • This sun-loving tree is a colonizer. Paper birch is more common and widespread now than 200 years ago, because clearing and burning have created many suitable sites.

• Paper birch is easily confused with **heart-leaved birch** or mountain paper birch *(B. cordifolia),* which some taxonomists classify as a variety of paper birch. Heart-leaved birch is distinguished by the notched bases of its conspicuously resin-dotted leaves (paper birch leaves have wedge-shaped to notched bases and inconspicuous or absent dots), and by the long, rounded (rather than short, pointed) middle lobe of its catkin scales. In Ontario, heart-leaved birch grows in cool, often moist sites from Sault Ste. Marie to western Lake Superior. • Both paper birch and heart-leaved birch can grow as single trunks or as multi-stemmed clumps, as shown by the 2 illustrations below.

ALSO CALLED: White birch, canoe birch, silver birch, spoolwood

FRENCH NAMES: Bouleau blanc, bouleau à papier, bouleau à canôt

SIZE AND SHAPE: Trees 15–25 m tall; crowns open, somewhat conical.

TRUNKS: Often leaning and clumped, 30–60 cm in diameter; young bark reddish, **thin, smooth,** with **horizontal pores** (lenticels); **mature bark white, peeling in large sheets;** wood moderately hard, pale, odourless.

BRANCHES: Ascending; **twigs slender,** dark reddish-brown, **with scattered, warty resin** glands; **buds resinous, with 3 brown-tipped, greenish scales.**

LEAVES: Alternate, simple, deciduous; blades 5–10 cm long, dull green, paler beneath, with **5–9 straight veins per side ending in large teeth with 3–5 smaller intervening teeth,** ovate, **widest below the middle,** slender-pointed; leaves yellow in autumn.

FLOWERS: Tiny; unisexual with male and female flowers on same tree; male flowers in clusters of 1–3 hanging catkins 7–9 cm long; female flowers in erect catkins 1–3 cm long; flowers form by autumn, mature next spring (before the leaves expand).

FRUITS: Small, flat, broadly 2-winged nutlets, 1.5–2.5 mm long, in axils of 3-lobed, usually hairy scales within hanging, 3–5 cm long catkins; seeds 1 per nutlet; nutlets mature in autumn, drop over winter.

HABITAT: Open, often disturbed sites and forest edges on a variety of substrates.

THIS TREE is too small to be commercially important, but it has been used for firewood. • Alaska birch was one of the first trees to migrate north behind receding glacial ice thousands of years ago. This fast-growing tree begins producing abundant seed each year after about 15 years. The winged nutlets (samaras) can be blown for long distances over snow. Birch seedlings thrive on exposed mineral surfaces free of competing vegetation, and burned trees quickly resprout from the base. • Many birch stands suffer 'birch dieback,' characterized by reduced resistance to insects, disease, drought, frost and other stresses, and by the gradual loss of twigs and branches. The cause of this dieback is not known. • This northern tree resembles paper birch (p. 110) and is sometimes considered a variety of that species. Paper birch and Alaska birch often hybridize to produce offspring with characteristics of both parents, making identification difficult. Alaska birch is distinguished by its hairy, densely glandular (rather than hairless, smooth or sparsely glandular) twigs. Also, its bark does not peel as readily as that of paper birch.

ALSO CALLED: Resin birch, Alaska white birch, Alaska paper birch • *B. resinifera*, *B. papyrifera* var. *neoalaskana*, *B. papyrifera* var. *humilis*, *B. alaskana*

FRENCH NAME: Bouleau d'Alaska

SIZE AND SHAPE: Small, stiffly upright trees 7–15 m tall; crowns narrow, oval.

TRUNKS: Slender, 10–20 cm in diameter; young bark reddish-brown, **thin, smooth,** with prominent **horizontal pores** (lenticels); **mature bark creamy white** or slightly pinkish, peeling in **papery sheets;** wood moderately hard and straight-grained.

BRANCHES: Slender, ascending; **twigs hairy, covered in crystalline resin glands** (sometimes concealing the surface); buds greenish-brown, resinous, slightly hairy, 3-scaled.

LEAVES: Alternate, simple, deciduous; blades 2–7 cm long, **triangular to broadly oval, slender-pointed,** shiny dark green above, pale yellowish-green and resin-dotted beneath, with **4–6 straight veins** per side **ending in large teeth with 3–5 smaller, often gland-tipped, intervening teeth;** leaves yellow in autumn.

FLOWERS: Tiny; unisexual with male and female flowers on same tree; male flowers in hanging catkins 2.5–4 cm long; female flowers in stout, erect catkins 1–2 cm long; flowers form by autumn, mature next spring (before the leaves expand).

FRUITS: Small, flat, broadly 2-winged nutlets in axils of 3-lobed scales within drooping catkins 2–3.5 cm long; seeds 1 per nutlet; nutlets mature in autumn, gradually drop over winter.

HABITAT: Bogs and poorly drained sites; also colonizes open, disturbed sites.

ALTHOUGH WATER BIRCH is too small to be of economic importance, it is sometimes used locally for firewood and fence posts. • In spring, the sweet sap can be tapped as a beverage, fermented to make beer or boiled down to make syrup. • The name 'water birch' refers to the habitat of this species, which grows almost exclusively along streams and near springs. The specific name, *occidentalis,* means 'western,' referring to the species' distribution (mostly from Manitoba west). • Canada's birches fall into 2 groups—the white birches (paper birch, grey birch, heart-leaved birch, blueleaf birch, water birch, Alaska birch and Kenai birch) and the yellow birches (yellow birch and sweet birch). Yellow birches have leaves with 8–12 veins per side (rather than 3–6), seed catkins that are erect and cone-like (rather than hanging and slender), and bark with a wintergreen taste and smell (absent in white birches). • Birches often hybridize, and identifying white birches can be especially difficult. Water birch is highly variable and sometimes hybridizes with paper birch (p. 110), complicating identification. Verified populations of water birch are sporadic in the Ontario range.

ALSO CALLED: Western birch, spring birch, black birch, red birch, mountain birch, river birch • *B. fontinalis*

FRENCH NAMES: Bouleau occidental, bouleau fontinal, merisier occidental, merisier rouge

SIZE AND SHAPE: Trees or tall shrubs 3–5 m (rarely 12 m) tall; crowns open, irregular.

TRUNKS: Often clumped, crooked, 10–35 cm in diameter; **young bark lustrous, blackish,** with **long horizontal pores** (lenticels); **mature bark purplish-brown to reddish-brown, not peeling easily;** wood moderately hard, susceptible to decay.

BRANCHES: Ascending, slender, with drooping tips; **twigs with dense, reddish, warty resin glands,** often hairy; buds slightly resinous, greenish-brown, 3-scaled.

LEAVES: Alternate, simple, deciduous; **blades 2–5 cm long,** shiny, deep yellow-green, paler and resin-dotted beneath, with **4–6 straight veins** per side **ending in large teeth with 3–4 smaller intervening teeth,** ovate, with rounded to wedge-shaped bases and pointed to blunt tips; stalks hairy, usually glandular; leaves yellow in autumn.

FLOWERS: Tiny; unisexual with male and female flowers on same tree; male flowers in hanging catkins 4–6 cm long; female flowers in stout catkins 2–3 cm long; flowers form by autumn, mature next spring (before the leaves expand).

FRUITS: Small, hairy, 2-winged nutlets in axils of sharply 3-lobed, fringed scales in hanging catkins 2–4 cm long; seeds 1 per nutlet; nutlets mature in autumn, drop over winter.

HABITAT: Moist sites on streambanks.

THE DURABLE WOOD of European white birch has been used for making skis, clogs and spindles, and as a source of cellulose and firewood. • This small, graceful tree is often planted as an ornamental. Many cultivars have been developed, including 'Fastigiata,' with a slender form like that of Lombardy poplar (p. 124); 'Purpurea,' with curly, twisted leaves; and 'Laciniata,' with deeply cut leaves on delicate, weeping branches. Unfortunately, birch trees are often attacked by birch leaf miner *(Fenusa pusilla),* a sawfly larva that disfigures the leaves. • The sweet spring sap can be boiled down to make syrup or fermented to make beer and vinegar. • In Europe, this fast-growing, sun-loving tree has been used as a nurse tree, to protect young plantations of hardwood trees such as beech. • The leaves were used traditionally to make medicinal teas for treating urinary tract infections and kidney stones. The resin glands are sometimes used in hair lotions. • European white birch is often mistaken for grey birch (p. 109), but grey birch has leaves with longer, more slender points and with more numerous teeth (18–47 vs. 9–28 per side). Also, grey birch has single or paired male catkins, densely hairy catkin scales and non-peeling bark.

Photo, bottom left: *B. pendula* 'Laciniata'

ALSO CALLED: European birch, weeping birch, European weeping birch, silver birch • *B. verrucosa*

FRENCH NAMES: Bouleau blanc d'Europe, bouleau verruqueux, bouleau commun, bouleau pleureur

SIZE AND SHAPE: Trees up to 15 m tall; crowns open, broad.

TRUNKS: Usually clumped, up to 30 cm in diameter, developing vertical, **black fissures near the base; young bark thin, smooth,** with horizontal pores (lenticels); **mature bark bright chalky-white,** peeling in **long strands;** wood yellowish-white, moderately hard.

BRANCHES: Spreading, with drooping tips; twigs reddish-tinged, **spindly, hairless, with tiny resin glands;** buds 3-scaled.

LEAVES: Alternate, simple, deciduous; blades 3–7 cm long, **hairless,** with **5–9 straight veins per side ending in large teeth with smaller intervening teeth,** triangular to broadly oval, slender-pointed; leaves turn yellow when shed, persisting 3–4 weeks longer than those of native birches.

FLOWERS: Tiny; unisexual with male and female flowers on same tree; male flowers in clusters of 2–4 hanging catkins 4–9 cm long; female flowers in stout catkins 1–3 cm long; flowers form by autumn, mature next spring (before the leaves expand).

FRUITS: Small, flat, 2-winged nutlets in axils of sparsely hairy, 3-lobed scales within hanging, 2–4 cm long catkins; seeds 1 per nutlet; nutlets mature in autumn, drop over winter.

HABITAT: Open, usually well-drained sites.

DISTRIBUTION: Introduced from Europe and Asia; grows wild in southern Ontario and occasionally becomes an aggressive weed.

ALDER WOOD is moderately strong, but the trunks are too small to be of economic importance. Green alder has been used for firewood. • This species is more shade tolerant than other alders, so it often grows in forest understoreys. Green alder starts producing seed at 5–10 years of age, with heavy crops about every 4 years or so. Alder flowers are wind pollinated, so they appear early, before most other plants have developed leaves that would interfere with wind currents. Young alders also reproduce vegetatively by sending up basal sprouts. • Alder roots have clusters of nodules containing nitrogen-fixing bacteria, which convert atmospheric nitrogen into a form usable by plants. Alders therefore thrive on nutrient-poor sites, and when these shrubs die and decompose, they release stored nitrogen and enrich the soil for other plants.

• Many birds and mammals eat alder buds, twigs and catkins. • The generic name, *Alnus,* is derived from a Celtic word meaning 'neighbour of streams.' The specific epithet, *viridis,* means 'green' and refers to the bright green leaves. The earlier name, *crispa,* means 'curly,' a reference to the leaf edges.

ALSO CALLED: Mountain alder, Sitka alder • *A. crispa*

FRENCH NAMES: Aulne vert, aulne crispé

SIZE AND SHAPE: Tall shrubs or occasionally small trees over 4 m tall.

TRUNKS: Often clumped; **young bark smooth,** with large, pale **horizontal pores** (lenticels); inner bark reddish; mature bark reddish-brown to grey, becoming rough; wood reddish-brown, light, soft.

BRANCHES: Spreading; **twigs sticky,** somewhat hairy; **pith 3-sided** (in cross-section); **buds stalkless,** with curved, sharp points and overlapping, often reddish scales.

LEAVES: Alternate, simple, deciduous; blades 4–9 cm long, bright shiny green, **paler and glandular beneath,** with 6–9 **prominent, straight veins** per side, ovate to oval, **often slightly wavy-edged,** with **small, sharp teeth, sticky when young.**

FLOWERS: Tiny; unisexual with male and female flowers on same tree; male flowers in stalked clusters of slender, hanging, 5–8 cm long catkins; female flowers in clusters of 3–5 **long-stalked, cone-like, 1–1.5 cm long catkins;** catkins form in autumn, persist over winter (female cones within buds), elongate and open in May–June (as the leaves expand).

FRUITS: Small, flat, 2-winged nutlets (samaras) with wings equal to or wider than nutlet, in axils of 5-lobed, **woody scales in erect, persistent cones;** seeds 1 per nutlet; nutlets drop in late summer to autumn.

HABITAT: Cool, wet depressions or dry uplands, often on rock, gravel or sand.

SPECKLED ALDER is too small to be of economic importance, but it does play an important ecological role in shading and stabilizing streambanks and enriching soil. • Inuit people and settlers extracted a dark dye from the bark for tanning and staining hides. The bark was also boiled to make medicinal teas for treating rheumatism, and it was applied to wounds as a poultice for reducing bleeding and swelling. Alder bark has astringent properties and contains salicin, a compound similar to aspirin. • This fast-growing, short-lived pioneer species readily invades land exposed by fire or clear-cutting. Speckled alder cannot tolerate shade, so other trees and shrubs soon replace it. • Speckled alder produces some of the earliest flowers each

spring, flowers eagerly sought by bees. • Sharp-tailed grouse and ptarmigan eat alder buds, and cottontail rabbits, deer and moose browse the twigs. • The 'speckled' in the common name refers to the conspicuous pores dotting the bark. 'Grey alder,' 'hoary alder' and *incana*, which means greyish or hoary, all refer to the pale undersides of the leaves.

ALSO CALLED: Tag alder, grey alder, hoary alder, red alder, river alder, rough alder • *A. rugosa*

FRENCH NAMES: Aulne rugueux, verne, aulne blanchâtre, aulne blanc, aulne à feuilles minces, aulne commun, vergne

SIZE AND SHAPE: Shrubs or small trees 2–4 m tall; crowns open, broad.

TRUNKS: Usually clumped, crooked, 6–10 cm in diameter; bark dark reddish-brown, **smooth,** with conspicuous **pale orange horizontal pores** (lenticels); inner bark reddish; wood reddish-brown, light, soft.

BRANCHES: Spreading; twigs zigzagged, hairy; **pith 3-sided** (in cross-section); buds reddish-brown, **stalked, blunt-tipped,** with 2–3 equal (not overlapping) scales.

LEAVES: Alternate, simple, deciduous; blades 5–10 cm long, **dull dark green above, paler green to hoary beneath,** thick, with 6–12 **conspicuous, straight veins** per side, **broadly ovate,** with rounded to notched bases and short-pointed tips, **edges sharply double-toothed and undulating, never sticky;** leaves green in autumn.

FLOWERS: Tiny; unisexual with male and female flowers on same tree; male flowers in stalked clusters of slender, hanging, 5–8 cm long catkins; female flowers in clusters of 2–5 **short-stalked, cone-like catkins;** catkins form in autumn, persist over winter (with **young female cones visible**), elongate and mature in April–May (before the leaves expand).

FRUITS: Small, flat, narrowly 2-winged nutlets (samaras) in axils of 5-lobed, **woody scales in hanging, 1.3–1.6 cm long cones that persist year-round;** seeds 1 per nutlet; nutlets drop in late summer to autumn.

HABITAT: Moist shores, streambanks, wetlands.

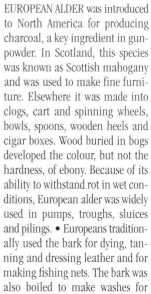

EUROPEAN ALDER was introduced to North America for producing charcoal, a key ingredient in gunpowder. In Scotland, this species was known as Scottish mahogany and was used to make fine furniture. Elsewhere it was made into clogs, cart and spinning wheels, bowls, spoons, wooden heels and cigar boxes. Wood buried in bogs developed the colour, but not the hardness, of ebony. Because of its ability to withstand rot in wet conditions, European alder was widely used in pumps, troughs, sluices and pilings. • Europeans traditionally used the bark for dying, tanning and dressing leather and for making fishing nets. The bark was also boiled to make washes for treating inflammation, especially around the throat. In the Alps, peasants applied bags of heated alder leaves as a cure for rheumatism. • In Ontario, European alder has been widely planted as an ornamental shade tree and as a companion tree for improving soil nitrogen in conifer plantations. • This tree readily sends up suckers, especially when the parent plant is cut back. In many parts of southern Ontario, European alder is an aggressive weed, displacing native trees and shrubs along streams and in wetlands.

ALSO CALLED: Black alder, European black alder

FRENCH NAME: Aulne glutineux

SIZE AND SHAPE: Trees up to 25 m tall; crowns rounded.

TRUNKS: Single or clumped, relatively straight, up to 30 cm in diameter; **young bark thin, smooth,** with large, pale **horizontal pores** (lenticels); inner bark reddish; mature bark dark brown, becoming rough; wood reddish-brown, light, soft.

BRANCHES: Spreading; twigs often **sticky,** somewhat hairy; **pith 3-sided** (in cross-section); **buds stalked, blunt-tipped,** with 2–3 equal scales.

LEAVES: Alternate, simple, deciduous; blades 4–8 cm long, smooth and dark green above, paler and finely hairy beneath, with **5–6 prominent, straight veins per side,** broadly ovate, widest above middle, blunt-tipped to notched, coarsely **double-toothed, sticky when young.**

FLOWERS: Tiny; unisexual with male and female flowers on same tree; male flowers in stalked clusters of hanging, 5–10 cm catkins; female flowers in small clusters of **short-stalked, cone-like catkins;** catkins form by autumn, mature in early spring (before the leaves expand).

FRUITS: Small, flat, narrowly 2-winged nutlets, in axils of 5-lobed, **woody scales in sticky, 1.5–2.5 cm long cones that persist year-round;** seeds 1 per nutlet; nutlets drop in late summer to autumn.

HABITAT: Floodplains and swampy sites.

DISTRIBUTION: Introduced from Europe; grows wild in southern Ontario.

Key to Genera in the Willow Family (Salicaceae)

1a Buds with a single scale; leaves typically lance-shaped to linear, more than 3 times as long as wide .... *Salix,* **willow** (key to species, below)
1b Buds covered by several overlapping scales; leaves ovate to round or triangular, less than 3 times as long as wide .... *Populus,* **poplar** (key to species, p. 119)

Key to the Willows (Genus *Salix*)

1a Leaves opposite to sub-opposite .... *S. purpurea,* **purple-osier willow** (p. 133)
1b Leaves alternate **2**

2a Leaf stalks with glands just below the blade **3**
2b Leaf stalks lacking glands near the blade **10**

3a Leaves linear to narrowly lance-shaped, more than 5 times as long as wide, widest below the middle **4**
3b Leaves broadly lance-shaped to ovate-oblong, up to 4 times as long as wide, widest at or above the middle **7**

4a Leaf tips gradually tapered and sharply curved to one side; stipules conspicuous on rapidly growing shoots .... *S. nigra,* **black willow** (p. 128)
4b Leaf tips variously pointed, not curved to one side; stipules slender, soon shed **5**

5a Branches slender, weeping with long, hanging tips; seed catkins often 2.5–3 cm long .... *S. babylonica* **hybrids, weeping willow** (p. 129)
5b Branches stouter, sometimes hanging but not long-drooping; seed catkins usually more than 4 cm long **6**

6a Mature leaves hairless, dark glossy green above; branchlets brittle-based, easily broken .... *S. fragilis,* **crack willow** (p. 131)
6b Mature leaves slightly hairy, dull green above; branchlets not brittle-based .... *S. alba,* **white willow** (p. 129)

7a Leaves whitish beneath with a dull waxy bloom **8**
7b Leaves green above and below, without a waxy bloom **9**

8a Flowers and fruits produced in late summer to autumn; young leaves hairless; mature leaves edged with gland-tipped teeth .... *S. serissima,* **autumn willow** (p. 130)
8b Flowers and fruits produced in spring to early summer; young leaves sparsely hairy; mature leaves edged with fine, sharp teeth .... *S. amygdaloides,* **peachleaf willow** (p. 134)

9a Leaves tapered to a long, slender point, paler and shiny beneath; twigs and young leaves without fragrant resin .... *S. lucida,* **shining willow** (p. 130)
9b Leaves more abruptly pointed, only slightly paler beneath; twigs and young leaves aromatic with fragrant resin .... *S. pentandra,* **bayleaf willow** (p. 135)

10a Mature leaves clearly hairy beneath **11**
10b Mature leaves mostly hairless beneath **13**

11a Leaves less than 5 times as long as wide, 3–7 cm long, regularly fine-toothed, with short, flat-lying, relatively inconspicuous hairs beneath; seed capsules sparsely hairy
.... ***S. arbusculoides,* littletree willow** (p. 127)
11b Leaves more than 5 times as long as wide, 4–20 cm long, with smooth or slightly wavy, down-rolled edges, silky-satiny beneath; seed capsules densely hairy........................ **12**

12a Leaves 5–20 cm long, crowded on branches; small branches few, flexible, shiny
.... ***S. viminalis,* basket willow** (p. 125)
12b Leaves 4–10 cm long, scattered or well-spaced on branches; small branches numerous, brittle, often coated with a waxy bloom.................... ***S. pellita,* satiny willow** (p. 126)

13a Leaves smooth-edged or with irregular, rounded teeth............................ **14**
13b Leaves with distinct, regular teeth... **16**

14a Leaf edges smooth, sometimes rolled under ...... ***S. planifolia,* tealeaf willow** (p. 136)
14b Leaf edges slightly wavy to indistinctly or irregularly toothed **15**

15a Capsules on visible slender stalks that are at least twice as long as the pale, yellowish scales, borne in loose catkins, appearing with the leaves; branchlets widely spreading; leaves dull green with raised veins beneath (especially when young)
.... ***S. bebbiana,* Bebb's willow** (p. 137)
15b Capsules on short stalks that are obscured by dark brown scales, forming dense catkins, appearing before the leaves; branchlets not wide-spreading; leaves shiny green above, relatively smooth beneath.................................... ***S. discolor,* pussy willow** (p. 136)

16a Mature leaves mostly 4–8 times as long as wide, gradually tapered to a long, slender point, rounded or notched at the base, 5–15 cm long; catkins with pale bracts shed before capsules mature
...... ***S. eriocephala,* heartleaf willow** (p. 132)
16b Mature leaves mostly 2–4 times as long as wide, more abruptly pointed; catkins with dark brown or blackish, persistent bracts **17**

17a Young leaves translucent, with whitish hairs; leaf bases rounded to notched, often obliquely asymmetrical
.... ***S. pseudomonticola,*
false mountain willow** (p. 138)

17b Young leaves not translucent, with reddish hairs; leaf bases wedge-shaped to rounded (rarely notched), symmetrical
.... ***S. myricoides,* blue-leaved willow** (p. 138)

Salix amygdaloides, peachleaf willow

Key to the Poplars (Genus *Populus*)

1a Leaf stalks round, often channelled above, usually shorter than the blade; leaf blades ovate, clearly longer than wide; buds sticky with fragrant resin
.... ***P. balsamifera*, balsam poplar** (p. 123)
1b Leaf stalks flattened (at least near the blade), usually equal to or longer than the blade; leaf blades triangular to heart-shaped or rounded, about as long as wide; buds with or without fragrant resin **2**

2a Mature leaves white- or greyish-woolly beneath, edged with 3–5 blunt, palmate lobes and/or a few irregular teeth; leaf stalks nearly round, flattened only near the blade
.... ***P. alba*, white poplar** (p. 120)
2b Mature leaves essentially hairless, regularly toothed, not lobed; leaf stalks flattened **3**

3a Leaves more or less triangular or 4-sided, edged with a definite translucent border created by callus-tipped teeth; buds sticky with fragrant resin; bark rough **4**
3b Leaves more or less round, without a translucent border, teeth blunt-tipped; buds neither sticky nor fragrant; bark smooth (rough near the trunk base with age).................... **5**

4a Leaves triangular, usually with 2–5 glands at the base of the blade, edged with coarse teeth (up to 2–5 mm); capsules splitting into 3–4 parts; a native, open-crowned tree
.... ***P. deltoides* ssp. *deltoides*, eastern cottonwood** (p. 124)
4b Leaves typically diamond-shaped (sometimes squared at the base), rarely glandular at the base, edged with fine teeth (up to 1–2 mm); capsules splitting in half; an introduced, usually columnar tree
.... ***P. nigra*, European black poplar** (p. 124)

5a Leaves edged with 20–30 fine (<1 mm), regular teeth, blades shorter than their stalks, essentially hairless
.... ***P. tremuloides*, trembling aspen** (p. 122)
5b Leaves edged with 7–15 coarse (up to 1.5–6 mm), wavy teeth, blades shorter than their stalks, conspicuously woolly beneath when young
...... ***P. grandidentata*, large-toothed aspen** (p. 121)

Populus nigra, European black poplar

WHITE POPLAR was among the first trees introduced to North America. It can withstand salt spray and was often used for shelter near the ocean. • Although still widely planted as an ornamental, this fast-growing tree may cause problems. The spreading roots raise sidewalks and clog sewers, and abundant suckers shoot up in undesirable places. White poplar can also be an aggressive weed, displacing native plants from natural environments such as dunes. • Poplars in Canada belong to 3 main groups: 1) the Tacamahaca or balsam poplars (black cottonwood, balsam poplar, narrowleaf cottonwood and the introduced Simon poplar); 2) the Aigeiros or cottonwoods (eastern cottonwood, plains cottonwood and the introduced Lombardy poplar); 3) the Leuce or aspen poplars (trembling aspen, large-toothed aspen and the introduced white poplar). Confusingly, some of the Tacamahaca are called cottonwoods, a name usually applied to the Aigeiros. • European white poplar often hybridizes with large-toothed aspen (p. 121) and trembling aspen (p. 122), producing offspring with intermediate characteristics. • At first glance, white poplar might be mistaken for a maple, but the poplar is easily distinguished by its woolly (not smooth), alternate (not opposite) leaves.

ALSO CALLED: Silver poplar, silver-leaved poplar, European white poplar

FRENCH NAMES: Peuplier blanc, abèle, érable argenté, peuplier argenté

SIZE AND SHAPE: Large trees 16–25 m tall; crowns rounded; roots wide-spreading.

TRUNKS: Straight, 60–100 cm in diameter; young bark smooth, greenish- to greyish-white with dark diamond-shaped pores (lenticels); mature bark darker, furrowed; wood pale, light, soft, straight-grained.

BRANCHES: Spreading; twigs white-woolly; **pith 5-pointed** (in cross-section); buds densely white-hairy, pointed, 5–7-scaled, with the **lowest scale directly above the leaf scar.**

LEAVES: Alternate, simple, deciduous; blades 5–12 cm long, dark green above, **densely white-woolly beneath, broadly ovate to round and palmately 3–5-lobed (maple leaf–like),** irregularly coarse-toothed; stalks flattened; leaf scars 3-sided, with 3 vein scars.

FLOWERS: Tiny; unisexual with male and female flowers on **separate trees,** borne in the axils of deciduous bracts in catkins; **catkins slender, hanging,** develop in early spring **(before the leaves expand).**

FRUITS: Tiny, pointed capsules in hanging catkins 10–15 cm long; seeds 1–3 mm long, tipped with a **tuft of silky white hairs; mature in early summer,** with the leaves.

HABITAT: Fields, fence lines and other disturbed sites, often on sandy soil.

DISTRIBUTION: Introduced from Europe and Asia; grows wild in southern Ontario, north to Ottawa.

THIS TREE'S WOOD is similar to the wood of trembling aspen (p. 122) but is usually harvested for pulp. • Large-toothed aspen and trembling aspen are both important for revegetating recently cut or burned land, holding soil in place and protecting other, slower-growing species of plants. These fast-growing, shade-intolerant pioneer trees live about 60 years. Mature trees (>20 years old) produce abundant seed every 4–5 years. The catkins mature 4–6 weeks after flowering. Although aspen seeds live only a few days, they are very numerous and sprout quickly on bare ground. These species will not grow from cuttings, but once a few trees become established, they spread rapidly by sending up suckers from their roots. • In spring, the whitish-downy twigs and buds make large-toothed aspen stand out among the other trees. • Grouse, quail and purple finches eat the buds and catkins. Moose, elk, deer, beavers, muskrats and rabbits all eat the buds, bark, twigs and leaves. • The specific epithet, *grandidentata,* means 'large-toothed,' in reference to the leaves. Because of their flattened stalks, these leaves tremble at the slightest breeze—hence the French name 'grand tremble.'

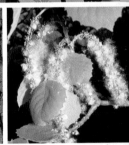

ALSO CALLED: Big-toothed aspen, big-tooth poplar, large-tooth poplar

FRENCH NAMES: Peuplier à grandes dents, grand tremble, tremble jaune

SIZE AND SHAPE: Trees 15–25 m tall; crowns short, rounded; roots shallow, spreading.

TRUNKS: Straight, 30–60 cm in diameter, self-pruning; young bark smooth, olive to yellow-grey with diamond-shaped marks about 1 cm wide; mature bark dark grey, furrowed; wood pale, soft, straight-grained.

BRANCHES: Spreading to ascending; twigs relatively stout, dull brownish-grey, downy to almost hairless, with orange pores (lenticels); **pith 5-pointed** (in cross-section); **buds dull brown, greyish-downy,** neither resinous nor fragrant, about 5–8 mm long, 5–7-scaled, the **lowest scale above the leaf scar.**

LEAVES: Alternate, simple, deciduous; **blades greyish-hairy at first,** soon hairless, dark green above, paler beneath, 5–10 cm long, **ovate to almost round,** usually short-pointed, with **7–15 coarse, uneven, blunt teeth per side; stalks flattened,** usually shorter than blades; leaves yellow in autumn.

FLOWERS: Tiny; unisexual with male and female flowers **in catkins on separate trees; catkins slender, hanging,** develop in early spring **(before the leaves expand).**

FRUITS: Downy, pointed, numerous, 6–7 mm long capsules in hanging, 10–12 cm catkins; seeds 1–3 mm long, tipped with a **tuft of silky white hairs; released in early summer** (as the leaves expand).

HABITAT: Upland habitats; largest on moist, fertile sites; scrubby on dry, poor sites.

FRESHLY CUT ASPEN is too heavy to float, so it must be transported by land. Aspen wood is an important source of fibre for chipboard, oriented strand board and paper. The wood is also used for excelsior, matchsticks, chopsticks, crates and fences. • Trembling aspen usually reproduces vegetatively. It sends up suckers from spreading roots, producing groups of genetically identical trees (clones) that can include thousands of trees covering areas up to 80 ha. Some clones are believed to have originated from trees that colonized land exposed by retreating Pleistocene glaciers, making the clones among the oldest and largest living organisms on earth. • About 500 species of plants and animals use aspens. The bark and twigs are a preferred food of deer, moose, beavers and snowshoe hares. Birds feed on the buds and catkins. • Many parasites infect aspens. Heart-rot fungus (*Fomes ignarius populinus*) produces hollow trunks used by cavity nesters such as flying squirrels, woodpeckers, ducks (e.g., wood ducks) and owls (e.g., northern saw-whet owls). • The trembling leaves of this tree gave rise to a number of Native names meaning 'woman's tongue' or 'noisy tree.'

ALSO CALLED: Quaking aspen, aspen poplar, golden aspen, popple, small-toothed aspen

FRENCH NAMES: Peuplier faux-tremble, fauxtremble, peuplier tremble, tremble

SIZE AND SHAPE: Trees 12–25 m tall; crowns short, rounded; roots shallow, wide-spreading.

TRUNKS: Straight, 30–60 cm in diameter, selfpruning; young bark smooth, **pale greenishgrey to almost white** with dark, diamondshaped marks, often whitish-powdery; mature bark dark grey, furrowed; wood pale, light, soft, straightgrained.

BRANCHES: Spreading to ascending; twigs slender, shiny dark green to brownish-grey, with orange pores (lenticels), **pith 5-pointed** (in cross-section); **buds shiny reddish-brown,** slightly resinous, not fragrant, 5–7 mm long, 6–7-scaled, the **lowest scale above the leaf scar.**

LEAVES: Alternate, simple, deciduous; blades dark green above, paler beneath, **broadly ovate to almost kidney-shaped,** short-pointed, **3–7 cm long,** with **20–30 fine, uneven, blunt teeth per side; stalks flattened,** slender, usually **longer than the blades;** leaves yellow in autumn.

FLOWERS: Tiny; unisexual with male and female flowers in **slender, hanging catkins on separate trees;** catkins develop in early spring **(before the leaves expand).**

FRUITS: Hairless, pointed, numerous, 5–7 mm long capsules, in hanging catkins up to 10 cm long; seeds 1–3 mm long, tipped with a **tuft of silky white hairs;** seeds released in **early summer** (as the leaves expand).

HABITAT: Upland habitats, including rocky, sandy, loamy and clayey sites.

BALSAM POPLAR hybridizes with several other poplars, including eastern cottonwood (p. 124), a cross that yields the **balm-of-Gilead *(Populus* x *jackii)*.** That hybrid rarely occurs in the wild, but a single female clone has been widely cultivated for medicinal and horticultural uses. • Balsam poplar wood resembles that of aspen and is used in similar ways. It has a pleasant odour when burned, but logs are often 'punky' with fungus. Wet balsam poplar is hard to split, but frozen logs (at −12° C or colder) split easily. • The bud resin was used traditionally in cough medicines and in antiseptic ointments for stopping bleeding. Balsam poplar buds have similar properties to balm-of-Gilead buds, which are sold in health-food stores. • Balsam poplar is often planted as a windbreak. This fast-growing pioneer tree usually lives about 70 years. It reproduces primarily by sending up sprouts from roots and stumps. Detached branches can also take root. • Grouse and songbirds eat the resinous buds. Deer, moose and small mammals (e.g., beavers, hares, porcupines) browse on the buds, twigs and leaves, and rodents also eat the bark.

ALSO CALLED: Hackmatack, tacamahac, balm poplar, balm tacamahac, liard, eastern balsam poplar, balsam, bam, hamatack, rough-barked poplar • *P. tacamahacca*

FRENCH NAMES: Peuplier baumier, peuplier, peuplier noir, baumier, laird

SIZE AND SHAPE: Trees 18–25 m tall; crowns narrow, irregular; roots wide-spreading.

TRUNKS: Straight, 30–60 cm in diameter, self-pruning; **young bark smooth, greenish-brown,** usually with dark markings; mature bark dark grey, furrowed; wood pale, light, soft.

BRANCHES: Few, ascending; twigs orange-brown; grey with age, stout, with large orange pores (lenticels), **pith 5-pointed** (in cross-section); **buds shiny orange-brown, sticky with a fragrant resin, pointed, 1.7–2.5 cm long,** 5-scaled, the **lowest scale above the leaf scar.**

LEAVES: Alternate, simple, deciduous; blades dark green above, **silvery-green to yellowish-green beneath (often brown-stained),** oval, tapered to a point, 6–15 cm long, edged with blunt teeth and with 2 warty glands at the base; **stalks 7–10 cm long, round** (not flattened); leaves yellow in autumn.

FLOWERS: Tiny; unisexual with male and female flowers **in slender, hanging catkins on separate trees;** male catkins 7–10 cm long; catkins appear in spring **(before the leaves expand).**

FRUITS: Egg-shaped, numerous, 6–7 mm long capsules, in hanging, 10–13 cm long catkins; seeds brown, 2 mm long, numerous, tipped with a **tuft of silky white hairs;** released in **early summer** (as the leaves expand).

HABITAT: Moist, low-lying sites such as ravines, river valleys and moist fields.

Eastern Cottonwood — *Populus deltoides ssp. deltoides* Willow Family

IN CANADA, the eastern cottonwood is found in a few small areas in southern Ontario and Quebec, whereas the **plains cottonwood *(P. deltoides* ssp. *monilifera)*** is widespread in the southern Prairie provinces. These 2 subspecies intergrade in Ontario. Plains cottonwood has minutely hairy buds, pale yellow twigs, and leaves with fewer (10–30) teeth and only 1–2 basal glands. • Cottonwood wood is soft, weak and tends to warp, but it has been used for construction timbers, chipboard, plywood, crates and excelsior, and in the production of methanol. • This amazingly fast-growing tree can reach 47 m in height in 30 years. Unfortunately, it is not suitable for city landscaping. Moisture-seeking roots often raise sidewalks and clog drainage pipes, and brittle branches litter the ground. • Hybrids between cottonwood and the distinctly columnar **European black poplar** or Lombardy poplar *(P. nigra)* are widely cultivated. One of these, **Carolina poplar *(Populus* x *canadensis),*** is grown for wood and bark fibre (in plantations) and as a fast-growing shade tree. The protein-rich leaves of hybrid poplars are fed to chickens, sheep and cattle. The leaf concentrate contains as much protein as meat does but is faster and cheaper to produce. Eventually, poplars could provide food for both humans and livestock.

ALSO CALLED: Necklace poplar, big cottonwood, common cottonwood, liard

FRENCH NAMES: Peuplier deltoïde, cotonnier, peuplier à feuilles deltoïde, peuplier du Canada

SIZE AND SHAPE: Trees 20–30 m tall; crowns broad (open grown) to narrow (in forests); roots shallow, spreading.

TRUNKS: Short (open grown) to long (in forests), 60–120 cm in diameter, sometimes massive; young bark smooth, yellowish-grey; mature bark dark grey, furrowed; wood pale, light, soft.

BRANCHES: Typically ascending at 45°; **twigs grey to reddish-brown,** stout, vertically ridged below buds, with sparse linear pores (lenticels); **pith 5-pointed** (in cross-section); **buds hairless,** shiny, yellowish-brown, fragrant, resinous, pointed, 1.5–2 cm long, 5–7-scaled, **3-sided at twig tips, pointing outwards below.**

LEAVES: Alternate, simple, deciduous; blades shiny green above, paler beneath, **rounded-triangular,** 5–17 cm long, **3–5 warty glands at the base** of the blade; leaf edges with **40–50 callus-tipped teeth; stalks slender, flat;** leaf scars 3-lobed, with fringed upper edges; leaves yellow in autumn.

FLOWERS: Tiny; unisexual with male and female flowers **in slender, hanging catkins on separate trees;** male catkins 5–7 cm long; catkins appear in early spring **(before the leaves expand).**

FRUITS: Egg-shaped, pointed, 8–12 mm long capsules in loose, hanging, 15–25 cm catkins; seeds 1–3 mm long, **tipped with silky white hairs,** released when capsules **split into 3–4 in early summer** (as the leaves expand).

HABITAT: Moist sites, usually on floodplains or on sand dunes near lakes.

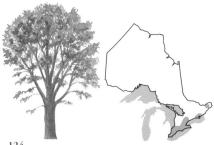

BASKET WILLOW has been cultivated since ancient times as a source of 'osiers' or withes. Its stout shoots, which can be up to 3.5 m long, were used in Europe to make large agricultural baskets and temporary fencing ('hurdles'). • This willow was introduced to many parts of Canada as a small, fast-growing ornamental shade tree and as a source of long, slender branches for basket weaving and wickerwork. For quantity and quality, young basket willow shoots are still considered the best source of wicker for furniture and baskets. • Willow seeds are dispersed by wind and water. Basket willow often grows by flowing water, and its seeds are readily carried to new locations by rivers and streams. However, seeds must reach a suitable landing quickly. Germination or death usually occurs 1–2 days after a seed is released. • The specific epithet, *viminalis,* means 'bearing withes' and refers to the traditional use of this species in wickerwork. • Basket willow could be mistaken for satiny willow (p. 126), but the latter has a whitish, waxy film on its young branchlets. Also, the new branches of satiny willow are less stiffly erect than those of basket willow.

ALSO CALLED: Silky osier, common osier, osier willow

FRENCH NAME: Saule des vanniers

SIZE AND SHAPE: Trees or shrubs up to 12 m tall; crowns spreading; roots shallow.

TRUNKS: Single or few; bark smooth, usually with raised pores (lenticels); wood soft, straight-grained, tough, odourless.

BRANCHES: Erect; **twigs yellowish-green** (usually) to reddish-brown, hairy at first, soon shiny, **long, slender, flexible; buds 1-scaled,** pressed to twigs.

LEAVES: Alternate, simple, deciduous; **blades dull green above, densely silky-satiny beneath, linear, 5–20 cm long,** 0.5–1.5 cm wide, with **smooth, down-rolled edges;** stalks 2–10 mm long, with swollen bases; stipules lance-shaped, glandular-toothed, soon shed; leaf scars V-shaped, with 3 vein scars.

FLOWERS: Tiny, in axils of small, **black, long-hairy bracts;** unisexual with male and female flowers forming catkins on separate trees; male flowers with 2 stamens; **catkins erect, 2–3 cm long, short-stalked,** appear April–May **(before the leaves expand).**

FRUITS: Silvery, short-hairy, 4–7 mm, short-stalked capsules in **dense, hanging, 4–6 cm catkins;** seeds tiny, green, silky white-hairy, released when capsules split in half in summer.

HABITAT: Streambanks and riverbanks.

DISTRIBUTION: Introduced from Europe and Asia; occasionally grows wild in southern Ontario north to Ottawa and Manitoulin Island.

MOST WILLOWS produce good seed crops almost every year. However, male satiny willow shrubs are rare in some regions, and in these areas shrubs must reproduce by vegetative means, rather than by seed. • Because of their rapidly spreading and branching root systems, many willows are important in controlling erosion, especially along streams and rivers. These very fast-growing trees and shrubs often reproduce by sprouting from roots and stumps. They also grow easily from cuttings and broken branches. • The name *pellita* means 'clad in skins,' probably in reference to the 'furry' undersurface of the leaves. • An essentially hairless variation, the form *psila* (*psila* means 'smooth'), grows in northeastern Canada, including parts of Ontario. It is characterized by dull blue-green leaves with hairless lower surfaces. • Satiny willow could be confused with Russian-olive (p. 181), because both trees have thick, similarly shaped leaves with smooth edges, dark green upper surfaces and silvery lower surfaces. Russian-olive, however, has shiny, silvery scales on its twigs, fruits and lower leaf surfaces. Also, its fruits are berry-like drupes, rather than tiny capsules in catkins.

ALSO CALLED: Silky willow

FRENCH NAME: Saule satiné

SIZE AND SHAPE: Small, shrubby trees or tall shrubs 3–5 m tall; roots shallow and spreading.

TRUNKS: Few; wood light, odourless, tough.

BRANCHES: Twigs brittle, yellowish-brown to dark reddish-brown, often with a bluish-white, waxy coating; **buds covered with 1 scale,** pressed to twigs.

LEAVES: Alternate, simple, deciduous; **blades dark green and hairless above** (often reddish when young), **satiny white-hairy with a prominent midvein beneath** and many parallel, impressed side-veins, thick, **narrow,** 4–10 cm long, 0.5–1.5 cm wide (sometimes to 13 cm long, 2.5 cm wide), **tapered at both ends,** with smooth to slightly wavy, **down-rolled edges;** stalks 2–10 mm long; stipules small or absent.

FLOWERS: Tiny, in axils of **dark brown or blackish, long-hairy bracts;** unisexual with male and female flowers forming catkins on **separate trees;** male flowers 2-stamened, forming catkins 2–3 cm long; **catkins erect, short-stalked, above small bracts,** appear May–June **(before or as the leaves expand).**

FRUITS: Pointed, 4–6 mm long, **densely white silky-hairy, essentially stalkless capsules in dense catkins 3–5 cm long;** seeds tiny, green, with silky white hairs, released June–July.

HABITAT: Riverbanks, lakeshores, fens, swamps and damp spruce forests.

LITTLETREE WILLOW is rare in Ontario, but it is one of the most common willows in the western boreal forest, with a range extending across the continent from Alaska to northwestern Ontario. A disjunct population has been discovered at Lac Mistassini in central Quebec. • The diamond-shaped patches on some branches are caused by fungal infection. Craftsmen often search out such branches and peel off the bark to expose orange-brown patterns in the pale wood. These branches can be used for making walking sticks. • Willows are shade-intolerant, and their extensive root systems often spread quickly, allowing them to revegetate disturbed sites. In many regions, littletree willow is one of the first shrubs to invade recently burned woodlands. It often forms dense, pure thickets on riverbanks and in burned areas, but it can also grow mixed with birch and spruce trees. • The specific epithet, *arbusculoides,* means 'like *arbuscula'* and refers to the similarity between this species and a species of northern Europe, **S. arbuscula.** • Over its vast range, littletree willow is highly variable, including low shrubs less than 30 cm tall and small trees 9 m tall.

ALSO CALLED: Shrubby willow

FRENCH NAME: Saule arbustif

SIZE AND SHAPE: Shrubs or shrubby trees 1–4 m tall (rarely to 9 m); roots shallow.

TRUNKS: Few to many; young bark smooth, sloughing off on older branchlets; mature bark often with diamond-shaped patches; wood light, soft, odourless, tough.

BRANCHES: Ascending; twigs shiny reddish-brown to greyish, slender; **buds 1-scaled,** flat-lying.

LEAVES: Alternate, simple, deciduous; **blades shiny deep green and hairless above,** paler with **short, flat-lying, roughly parallel, silvery hairs beneath,** 2–7 cm long, 0.5–1.5 cm wide, **tapered at both ends, edged with small, gland-tipped teeth;** stalks 2–6 mm long; stipules tiny, soon shed; leaves yellow in autumn.

FLOWERS: **Tiny,** in axils of small, brown, hairy bracts; unisexual with male and female flowers in catkins on separate trees; male flowers with 2 stamens, in catkins 1–2 cm long; catkins **erect, stalkless or on very short shoots** above several small leaves, appear May–June (**as the leaves expand** or slightly before).

FRUITS: Conical, **sparsely silky-hairy, 4–6 mm capsules** on short stalks in loosely irregular catkins 2–6 cm long; seeds tiny, green, silky-hairy, released June–August.

HABITAT: Riverbanks, peat bogs and recently burned areas.

127

THIS COMMON TREE is North America's largest native willow. It is the only tree willow in Ontario with leaves that are fairly uniformly green on both surfaces and with conspicuous stipules on fast-growing shoots in late summer. • Black willow has little commercial value, but it has been used locally for construction timbers and fuel and for making wicker baskets and furniture. During the American Revolution, the wood of black willow (and of other willows) was made into fine charcoal, which was then used to make gunpowder. • The brittle-based branches of black willow are easily broken by wind, and on moist ground they often take root. This form of vegetative reproduction is especially effective along rivers and streams, where flowing water can carry branches great distances and establish colonies in new locations. Black willow cuttings can be embedded in riverbanks to control erosion. • The tiny, fluffy seeds

disperse in wind and water, and they grow readily in moist, sunny sites. However, they must germinate within 24 hours of falling or die. • The species name, *nigra,* means 'black' and refers to the striking black bark of mature trees.

ALSO CALLED: Swamp willow

FRENCH NAME: Saule noir

SIZE AND SHAPE: Trees or tall shrubs **3–20 m tall;** crowns broad, irregular; roots dense, spreading.

TRUNKS: **Often leaning and forked into 2–4 trunks,** up to 50 cm in diameter; mature bark dark brown to blackish, flaky, deeply furrowed; wood light, tough and springy.

BRANCHES: Spreading; twigs pale yellowish-brown to reddish- or purplish-brown, ridged lengthwise below leaf scars, **tough and flexible but brittle-based;** buds 1-scaled, sharp-pointed, flat-lying.

LEAVES: Alternate, simple, deciduous; **blades uniformly green above and below, thin, 5–15 cm long,** typically **tapered to an abruptly curved (scythe-like) tip,** rounded to wedge-shaped at the base, **fine-toothed;** stalks 3–10 mm long, hairy, usually with glands near the blade; **stipules large, persistent,** fine-toothed; leaves yellow in autumn.

FLOWERS: **Tiny,** in axils of **pale yellow, hairy, deciduous bracts;** unisexual with male and female flowers in catkins on separate trees; male flowers with 3–7 (usually 6) stamens; **catkins on leafy, 1–3 cm shoots** in May–June **(as the leaves expand).**

FRUITS: **Light brown, hairless, 3–5 mm capsules** in loose, hanging catkins 2–8 cm long; seeds tiny, green, silky-hairy, released June–July.

HABITAT: Moist to wet habitats on floodplains and in swamps and low meadows.

THE SILVER-GREY LEAVES of this attractive shade tree often sweep the ground. White willow is the most common willow in Europe and the most frequently planted in Canada. Unfortunately, it is plagued by many diseases and insects. Also, its fallen leaves and branches often litter the ground, and its rapidly spreading roots can clog drains. • White willow wood does not split, so it has been used to make clogs, carvings, and balls and mallets for croquet and cricket. • White willow trees are often pollarded to produce tufts of straight shoots suitable for weaving. • Large willows with pendulous branches are called weeping willows. The **true weeping willow (S. babylonica)** is not in Ontario,

but hybrids of *S. babylonica* and *S. alba* (**weeping willow, Salix x sepulcralis**), and of *S. babylonica* and *S. fragilis* (**Wisconsin weeping willow, Salix x pendulina**), occasionally grow wild here. Also, *S. alba* frequently crosses with *S. fragilis* to produce **hybrid crack willow (Salix x rubens).** This hybrid is probably more common than either parent. • A popular cultivar of *S. alba,* **golden weeping willow (S. alba var. vitellina 'Pendula'),** has flexible, hairless yellow twigs, and leaves with hairless upper surfaces.

ALSO CALLED: Golden willow, common willow, European white willow, French willow

FRENCH NAMES: Saule blanc, saule pleureur doré, saule jaune, osier jaune, saule argenté

SIZE AND SHAPE: Trees or shrubs to 15 m tall; crowns broad; roots deep, spreading.

TRUNKS: Straight, 60–120 cm in diameter; mature bark light brown to dark grey, corky, furrowed; wood light, even, resilient.

BRANCHES: Ascending; **twigs greenish-brown to yellow, slender, flexible but brittle-based, often hanging; buds 1-scaled,** hairy, flattened.

LEAVES: Alternate, simple, deciduous; blades bright to greyish-green above, whitish with a waxy bloom beneath, **silky-hairy (especially when young), lance-shaped,** tapered at both ends, 4–12 cm long, **with fine, gland-tipped teeth;** stalks hairy, often glandular near the blade; stipules small, soon shed; leaves yellow in autumn.

FLOWERS: Tiny, in axils of **small, greenish-yellow, hairy bracts that are soon shed;** unisexual with male and female flowers in catkins

on separate trees; male flowers with 2 (sometimes 3) stamens, in catkins 3–5 cm long; **catkins erect, on 1–4 cm shoots with 2–4 small leaves,** appear May–June **(as the leaves expand).**

FRUITS: Hairless, **3–6 mm long, essentially stalkless capsules** in catkins 4–6 cm long; seeds tiny, green, silky-hairy, released May–June.

HABITAT: Moist to wet sites along streams and in disturbed sites.

DISTRIBUTION: Introduced from Europe and central Asia; widely naturalized in Ontario.

S. babylonica hybrids   S. alba

THIS ATTRACTIVE NATIVE WILLOW is often planted as an ornamental. • Many animals, such as moose, deer, squirrels, rabbits and porcupines, feed on the leaves, buds, catkins and bark of shining willow. • The name *lucida*, 'shining,' refers to the shining leaves and the lustrous twigs. • The leaves of shining willow resemble those of **autumn willow (S. serissima)** and peachleaf willow (p. 134), but autumn willow has a white, waxy coating on its lower leaf surfaces, and peachleaf willow has less glossy leaves with prominent, pale midveins. Yet another similar species, bayleaf willow (p. 135), is distinguished by its relatively short-pointed leaves, its yellow-green (rather than green to brownish) female flowers and its consistently 5-stamened male flowers. • In our province, willows are the only alternate-leaved woody plants with flat-lying buds each covered by a single scale. American sycamore (p. 70) and cucumber-tree (p. 67) also have single bud scales, but their buds stick out from the twigs. • A hairy variety, **S. lucida var. intonsa,** has persistent reddish hairs on its leaves and twigs. It has been found on the shores of Lake Abitibi and eastern Lake Superior and on the Bruce Peninsula. The epithet *intonsa* means 'not shaved.'

ALSO CALLED: Yellow willow

FRENCH NAMES: Saule brilliant, saule laurier, saule luisant

SIZE AND SHAPE: Small trees or tall shrubs 3–5 m tall; crowns broad.

TRUNKS: Short, small, rarely to 20 cm in diameter; young bark smooth; mature bark brown, irregularly furrowed; wood light, soft.

BRANCHES: Upright; **twigs shiny yellowish to chestnut-brown, rusty hairy at first,** soon hairless, slender; **buds 1-scaled,** pale brown, flat-lying.

LEAVES: Alternate, simple, deciduous; blades reddish and **rusty-hairy when young, dark shiny green** and hairless when mature, **shiny but paler beneath,** lance-shaped, **slender-pointed,** 4–15 cm long, with rounded or wedge-shaped bases, edged with **fine, gland-tipped teeth;** stalks 5–15 mm, **glandular near the blade; stipules glandular-toothed,** semi-circular, sometimes absent.

FLOWERS: Tiny, in the axils of small, yellowish, thinly hairy bracts (shed before capsules ripen); unisexual with male and female flowers in catkins on separate trees; male flowers with 3–6 stamens; catkins erect, 1.5–5 cm long, **on 1–2.5 cm long, leafy shoots** in May–June (as the leaves expand).

FRUITS: Pale brown, hairless, 4–7 mm long capsules on 0.5–1 mm stalks in catkins 1.5–5 cm long and 1–1.5 cm wide; seeds tiny, silky-hairy, released when capsules split in half in June–July.

HABITAT: Marshes, bogs, shorelines, floodplains and other wet sites.

MAP: Dark green, *S. lucida/S. serissima* overlap.

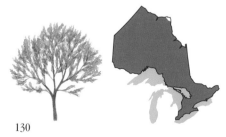

CRACK WILLOW is one of the largest willows in the world, but it is not economically important. It is sometimes cut for firewood, and in colonial times it was imported for making high-quality charcoal to use in cannon powder. In Scotland, the attractive wood has been used in boat finishing. • Brittle branches from this tree often litter the ground after windy weather. Given a little moisture, fallen branches may root. Streams also help to spread the species by carrying twigs to new locations. • The specific epithet, *fragilis,* means 'brittle or fragile' and refers to the brittle, easily broken branches of this species. • Crack willow is widely planted as an ornamental shade tree. It commonly escapes in southern Ontario, but pure specimens are rare. Hybrids between crack willow and white willow, called hybrid crack willow (p. 129), are much more common and display characteristics of both parents. • Crack willow branches and twigs spread at an angle of 60–90°, whereas those of white willow spread at 30–45°. • Crack willow is commonly confused with black willow (p. 128). Black willow leaves have green lower surfaces, finely toothed edges and large, persistent stipules.

ALSO CALLED: Brittle willow, snap willow

FRENCH NAMES: Saule fragile, saule cassant

SIZE AND SHAPE: Trees 20–30 m tall; crowns spreading; **roots reddish,** often conspicuous on eroded shores.

TRUNKS: Up to 1–2 m in diameter; mature bark deeply furrowed, narrow-ridged; wood soft, reddish, tough.

BRANCHES: Spreading; **twigs yellowish, greenish or dark reddish-brown, shiny, slender, stiff, brittle-based; buds 1-scaled,** gummy, flat-lying.

LEAVES: Alternate, simple, deciduous; blades green above, paler with a whitish bloom beneath, lance-shaped, 7–15 cm long (larger on rapidly growing shoots), tapered at both ends, **edged with coarse (4–7 per cm), irregular, gland-tipped teeth;** stalks usually with prominent glands near the blade; stipules tiny or absent.

FLOWERS: **Tiny,** in the axils of **small, pale yellow to yellowish-green, hairy bracts** (soon shed); unisexual with male and female flowers in catkins on separate trees; male flowers with 2 (sometimes 3–4) stamens, in 3–6 cm catkins; **catkins hanging, on leafy, 1–5 cm shoots** in May–June **(as the leaves expand).**

FRUITS: Hairless, lance-shaped, 4–5 mm capsules in 5–8 cm catkins; seeds tiny, silky-hairy, released June–July.

HABITAT: Streambanks, lakeshores, wet woodlands, roadsides and pastures.

DISTRIBUTION: Introduced from Europe and Asia Minor; grows wild in southern Ontario, but less common northward.

HEARTLEAF WILLOW typically has silvery galls caused by small insects. In the past, galls were steeped to make a medicinal tea for stimulating urination and relieving fluid retention. • The name *eriocephala* is derived from the Greek *erion,* 'wool,' and *kephale,* 'head,' in reference to the woolly seed catkins. • Willows are easily recognized as a group, but individual species are often difficult to identify. For one thing, many trees may not have all of the features necessary to make a positive identification. In cases where fruit characteristics are important for identification, immature trees and male trees are especially troublesome. As well, leaves can vary greatly with age and habitat. For example, leaves on young, vigorous shoots may be much larger and hairier or less regularly toothed than those on mature trees. To further complicate matters, willows often hybridize, producing offspring with intermediate characteristics. • Heartleaf willow is a highly variable, complex species. Some taxonomists consider it a single species with many highly variable forms, while others treat it as a group of similar species that are difficult to tell apart. For example, **yellow willow (*S. lutea*)** is often listed as a separate species, but it is included in *S. eriocephala* here.

ALSO CALLED: Diamond willow, Missouri River willow, Missouri willow, erect willow, yellow willow • *S. rigida, S. cordata, S. lutea*

FRENCH NAMES: Saule à tête laineuse, saule rigide

SIZE AND SHAPE: Shrubby trees or tall shrubs 2–4 m tall; crowns spreading.

TRUNKS: Clumped, 8–15 cm in diameter; mature bark thin, grey to black, scaly; wood light, soft.

BRANCHES: Upright; **twigs yellowish-green and downy when young, reddish-brown and hairless with age; buds 1-scaled,** reddish-brown, flat-lying.

LEAVES: Alternate, simple, deciduous; **blades reddish and white-hairy when young, hairless and dark purplish-green above when mature, silvery-whitish beneath with reddish hairs along some veins, stiff,** oblong-lance-shaped, **rounded to notched at the base,** 5–15 cm long, finely glandular-toothed; stipules glandular-toothed, 5–20 mm long, persistent; leaves deep red and veiny when shed in autumn.

FLOWERS: **Tiny,** in axils of dark brown, 1–1.5 mm, crinkly-hairy bracts; unisexual with male and female flowers in catkins on separate trees; male flowers 2-stamened, in 1–3 cm catkins; catkins stalkless or (usually) on **leafy shoots** up to 1 cm long, often numerous in long series, appear April–May **(as or slightly before the leaves expand).**

FRUITS: Brown **(reddish when young), hairless or hairy, lance-shaped, 4–6 mm capsules on 1–2 mm stalks (stalks longer than bracts); capsules crowded and spreading in 2–8 cm catkins;** seeds tiny, silky-hairy, released in summer.

HABITAT: Streambanks, floodplains, shores, ditches and swamps.

THE MOSTLY OPPOSITE LEAVES of this species are unique among Ontario willows. • Purple-osier willow has been widely planted in Ontario and has escaped cultivation in many, widely separated locations. It is hardy as far north as southern Lake Superior and Quebec City. • This attractive willow has been culti-vated since ancient times as a source of withes for making baskets. Its striking purplish shoots can be woven with branches from other wil-lows to produce contrasting patterns and trims. Many willows produce strong, slender, flexible withes ideal for weaving. • Most wil-lows grow readily from cuttings, and thou-sands of offspring can be propagated from an individual tree. This property is particularly useful for preserving individual trees that have desirable attributes. Some willows have been perpetuated for centuries in this way, each genetically identical to the original parent tree. • Willow bark has been used for years to relieve pain, inflammation and fever. It contains salicin, from which was derived acetylsalicylic acid (Aspirin). Both of these compounds are named after the genus *Salix*. • The generic name, *Salix*, is derived from the Celtic words *sal*, 'near,' and *lis*, 'water,' in reference to the usual habitat of most willows.

ALSO CALLED: Purple willow

FRENCH NAME: Saule pourpre

SIZE AND SHAPE: Shrubs or shrubby trees up to 5 m tall; crowns spreading.

TRUNKS: Clumped; young bark smooth; wood light, soft, odourless.

BRANCHES: Upright; twigs yellowish-green to **dark purple,** hairless, slender, flexible; **buds essentially opposite, 1-scaled,** purplish, small, flat-lying.

LEAVES: Essentially **opposite** (at least near twig tips), simple, deciduous; **blades dull green and often purplish** above with **prominent pale mid-veins, paler with a whitish bloom beneath,** essentially hairless, lance-shaped, **usually widest above the middle,** 2–6 cm long, smooth-edged or with fine gland-tipped teeth near the tip; stalks 1–4 mm long.

FLOWERS: Tiny, in axils of small, hairy, blackish bracts (sometimes pale centred and/or becom-ing hairless); unisexual with male and female flowers in catkins on separate trees; male flow-ers 2-stamened, with filaments (and sometimes anthers) fused, in catkins 2–3 cm long; **catkins often paired,** stalkless or on short, leafy shoots, appear in spring **(before the leaves expand).**

FRUITS: Densely short-hairy, egg-shaped, plump, stalkless capsules 2–3 mm long, in catkins 2–3 cm long; seeds tiny, silky-hairy, released in summer.

HABITAT: Low, wet sites near streams and pools and on sandy beaches.

DISTRIBUTION: Introduced from Eurasia; grows wild in southern Ontario, with both frequency and range increasing.

LIKE MOST WILLOWS, peachleaf willow has little commercial value. Because of its drooping branch tips, it is sometimes popular in landscape plantings. It is rarely cut for timber but is sometimes used for firewood or as a source of charcoal. The tannin-rich bark produces a pale brown dye. • The dense, tenacious roots of peachleaf willow have saved many streambanks from erosion. • Willows provide food and shelter for many birds and mammals. Deer browse on the leaves and twigs, while squirrels and rabbits eat the tender shoots and bark. The early-blooming flowers can be an important source of spring nectar for bees. • The specific epithet, *amygdaloides,* comes from the Greek *amugdalos,* 'almond,' and *öides,* 'resembling,' in reference to the almond-shaped leaves of this species. • Peachleaf willow could be confused with black willow (p. 128), but black willow has smaller, narrower leaves with curved tips and pale green (not waxy whitish) lower surfaces. Also, black willow has brittle-based branches, hairy young leaves and large, persistent stipules. • Peachleaf willow and shining willow (p. 130) have similar leaves, but the lower surfaces of shining willow leaves are pale, shiny green.

ALSO CALLED: Peach willow

FRENCH NAMES: Saule à feuilles de pêcher, saule amygdaloïde

SIZE AND SHAPE: Trees or tall shrubs **3–20 m tall;** crowns spreading, irregular.

TRUNKS: Often leaning, in clumps of 1–4, up to 30–40 cm in diameter; young bark reddish or yellowish, smooth; mature bark greyish-brown, with flat, shaggy ridges; wood light, soft.

BRANCHES: Often upcurved with nodding tips; twigs yellowish-brown with lighter pores (lenticels), **slender, flexible;** buds shiny yellowish-brown, **sharp-pointed, 1-scaled,** flat-lying.

LEAVES: Alternate, simple, deciduous; **blades reddish and sparsely hairy when young,** dark green to yellowish-green and hairless when mature, whitish with a waxy bloom beneath, thin, with a **prominent midvein, lance-shaped, slender-pointed,** unevenly rounded at the base, 5–14 cm long, **fine-toothed;** stalks usually lacking glands.

FLOWERS: Tiny, in the axils of **deciduous, pale yellow, hairy bracts;** unisexual with male and female flowers on separate trees; male flowers with 3–7 (typically 5) stamens, in 3–6 cm catkins; catkins on leafy shoots in May–June **(as the leaves expand).**

FRUITS: Reddish or yellowish, hairless, short-beaked, lance-shaped, 4–7 mm capsules in loose, 4–9 cm catkins; seeds tiny, silky-hairy, released June–July.

HABITAT: Moist sites on floodplains and lakeshores; characteristic of many swamps south of the Shield.

BAYLEAF WILLOW was introduced to Canada as a hardy ornamental shrub whose fragrant leaves were sometimes used to flavour food. It is still cultivated in Ontario, and it is especially popular in regions with acidic soils. Bayleaf willow can be grown in many parts of northern Ontario. • Willows have been cultivated since at least the time of ancient Greece and Rome. Many species are highly valued in landscaping and are easily propagated from cuttings. • The epithet, *pentandra,* comes from the Greek *penta,* 'five,' and *andron,* 'male,' and refers to the 5-stamened male flowers. • This species could be confused with shining willow (p. 130), but the leaves of shining willow have long, slender, tapered tips, whereas those of bayleaf willow are relatively short-pointed. • Bayleaf willow is also very similar to autumn willow (p. 130), a native shrub that can reach 4 m in height. However, the leaves of autumn willow have whitish lower surfaces with a thin, waxy bloom. Also, the bracts of autumn willow catkins are hairy from base to tip, whereas those of bayleaf willow have hairless tips.

ALSO CALLED: Laurel willow

FRENCH NAME: Saule laurier

SIZE AND SHAPE: Small trees or tall shrubs up to 7 m tall; crowns broad.

TRUNKS: Usually clumped and often leaning; mature bark grey-brown; wood light, soft.

BRANCHES: Upright to spreading; twigs shiny reddish-brown, slender; **buds 1-scaled,** yellow, flat-lying.

LEAVES: Alternate, simple, deciduous; **blades dark shiny green above** with yellow midveins, **green or slightly paler beneath,** hairless, **fragrant, ovate,** with **pointed** tips and rounded to wedge-shaped bases, 4–10 cm long, edged with gland-tipped teeth; stalks with glands near the blade; stipules small, glandular.

FLOWERS: **Tiny,** in the axils of **deciduous, pale yellow, hairy bracts with hairless tips;** unisexual with male and female flowers in catkins on separate trees; male flowers with 4–9 (usually 5) stamens, in catkins 3–6 cm long; **catkins on short, leafy shoots,** appear in May–June **(as or slightly after the leaves expand).**

FRUITS: Yellow-green capsules 5–8 mm long, on 0.5–1.5 mm stalks in 3.5–7 cm catkins; seeds tiny, green, silky-hairy, released in June–July.

HABITAT: Moist sites such as riverbanks; prefers acidic soils.

DISTRIBUTION: Introduced from Europe and Asia; grows wild in Ontario in a few isolated locations.

THE FUZZY, IMMATURE CATKINS of this well-known willow have been likened to the soft paws or toes of a cat, hence the name 'pussy willow.' Pussy willow catkins are the first willow catkins to appear each year and are recognized as a sign of spring. Catkin-bearing branches from female shrubs are often gathered for use in bouquets. Male pussy willows should not be collected, because they will open and shed their pollen in the house. If bud-bearing twigs are brought indoors in late winter and set in water, they can be 'forced' to produce pussy willows early. • Pussy willow is sometimes planted as a hardy, fast-growing ornamental shrub. • The catkins provide important food for bees and other insects in early spring. Pollen and nectar in the catkins attract insects, which in turn pollinate hundreds of the tiny willow flowers. • The name *discolor,* 'of a different colour,' refers to the contrasting upper and lower leaf surfaces. • Pussy willow could be confused with **tealeaf willow *(S. planifolia)*,** also called diamondleaf willow, which occasionally reaches 4 m in height. Tealeaf willow has smooth-edged, hairless leaves and smaller (5–7 mm) capsules with prominent styles and short (<0.5 mm) stalks.

Photo, bottom left: *S. planifolia*

ALSO CALLED: Tall pussy willow, glaucous willow, pussy feet

FRENCH NAMES: Saule discolor, minous, petit minous, châtons, petits-chats

SIZE AND SHAPE: Trees or tall shrubs 2–6 m tall; crowns rounded.

TRUNKS: Few, clumped, 10–20 cm in diameter; mature bark grey-brown, furrowed; wood light, soft.

BRANCHES: Upright, rather stout; twigs dark reddish-brown with pale pores (lenticels), shiny, sometimes with a waxy bloom, becoming hairless; **buds 1-scaled,** reddish-purple, 7–10 mm long, flat-lying.

LEAVES: Alternate, simple, deciduous; highly variable, **blades reddish-hairy at first,** becoming **green and hairless above** with **hairless (or persistently few-haired) undersides coated in a waxy bloom,** oblong to elliptic, 3–10 cm long, wedge-shaped at the base, toothless to **irregularly toothed or almost wavy-edged** (especially above midleaf); stalks green, 5–15 mm long; stipules large on vigorous shoots.

FLOWERS: Tiny, in axils of dark brown, white-hairy, 1.5–2.5 mm bracts; unisexual with male and female flowers on separate trees; male flowers 2-stamened, in 2–4 cm catkins; **catkins densely hairy,** stalkless or on short, bracted shoots, appear in April–June **(before the leaves expand).**

FRUITS: Minutely grey-hairy, 7–12 mm long capsules, long-beaked, with **<1 mm styles,** hanging in **dense, 5–9 cm catkins;** seeds tiny, silky-hairy, released in late May–June.

HABITAT: Ditches, wet meadows, wooded swamps, lakeshores and streambanks.

MAP: Pale green, *S. discolor;* pink, *S. planifolia;* dark green, overlap.

THE WOOD OF BEBB'S WILLOW has been used for baseball bats and wickerwork. It was also once used to make charcoal for gunpowder. • The diamond-shaped patches on some branches are caused by fungal infections, which produce attractive reddish-orange to brown patterns in the pale wood. Peeled and sanded, such 'diamond willow' branches are used to make walking sticks, lampposts, furniture and rustic plaques and clock faces. • A pioneer species, Bebb's willow is often among the first woody plants to appear after a fire. It can live about 20 years. • This common, widespread willow is an important source of food and shelter for many birds and mammals. Moose, white-tailed deer, beavers, muskrats and hares eat the twigs and bark, while ptarmigan, grouse and grosbeaks feed on the buds and leaves. • The specific epithet, *bebbiana*, honours Michael Schuck Bebb (1833–95), an American botanist who studied willows. • Bebb's willow has extremely variable leaf form and twig hairiness among varieties, over one plant at a given time and among plants of different ages. Several weakly defined varieties have been described.

ALSO CALLED: Beaked willow, long-beak willow, diamond willow, grey willow

FRENCH NAMES: Saule de Bebb, châtons, petit minou

SIZE AND SHAPE: Trees or tall shrubs 1–6 m (rarely 8 m) tall; crowns broad, rounded.

TRUNKS: Clumped, 6–15 cm in diameter; young bark reddish-brown to grey; mature bark greyish-brown, furrowed; wood light, soft, tough.

BRANCHES: Upright to spreading; twigs reddish-purple to orange-brown with pale pores (lenticels), eventually hairless; **buds 1-scaled,** shiny brown, blunt, flat-lying.

LEAVES: Alternate, simple, deciduous; blades silky-hairy and sometimes reddish when young, **dull green above** when mature and **whitish with a waxy bloom, hairy and prominently net-veined beneath,** often widest above midleaf, 2–8 cm long, smooth- to wavy-edged, may be irregularly glandular-toothed towards the base; stipules tiny, soon shed, larger and persistent on vigorous shoots.

FLOWERS: Tiny, in the axils of **yellowish or straw-coloured** (often reddish-tipped), sparsely hairy, 1–3 mm bracts; unisexual with male and female flowers on separate trees; male flowers 2-stamened, in 1–3 cm catkins; catkins on leafy, 5–20 mm shoots, in May–June **(as the leaves expand).**

FRUITS: Finely grey-hairy, long-beaked, 6–8 mm capsules on 2–5 mm stalks in **loose, 2–7 cm catkins;** seeds tiny, silky-hairy, released in June–July.

HABITAT: Low-lying, moist to wet sites; also in forests on limestone flats and sand plains.

FALSE MOUNTAIN WILLOW sometimes forms thickets from root suckers. As with many other willows, these suckers may grow over 1 m in a year, and they form long, straight, slender shoots excellent for basket weaving. • The specific epithet, *pseudomonticola* or 'false *monticola*,' refers to the confusion between this species and **mountain willow *(S. monticola)*,** until recently considered part of the same species. *S. monticola* is a western species found in Wyoming, Colorado, Utah, New Mexico and Arizona. • False mountain willow could be confused with **blue-leaved willow *(S. myricoides)*,** also called bayberry willow and *S. glaucophylloides,* a similar shrub that occasionally reaches the size of a small tree (5 m tall). Both species have reddish-tinged young leaves, but those of blue-leaved willow are not translucent and their hairs are rusty red (not light-coloured). Mature blue-leaved willow leaves have wedge-shaped to rounded, symmetrical leaf bases that are usually not notched. Also, blue-leaved willow has a relatively heavy white, waxy coating on its lower leaf surfaces, and dried plants turn black. Blue-leaved willow grows on sandy or gravelly sites on dunes, floodplains and shores from the southern tip of Ontario to the shores of James Bay.

ALSO CALLED: White mountain willow • *S. barclayi* var. *pseudomonticola*

FRENCH NAME: unknown

SIZE AND SHAPE: Small trees or tall shrubs **1–6 m tall;** crowns broad, rounded.

TRUNKS: Usually clumped; bark shiny yellowish-brown to dark reddish-brown, smooth; wood light, soft.

BRANCHES: Upright to spreading; twigs glossy yellowish-green, hairless or sparsely hairy; **buds 1-scaled,** blunt, flat-lying.

LEAVES: Alternate, simple, deciduous; **blades** sparsely pale-hairy, translucent and reddish-tinged when young, dark green when mature with a **whitish waxy bloom beneath,** essentially hairless, **elliptic to ovate,** often widest above midleaf, **3–10 cm long,** abruptly pointed, **rounded to notched and often asymmetrical at the base,** glandular-toothed; stalks and adjacent midvein reddish, stalks 6–20 mm long; **stipules prominent, 5–10 mm long,** ovate, toothed.

FLOWERS: Tiny, in axils of **brown to blackish, long-hairy, 0.5–2.5 mm bracts;** unisexual with male and female flowers on separate plants; male flowers 2-stamened, in 1.5–4 cm catkins; **catkins stalkless or on short, leafy shoots,** in May **(before the leaves expand).**

FRUITS: Yellowish-brown, hairless, 4–6 mm capsules on 1–2 mm stalks in dense 2–9 cm long catkins; seeds tiny, silky-hairy, released in June (often before the leaves expand fully).

HABITAT: Shorelines and moist sites in ravines, aspen stands and gravelly clearings.

MAP: Pale green, *S. pseudomonticola;* pink, *S. myricoides;* dark green, overlap.

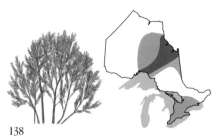

Key to Genera in the Rose Family (Rosaceae)

1a Leaves compound, divided into leaflets ...... ***Sorbus,* mountain-ash** (key to species, below)
1b Leaves simple, not divided into leaflets **2**

2a Fruits fleshy drupes .... ***Prunus,* cherry, plum, peach** (key to species, pp. 140–141)
2b Fruits fleshy pomes (apple-like)... **3**

3a Branches usually thorny; fruits containing 1–5 bony, seed-like stones
.... ***Crataegus,* hawthorn** (discussion and key to species, pp. 141–143)
3b Branches lacking thorns; fruits otherwise **4**

4a Pith 5-pointed (in cross-section); fruits dark reddish-purple to blackish, berry-like, usually 10-seeded, borne in elongated clusters .... ***Amelanchier,* serviceberry** (pp. 169–170)
4b Pith round (in cross-section); fruits green or yellow to reddish, apple-like, containing 2–5 papery or leathery compartments that are easily opened to expose the seeds, borne singly or in small, rounded clusters **5**

5a Young leaves folded in bud, expanding from lengthwise pleats; branches often thorny; mostly native species............................... ***Malus,* crabapple** (key to species, p. 143)
5b Young leaves expanding from rolled edges; branches not thorny; introduced fruit trees **6**

6a Young leaves with up-rolled edges gradually revealing the upper leaf surface; twigs hairless; fruits broad-based, with many grit cells in the flesh...................... ***Pyrus,* pear** (p. 153)
6b Young leaves with down-rolled edges gradually revealing the lower surface; fruits round, lacking grit cells .... ***Malus,* crabapple** (key to species, p. 143)

Key to the Mountain-Ashes (Genus *Sorbus*)

1a Twigs, leaf stalks and flower stalks densely white-woolly (at least at flowering time); leaves usually permanently hairy beneath; winter buds with silky white hairs, not sticky
.... ***S. aucuparia,* European mountain-ash** (p. 159)
1b Twigs, leaves and flower stalks essentially hairless (sometimes with a few sparse hairs); winter buds hairless, gummy **2**

2a Leaflets usually 3–5 times as long as wide, tapered to a long, slender point, broadest below the middle; fruits 4–6 mm in diameter
.... ***S. americana,* American mountain-ash** (p. 157)
2b Leaflets usually 2–3 times as long as wide, more abruptly pointed, broadest near the middle; fruits 8–12 mm in diameter .... ***S. decora,* showy mountain-ash** (p. 158)

Key to the Cherries, Plums and Peaches (Genus *Prunus*)

1a Branches usually with rough thorns, not tipped with buds; leaves edged with prominent, outward-pointing teeth; fruits large, slightly oblong drupes (plums)............................. **2**

1b Branches lacking thorns, tipped with buds; leaves edged with very fine, oblique teeth; fruits smaller, round drupes (cherries) **5**

2a Flowers and fruits usually solitary; leaves widest above the middle; mature fruits dark blue to almost black.. **3**

2b Flowers and fruits in round clusters of 2–5; leaves widest at or below the middle; mature fruits red to yellow, 2–3 cm long **4**

3a Branches unarmed or somewhat thorny; fruits 2–3 cm long, juicy and sweet .... *P. domestica*, **garden plum** (p. 152)

3b Branches rather thorny; leaves 2–4 cm long; fruits 1–1.5 cm long, inedible .... *P. spinosa*, **blackthorn** (p. 152)

4a Leaf teeth sharp, not gland-tipped; sepals without glands; buds reddish-brown .... *P. nigra*, **Canada plum** (p. 151)

4b Leaf teeth rounded, some usually gland-tipped; sepals edged with gland-tipped teeth; buds blackish .... *P. americana*, **American plum** (p. 150)

5a Flowers and fruits in elongated clusters **6**

5b Flowers and fruits in small, rounded, usually tassel-like clusters **8**

6a Flowers with elliptic, 6–10 mm long petals, borne on long (1–1.5 cm) stalks; fruits 6–8 mm across, with a sculpted stone, inedible; introduced species .... *P. padus*, **European bird cherry** (p. 145)

6b Flowers with rounded, <5 mm long petals, borne on short (5–8 mm) stalks; fruits 8–10 mm across, with a smooth stone, edible; native species **7**

7a Leaves leathery, edged with incurved teeth, brownish-hairy beneath along the midvein; sepals pointed, usually longer than wide, smooth-edged or with inconspicuous, irregular, gland-tipped teeth, persisting at the base of the fruit .... *P. serotina*, **wild black cherry** (p. 144)

7b Leaves thinner (not leathery), edged with straight teeth, hairless beneath; sepals blunt, usually wider than long, conspicuously glandular-toothed, soon shed .... *P. virginiana*, **chokecherry** (p. 145)

8a Flowers and fruits stalkless, usually single or paired **9**

8b Flowers and fruits distinctly stalked **10**

9a Fruit a peach, up to 10 cm across; leaves hairless, lance-shaped to oblong-lance-shaped, up to 20 cm long; flowers pink, up to 5 cm across .... *P. persica*, **peach** (p. 147)

9b Fruit a slightly hairy cherry; leaves woolly beneath, oval to egg-shaped, widest at or above the middle, less than 7 cm long; flowers white or pink, up to 2 cm across .... *P. tomentosa*, **Manchu cherry** (p. 147)

10a Flowers rarely >1.5 cm across, petals 4–7.5 mm long; fruits <1 cm in diameter. **11**
10b Flowers 2–3 cm across, petals 9–15 mm long; fruits 1.5–2.5 cm in diameter **12**

11a Flower and fruit clusters tassel-like, naked at the base (without leafy bracts); petals hairy beneath; cherries bright red; leaf blades usually more than twice as long as wide
. . . . *P. pensylvanica,* **pin cherry** (p. 146)
11b Flower and fruit clusters with a short, branched central stalk, leafy-bracted at the base; petals hairless; cherries nearly black; leaf blades less than 1.5 times as long as wide
. . . . *P. mahaleb,* **mahaleb cherry** (p. 147)

12a Leaves soft and rather droopy, somewhat hairy beneath; calyx lobes smooth-edged, constricted below the base; mature leaves hairy beneath on the midvein, with glands on the stalk just below the 6–12 cm long blade; fruit sweet . . . . *P. avium,* **sweet cherry** (p. 148)
12b Leaves firm, ascending, hairless; calyx lobes glandular-toothed, not constricted below the base; mature leaves hairless, with glands on the edges of the 4–9 cm long blade (not on the stalk); fruit sour. . . . . *P. cerasus,* **sour cherry** (p. 149)

Hawthorns (Genus *Crataegus*)

When it comes to taxonomic problems, few groups are thornier than the hawthorns. The shrubs and small trees in this large, complex group have been classified and reclassified over the years, with the number of named species in Ontario ranging from 91 (Sargent 1908) to 8 (Soper 1949). The most widely accepted treatment, which identified 39 'good' species in the province, resulted from a detailed, 6-year taxonomic study in the 1970s (Phipps and Muniyamma 1980). Even with such intensive work, many taxa still require further study, and revisions continue. For example, 7 of the species described by Phipps and Muniyamma (1980) are now included in other species according to the Integrated Taxonomic Information System of Agriculture and Agri-Food Canada (ITIS 2000). Similarly, 3 of Ontario's 22 rare hawthorns (*Crataegus dilatata, C. dissona* and *C. persimilis*), as determined by ONHIC, were not described as species by Phipps and Muniyamma (1980) (see p. 23 of the introduction for a full list of rare species).

Much of the confusion with the hawthorns stems from their tendency to hybridize, producing off-spring with intermediate characteristics, and from their ability to produce seed without fertilization (apomixis). Some species are relatively static and clearly defined, while others are highly variable and difficult to typify. Also, many species are very similar to one another and can only be distinguished when specimens are of excellent quality. In some cases, fruit may be necessary to correctly identify a species, while in others flower characteristics are most important. Trees without flowers or fruits often cannot be identified to species, even by experts.

Because of the identification difficulties associated with hawthorns, and the large number of taxa found in Ontario, not all species are discussed in detail in this guide. Instead, 16 of the most widely recognized species are described, representing 11 of Ontario's 14 series. A series is a set of very closely allied species. All 14 series can be distinguished using the following key, based on the work of Phipps and Muniyamma (1980).

Key to the Series of Ontario Hawthorns (Genus *Crataegus*)

1a Leaves deeply 3–7-lobed, with main veins extending to both the lobe notches and lobe tips; fruits containing 1 stone; anthers red
.... **Series Oxyacanthae** (*C. monogyna*, **oneseed hawthorn,** p. 160)
1b Leaves toothed or shallowly lobed, with main veins extending to lobe or tooth tips only; fruits containing 2 or more stones; anthers usually white, pink or yellow **2**

2a Leaves 2–3 times as long as wide, narrowly wedge-shaped at the base, finely toothed and some- times also shallowly lobed; thorns long and slender **3**
2b Combination of leaves and thorns not as above **4**

3a Leaves glossy dark green, finely toothed and only slightly lobed; flower clusters lacking dense hairs; fruits with 2–3 styles and stones
.... **Series Crus-galli** (*C. crus-galli*, **cockspur hawthorn,** p. 162)
3b Leaves dull to slightly glossy, regularly shallow-lobed; flower clusters with dense, short hairs; fruits with 3–5 styles and stones .... **Series Punctatae** (*C. punctata*, **dotted hawthorn,** p. 163)

4a Thorns relatively short (<3 cm); fruits blackish; stones with a cavity on the lower surface
.... **Series Douglasiannae** (*C. douglasii*, **black hawthorn,** p. 161)
4b Plants without the above combination of characteristics............................. **5**

5a Leaves relatively small (<4 cm long), about as wide as long (triangular, circular) or diamond- shaped, usually with distinct lobes, rarely broadest above midleaf and scarcely lobed; leaf stalks often with a few glands; flowers <1.5 cm across; thorns 4–8 cm long, thin when long; ripe fruits typically dull red, round and 8–10 mm across
.... **Series Rotundifoliae** (*C. chrysocarpa*, **fireberry hawthorn,** p. 165)
5b Leaves either clearly longer than wide, or if broad then >5 cm long when mature **6**

6a Mature fruits round, about 8–12 mm across, pink to mauve or crimson, coated with a waxy white bloom; green and ripe fruits often present; persistent sepals at the fruit tip strongly elevated
.... **Series Pruinosae** (*C. pruinosa*, **frosted hawthorn,** p. 167)
6b Mature fruits red, without a waxy white bloom, or large (>1.5 cm) fruits occasionally with a bloom; persistent sepals only slightly elevated (if at all) **7**

7a Mature fruits at least 1 cm long, round to ellipsoidal; mature leaf blades broad (>5 cm long)... **8**
7b Mature fruits generally <1 cm long; mature leaf blades generally <5 cm long **10**

8a Flowers large (2.2–2.8 cm across); fruits large (>1.5 cm), with a whitish waxy bloom
.... **Series Dilatatae** (rare, not described in this guide)
8b Flowers smaller; fruits without a waxy bloom **9**

9a Mature leaves firm, with stout stalks and hairy lower leaf surfaces; anthers whitish, on relatively short stalks (filaments); thorns relatively slender
.... **Series Molles** (*C. mollis*, **downy hawthorn,** p. 168)
9b Mature leaves relatively thin, with slender stalks and essentially hairless lower leaf surfaces; anthers pink to red, on relatively large stalks (filaments); thorns relatively stout
.... **Series Coccineae** (*C. pedicellata*, **scarlet hawthorn,** p. 167)

10a Fruit stones with cavities on the lower side; leaves hairy beneath; thorns stout or absent; young growth with conspicuous coral-red buds; flowers clusters densely hairy; fruits glossy scarlet, often succulent . . . . **Series Macracanthae (*C. succulenta*, fleshy hawthorn,** p. 164)
10b Plants without the above combination of characteristics **11**

11a Shrubs extremely thorny, with many stout thorns; ripe fruits usually bright red and rather dry; leaves thin **12**
11b Shrubs moderately thorny; ripe fruits usually dull red, sometimes more or less succulent; leaves various **13**

12a Flower clusters clearly bracted when the flowers mature; sepals edged with glandular teeth; leaves elliptic; thorns often long and slender
. . . . **Series Intricatae** (presence questionable; not described in this guide)
12b Flower clusters with few noticeable bracts when the flowers mature; sepals usually smooth-edged; leaves elliptic to triangular-egg-shaped; thorns stout, of various lengths
. . . . **Series Tenuifoliae (*C. flabellata*, fanleaf hawthorn,** p. 166)

13a Leaf blades firm, elliptic to egg-shaped; thorns stout; fruit stones with a central cavity
. . . . **Series Brainerdianae (*C. brainerdii*, Brainerd hawthorn,** p. 165)
13b Leaf blades thin, diamond-shaped, sometimes as wide as long; thorns slender; fruit stones lacking a central cavity . . . . **Series Suborbiculatae** (rare species; not described in this guide)

Key to the Apples and Crabapples (Genus *Malus*)

1a Flowers brightly rose-coloured (fading to white) with red anthers; leaves pleated lengthwise in bud, sharply toothed and often more or less lobed when mature, soon hairless; native species
. . . . **M. coronaria, wild crabapple** (p. 154)
1b Flowers whitish or pinkish with yellow anthers; leaves expanding from down-rolled edges, never lobed; introduced species **2**

2a Leaves blunt-toothed, rounded or notched at the base, more or less woolly beneath; leaf stalks, young twigs and calyx lobes woolly; apples 6–12 cm in diameter
. . . . **M. pumila, common apple** (p. 156)
2b Leaves sharp-toothed, wedge-shaped at the base, nearly hairless beneath; leaf stalks, young twigs and calyx lobes soon hairless; crabapples about 1 cm in diameter
. . . . **M. baccata, Siberian crabapple** (p. 155)

Crataegus cultivar   *Malus pumila*, common apple   143

WILD BLACK CHERRY wood is easily worked and polishes beautifully. It is considered equal in quality to black walnut, with a rich, red colour similar to mahogany. Black cherry was once very popular in furniture and in frames for engravings and etchings. It has also been used in cabinets, panelling, veneers, interior trim, musical instruments and tool handles. Because of its early popularity, this tree is now scarce throughout its range. • In 1629, wild black cherry became one of the first trees introduced to English horticulture from North America. • Wild black cherry fruits can be eaten raw or used in jelly, syrup, wine, juice and pies. • The leaves and inner bark were once used in tonics, sedatives and cough syrups. **Caution:** All parts of this tree except the cherry flesh contain hydrocyanic acid. Wilted leaves have poisoned cattle, and children have died from chewing on twigs. • The cherries provide food for many game birds, songbirds and small mammals. Chipmunks and deer mice cache the pits (which are poisonous to us). White-tailed deer eat the fresh green leaves in spring but may be poisoned by wilted leaves in autumn.

ALSO CALLED: Black chokecherry, rum cherry, cabinet cherry, timber cherry, wine cherry

FRENCH NAMES: Cerisier tardif, cerisier noir, cerisier d'automne

SIZE AND SHAPE: Trees or tall shrubs 20–30 m tall; crowns rounded.

TRUNKS: Straight, 30–100 cm in diameter; young bark dark reddish-brown to almost black, smooth, with conspicuous pores (lenticels); mature bark rough with **outcurved, squared scales,** reddish-brown beneath; wood reddish-brown, fine-grained, hard.

BRANCHES: Arched with drooping tips; twigs slender, reddish-brown, smelly when broken; **buds chestnut-brown, often greenish-tinged,** 3–4 mm long, pointing outwards slightly.

LEAVES: Alternate, simple, deciduous; **blades thick, waxy dark green above,** paler beneath with **fine, white (eventually rusty) hairs on each side of the lower midvein,** 5–15 cm long, widest near midleaf and tapered to both ends, edged with incurved teeth.

FLOWERS: White, cupped, on 5 mm stalks, bisexual; petals 5, sepals 5; flowers hanging from the tips of short, new, leafy shoots, forming narrow, elongated, 10–15 cm clusters in May (as the leaves expand fully).

FRUITS: **Reddish to blackish cherries** (drupes) with dark purple flesh, juicy, 8–10 mm across, **with persistent sepals at the base;** seeds single, within a 6–8 mm stone; cherries hang in elongated clusters of 6–12, ripen August–September.

HABITAT: Open woodlands on rocky terrain; various disturbed sites, e.g., burned or logged areas.

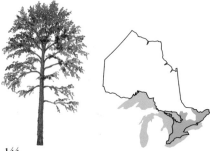

CHOKECHERRY fruits are edible raw, but even fully ripe fruits are rather astringent. Green chokecherries cause severe puckering and even choking, hence the common name. Usually, chokecherries are cooked and used to prepare jellies (especially mixed with apples), sauces, preserves and wines. • Native peoples and settlers used chokecherry bark and roots to make sedatives, blood-fortifying tonics, appetite stimulants and medicinal teas for treating coughs, tuberculosis, malaria, stomachaches and intestinal worms. • **Caution:** All parts of this tree except the cherry flesh contain the toxin hydrocyanic acid. • Chokecherry grows prolifically from sprouting stumps and root suckers. This fast-growing, light-loving, short-lived tree quickly invades logged land, abandoned farms and exposed streambanks, stabilizing soil and reducing erosion. • Game birds and more than 25 species of songbirds eat and disperse chokecherries. • **European bird cherry (P. padus)** is a small, introduced tree similar to chokecherry but distinguished by larger (6–10 mm) petals, longer (10–15 mm) flower stalks and smaller (6–8 mm), inedible fruits with sculpted stones. European bird cherry occasionally grows wild in the Ottawa-Carleton and York regions and in Wellington County.

Photo, bottom right: *P. padus*

ALSO CALLED: Eastern chokecherry, Virginia chokecherry, chuckley-plum, common chokecherry, red chokecherry, sloetree, wild cherry

FRENCH NAMES: Cerisier de Virginie, cerisier à grappes, cerisier, cerisier sauvage

SIZE AND SHAPE: Trees or tall shrubs 4–10 m tall, **often forming thickets;** crowns rounded.

TRUNKS: Often twisted and/or inclined, 5–10 cm in diameter; **bark dark grey-brown,** smooth or finely scaly, with prominent lenticels; wood light brown, fine-grained, hard, heavy.

BRANCHES: Slender, ascending; twigs smooth, reddish- to greyish-brown, **strong-smelling** when crushed; buds 3–4 mm long, **dark brown with pale-edged scales.**

LEAVES: Alternate, simple, deciduous; blades deep green above, paler beneath, thin, usually **widest at or above midleaf, abruptly sharp-pointed,** 4–12 cm long, **edged with small, slender, sharp teeth;** stalks with 1 to several glands near the blade.

FLOWERS: Small, white, saucer-shaped, on 5–8 mm stalks, bisexual; petals 5, round, 4 mm long; sepals 5; flowers in **cylindrical, 5–15 cm long clusters** of 10–25, **hanging from the tips of short new leafy shoots** in May–June **(before the leaves expand fully).**

FRUITS: Shiny, yellow to **deep red or black cherries** (drupes) 8–10 mm across, with tiny persistent sepals at the base; seeds single, within a stone; cherries hang in **elongated clusters,** ripen August–September.

HABITAT: Exposed areas and open woodlands, on substrates ranging from rich soil to rock.

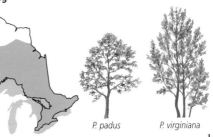

P. padus   *P. virginiana*

PIN CHERRY wood is seldom used, except as firewood. • The little cherries are edible but sour. Mashed and strained, they make excellent jellies and cold drinks. • **Caution:** The leaves, bark and stones are toxic. • Pin cherry can live about 40 years, and once mature it usually produces abundant fruit each year. The stones remain viable for decades on the ground, waiting for the proper conditions (fluctuating temperatures and light exposure) to trigger germination. • This attractive shrub is sometimes planted as an ornamental, but it spreads quickly via suckers from underground runners. Because of this tendency, pin cherry is sometimes planted to stabilize soil. After fire, the shrub grows rapidly, reducing erosion and improving conditions for the establishment of other species. It soon disappears under a forest canopy. • The heavy, succulent fruits depend on animals (mainly birds) for dispersal and propagation. The name 'bird cherry' refers to the popularity of the fruits among songbirds. • The clusters of small, round, shiny fruits have been likened to clusters of glass-headed pins stuck into a pincushion, hence the name 'pin cherry.'

ALSO CALLED: Bird cherry, fire cherry, wild red cherry, hay cherry, pigeon cherry

FRENCH NAMES: Cerisier de Pennsylvanie, cerises d'été, petit merisier, arbre à petites merises

SIZE AND SHAPE: Small trees or tall shrubs up to 12 m tall; crowns narrow, rounded.

TRUNKS: Straight, up to 25 cm in diameter; **mature bark shiny reddish-brown,** smooth, peeling in thin horizontal strips, with **conspicuous, orange-powdered, horizontal pores** (lenticels); wood light brown, soft, porous.

BRANCHES: Ascending when young, horizontal with age; twigs reddish, slender, sour-smelling when bruised or broken; **buds 1–2 mm long,** rounded, **several clustered at twig tips.**

LEAVES: Alternate, simple, deciduous; blades shiny green, hairless, thin, **lance-shaped,** slender-pointed, rounded at the base, 4–15 cm long, edged with **tiny, uneven teeth;** stalks with **glands near the blade;** leaves turn purplish-red in autumn.

FLOWERS: White, about 1 cm across, on 1–2 cm stalks, bisexual; petals 5, round, 5–7 mm long, **hairy at the base;** sepals 5; flowers borne in tassel-like clusters (umbels) of 2–7 in spring (as the leaves expand).

FRUITS: Bright red cherries (drupes), **6–8 mm** in diameter, hanging on slender stalks in **small, flat-topped clusters;** seeds single, within a round stone; cherries ripen July–September.

HABITAT: Open woodlands or recently disturbed sites; often abundant.

THE PEACH has been cultivated since ancient times for its sweet, juicy fruits. Many varieties have been developed, including the freestone peach, favoured for its thick fruits with flesh that separates readily from the stone. Clingstone peach fruits do not separate readily, but the firmer flesh makes excellent preserves. Nectarines have hairless, usually smaller fruits. Some peaches are planted for their flowers, and various cultivars have single or double corollas in colours ranging from red to white. • The heavy fruits limit dispersal, but wild peach trees occasionally spring up from discarded pits near roads, trails and rivers. • Many *Prunus* species have been brought to Canada, and some occasionally escape from cultivation in southern Ontario. **Mahaleb cherry** or perfumed cherry *(P. mahaleb)* is usually cultivated for its prolific, fragrant flowers and dark red, aromatic wood. Mahaleb cherry resembles pin cherry (p. 146) but is distinguished by its relatively broad leaves, hairless petals and deep red to black fruits. Like peach, **Manchu cherry** or Nanking cherry *(P. tomentosa)* is a small, spreading tree with stalkless flowers and fruits and finely sharp-toothed leaves. However, peach leaves are hairless, whereas Manchu cherry leaves are woolly underneath.

FRENCH NAME: Pêche

SIZE AND SHAPE: Small, spreading trees up to 10 m tall; crowns broad and rounded.

TRUNKS: Short, often crooked, up to 30 cm in diameter, usually marked with horizontal streaks; bark dark reddish-brown, smooth at first, rough with age.

BRANCHES: Spreading; twigs green to dark reddish-brown, smooth, long, slender, with short spur-shoots.

LEAVES: Alternate, simple, deciduous; blades shiny green, paler beneath, **8–15 cm long, lance-shaped,** slender-pointed, rounded to wedge-shaped at the base, finely saw-toothed, **often with sides upcurved from the midvein;** stalks short, with small glands near the blade.

FLOWERS: Usually **pink, 2.5–3.5 cm across,** bisexual; petals 5, rounded; sepals 5; **flowers single** (sometimes paired), appear in April-May **(before the leaves expand).**

FRUITS: Velvety, yellowish to pink peaches (drupes), round, slightly grooved, up to 10 cm across and soft-fleshed in cultivation, **5–7.5 cm across** and harder in the wild; seeds single, within a somewhat flattened, **deeply sculpted stone;** fruits single on **very short stalks,** mature in summer.

HABITAT: Open, often disturbed sites on roadsides, in thickets and near abandoned homes.

DISTRIBUTION: Introduced from Eurasia; grows wild in Essex County and the Niagara Regional Municipality.

SWEET CHERRY has large and luscious fruits—the common, commercially available cherries. This popular *Prunus* has been cultivated in North America for over a century, and many varieties are grown in orchards in warm parts of Canada. The cherries are larger and sweeter and keep longer than those of most other species. They are delicious fresh from the tree. • The strong, hard wood takes a polish well. In Europe, it has been used in interior finishing and for making furniture, musical instruments and small household items. • Unlike many other cherries, sweet cherry does not produce suckers. • Sweet cherry is one of the most common domestic cherries growing wild in Ontario. Next to humans, birds are its most important dispersal agent. Many birds, including grouse, thrashers, robins and cedar waxwings, enjoy eating the cherries. When ripe fruits hang on the trees, farmers face a never-ending battle with the persistent winged bandits. At other times of the year, white-tailed deer and rabbits can damage trees by eating the leaves and twigs. • The epithet, *avium,* from the Latin *avis* or 'bird,' refers to the popularity of the fruits among birds. • 'Bing cherry' is the name for the most widely grown cultivar of sweet cherry. It was developed in 1875 by Ah Bing, a Chinese nursery worker in Oregon.

ALSO CALLED: Mazzard cherry, gean, Bing cherry

FRENCH NAMES: Cerisier sauvage, cerisier de France

SIZE AND SHAPE: Trees up to 20 m tall; crowns cylindrical to pyramidal.

TRUNKS: Tall and reaching 60–90 cm in diameter in the wild, shorter and smaller in orchards; bark reddish-brown, smooth, with conspicuous horizontal pores (lenticels), sometimes peeling; wood yellowish-red, strong.

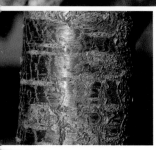

BRANCHES: Stout, spreading; twigs reddish-brown under a greyish film, smooth; buds shiny brown, some **clustered at tips of short spur-shoots.**

LEAVES: Alternate, simple, deciduous; blades dull dark green above, paler and **hairy on veins beneath, 6–12 cm long,** widest above midleaf, pointed, with sharp, gland-tipped double teeth; **stalks 2–4 cm long, with 2 glands near the blade.**

FLOWERS: White, 2–3 cm across, bisexual; petals 5; sepals 5, **hairless;** flowers in small, **tassel-like clusters** (umbels) of 1–5 on leafy spur-shoots in May (before or as the leaves expand).

FRUITS: Dark red to almost black (sometimes yellow), fleshy **cherries** (drupes), **round to heart-shaped, 1.5–2.5 cm across;** seeds single, within round stones; cherries hang on slender, 2–3 cm stalks in small, flat-topped clusters on spur-shoots; ripen June–July.

HABITAT: Open, often disturbed sites along fence lines and roads and in woods.

DISTRIBUTION: Introduced from Asia Minor; grows wild in southern Ontario, especially in the Niagara Regional Municipality.

SOUR CHERRY is widely grown in orchards in mild regions of Canada. Some double-flowered cultivars are grown as ornamentals, but usually this species is cultivated for the fruit. The tart, juicy cherries are sweetened and baked in pies and cakes; mashed and boiled to make jams and jellies; or canned in syrup. • Sour cherry can reproduce vegetatively by sending up numerous shoots (suckers) from underground runners. However, it usually escapes cultivation and spreads to new regions as seeds. Birds often swallow the hard, protective stones and deposit them, undigested, in new sites.

• Game birds, songbirds, raccoons and foxes all eat the cherries, and rabbits and white-tailed deer browse on the leaves and twigs. • The specific epithet, *cerasus,* is a Greek word meaning 'cherry tree.' It is also the name of the town, Cerasus of Pontus, in the region where this cherry originated. • Sour cherry could be confused with sweet cherry (p. 148), but sweet cherry leaves have hairs on the underside of the veins, and glands on the stalks just below the blades. Also, sweet cherry fruits are larger, sweeter and more deeply coloured.

ALSO CALLED: Pie cherry, mazzard cherry, morello cherry
FRENCH NAME: Cerisier aigre
SIZE AND SHAPE: Small trees up to 10 m tall; crowns usually broadly rounded.
TRUNKS: Short, soon branched; bark greyish.
BRANCHES: Stout; twigs with stubby spur-shoots; buds shiny reddish-brown, some clustered at the tips of short spur-shoots, pointing outwards.
LEAVES: Alternate, simple, deciduous; **blades dark green, lustrous, hairless beneath** (when mature), firm, elliptical to ovate and widest above the middle, **4–9 cm long, tipped with a blunt point,** edged with **double or single, rounded teeth** and with a **gland on the blade near the stalk;** stalks usually less than 2 cm long, lacking glands.

FLOWERS: White, 2–3 cm across, bisexual; petals 5; sepals 5, **hairless;** flowers borne in small, flat-topped clusters of 2–5 at tips of leafy spur-shoots, in May (before or as the leaves expand).
FRUITS: Bright red cherries (drupes), juicy, round, **1–2 cm across;** seeds single, within a round stone; cherries borne in small, flat-topped clusters at the tips of leafy spur-shoots; ripen in July.
HABITAT: Open, often disturbed sites such as fence lines, roadsides and woodland borders.
DISTRIBUTION: Introduced from southern Europe, but probably from Asia Minor originally; grows wild in southern Ontario.

American Plum
Prunus americana

Rose Family

AMERICAN PLUM wood is hard and attractive but is not commercially valuable because of the tree's small size. • American plum is widely planted as an ornamental across Canada, frequently in regions outside its natural range. This small, attractive tree grows quickly but doesn't live long. It has been cultivated in orchards, parks and gardens for its beautiful, fragrant flowers and edible fruits. Hundreds of large-flowered cultivars have been developed. • The fruits have tough, sour outer skins, but their sweet, juicy flesh is delicious, making excellent jams, jellies, preserves and pies. The plums can also be halved, then pitted and dried like prunes; or puréed, spread in a thin sheet and dried as fruit leather. • **Caution:** All parts of this tree, except the flesh and skin of the plums, contain the toxin hydrocyanic acid. • This small tree or tall shrub often spreads from the roots, sending up suckers to form dense thickets. Along streams, the plants help stabilize the banks and reduce erosion. • White-tailed deer, black bears (historically), foxes, raccoons, squirrels and many birds eat American plum fruits and disperse the seeds.

ALSO CALLED: Wild plum, brown plum, red plum, yellow plum

FRENCH NAMES: Prunier d'Amérique, guignier, prunier de la Gallissonnière, prunier sauvage

SIZE AND SHAPE: Trees or shrubs 6–10 m tall, often forming thickets; crowns broad.

TRUNKS: Short, 12–20 cm in diameter; young bark smooth, with horizontal pores (lenticels); mature bark reddish-brown to grey-brown or nearly black, rough with plates; wood reddish-brown, hard, strong.

BRANCHES: Spreading, somewhat **thorny** with

spine-like dwarf twigs; twigs reddish- to greyish-brown, with a **bitter almond flavour;** buds greyish, 3–8 mm long, with 2-coloured, chestnut to greyish-brown scales.

LEAVES: Alternate, simple, deciduous; blades dark green above, paler beneath, oval, 4–12 cm long, edged with **fine, sharp, slender-pointed teeth** often tipped with a callus or bristle (not a gland); stalks often with 2 glands near the blade.

FLOWERS: White, 1.5–2.5 cm across, saucer-shaped, very fragrant, on 1–2.5 cm long stalks, bisexual; petals 5, 1–1.5 cm long; flowers borne in flat-topped clusters of 2–4 in late April to early June **(before or as the leaves expand).**

FRUITS: Yellow to red plums (drupes) with a thin, waxy bloom, 2–3 cm long, yellow-fleshed; seeds single, within a flattened stone; plums single or 2–4 together, mature in August–September.

HABITAT: Rocky or sandy soils in moist woods and along streams, roads and fence lines; not common.

CANADA PLUM is often planted as an ornamental for its beautiful, fragrant spring blossoms and its attractive, edible fruit. The cultivar 'Princess Kay' has showy double flowers. • The skins of the plums are usually tough and astringent, and the flesh can also be very sour, especially when still firm. After the first frosts, the fruits become soft and juicy. They can be eaten fresh, stewed to make jelly or jam, puréed to make juice or baked in pies.
• **Caution:** Children have died from eating too many plums without removing the stones. As with other plums, all parts of this tree (except the skin and flesh of the fruits) contain the toxin hydrocyanic acid. • Canada plum seems to prefer basic soils, but it is not restricted to calcareous regions. • White-tailed deer, black bears, foxes, bobcats, raccoons, muskrats, squirrels, small rodents and large birds all feed on the succulent fruits.
• Plum trees often harbour an aphid that is deadly to potatoes, so gardeners avoid planting plums and potatoes together.
• The specific epithet, *nigra*, means 'black' and refers to the dark, almost black bark of the branches.

ALSO CALLED: Red plum, black plum, wild plum, horse plum

FRENCH NAMES: Prunier noir, prunier sauvage, guignier, prunier canadien

SIZE AND SHAPE: Straggly trees or tall shrubs 6–10 m tall, usually forming thickets; crowns irregular, flat-topped.

TRUNKS: Short, 12–25 cm in diameter, often clumped; young bark dark reddish-brown to blackish with grey horizontal pores (lenticels), soon splitting and curling; mature bark grey-brown, rough with outcurved scales; wood rich reddish-brown, heavy, hard, fine-grained.

BRANCHES: Upright, crooked and somewhat **thorny** with spine-like dwarf twigs; twigs reddish-brown, **bitter almond–flavoured;** buds greyish-brown, 4–8 mm long.

LEAVES: Alternate, simple, deciduous; **blades dark, dull green above,** paler beneath, broadly oval, 6–14 cm long, abruptly slender-pointed, thin, with **rounded, mostly gland-tipped, double teeth; stalks stout, with 1–2 large, dark glands** near the blade.

FLOWERS: White, turning pinkish, saucer-shaped, 1.5–3 cm across, fragrant, on reddish, 1–2 cm stalks, bisexual; petals 5; sepals 5; flowers borne on year-old twigs in flat-topped clusters of 2–4 in late April to early June **(before or as the leaves expand).**

FRUITS: Red, scarlet or yellow plums (drupes) **without a waxy bloom,** 2.5–3 cm long, thick-skinned, yellow-fleshed; seeds single, within flattened stones 2–2.5 cm long; plums single or 2–4-clustered, ripen August–September.

HABITAT: Common in moist, open woodlands, thickets and pastures and along fence lines.

PLUM WOOD is hard and takes a polish well. In Europe, it has been used to make cabinets and musical instruments. • The garden plum has been cultivated in Eurasia for many years. British and French settlers brought it to North America, and it is now widely grown as a fruit tree in Canada. Many varieties with improved fruits have been developed. Cultivars with showy, double (10-petalled) flowers are planted as ornamentals in parks and gardens. • The ripe plums are delicious fresh from the tree. They also make excellent jams, preserves, pies and fruit leather. The prunes commonly available in grocery stores are made from these large, firm, readily dried plums. • **Blackthorn** or sloe *(P. spinosa)* is another introduced shrub that occasionally escapes cultivation in Ontario. It was brought to North America from Europe and northern Asia for planting as an ornamental and in hedgerows. Blackthorn grows wild in Essex County and Waterloo Regional Municipality. It is very similar to the garden plum, but blackthorn is a smaller, spinier tree with smaller (2–4 cm) leaves and smaller (1–1.5 cm), inedible fruits. Blackthorn fruits have been used to flavour and colour gin.

ALSO CALLED: European plum, Damson plum

FRENCH NAMES: Bullace, prunier de l'Islet

SIZE AND SHAPE: Bushy small trees or tall shrubs to 8 m tall, usually forming thickets; crowns rounded, open.

TRUNKS: Short, up to 30 cm in diameter; mature bark greyish to almost black; wood reddish-brown, hard, fine-grained.

BRANCHES: Many, usually **thorny** with spine-like dwarf twigs; twigs reddish, often hairy.

LEAVES: Alternate, simple, deciduous; blades dark green above, **paler, prominently veined and hairy beneath,** oval, rounded to broadly pointed at the tip, 4–7 cm long, **thick, edged with coarse, irregular saw-teeth.**

FLOWERS: White, saucer-shaped, 2–2.5 cm across, bisexual; petals 5; sepals 5; flowers borne **singly or in pairs** (sometimes 3s), in early spring.

FRUITS: Dark blue to near black plums (drupes), somewhat egg-shaped, 2–3 cm long, juicy; seeds single, within a large stone; plums mature in late summer.

HABITAT: Roadsides, fence lines, old orchards.

DISTRIBUTION: Introduced from Europe and western Asia; rarely grows wild in southern Ontario.

COMMON PEAR wood is very hard and fine-grained. It has been used to make drawing instruments, rulers, tool handles, carvings and wood engravings. It also makes excellent fuel. • For centuries, people have used and propagated pears. Today, cultivars developed from the original Eurasian species are grown in many parts of North America. Usually, the trees are heavily pruned to improve fruit production and make harvesting easier, so they rarely reach their full height. • This long-lived, slow-growing tree produces fruit each year, but heavy crops are often followed by a year with low production. Common pear can reproduce by sending up shoots (suckers) from underground runners, sometimes creating dense thickets in abandoned farmyards or orchards. • Small mammals, deer and cattle eat the fruit, especially when it has ripened and fallen to the ground. Pear seeds are dispersed via animal droppings and discarded pear cores. • Like their domestic counterparts, wild-growing pear trees have edible fruits, but the fruits are usually smaller (less than 6 cm long), inconspicuous, drier and grittier. • Some taxonomists have classified the pears (*Pyrus* spp.), apples (*Malus* spp.) and mountain-ashes (*Sorbus* spp.) together as species of the genus *Pyrus*.

FRENCH NAME: Poirier commun

SIZE AND SHAPE: Trees or shrubs to 15 m tall; crowns round to cylindrical.

TRUNKS: Straight, up to 30 cm in diameter; mature bark dark brown to blackish, with small, squared scales; wood reddish-brown, fine-grained.

BRANCHES: Short, stout, ascending, often with **spine-like spur-shoots;** twigs reddish-brown to olive-brown, with yellow pores (lenticels); buds chestnut-brown to greyish, hairy.

LEAVES: Alternate, simple, deciduous; **blades thick and leathery,** shiny dark green above, paler beneath, sharp-pointed, rounded at the base, 3–8 cm long, finely blunt-toothed, **twisted in bud; stalks often equal to or longer than blade;** leaves yellow in autumn.

FLOWERS: Showy, fragrant, pink fading to white, about 2.5–3.5 cm wide, bisexual; sepals hairy; **anthers 20–30, purple;** flowers in flat-topped clusters on spur-shoots in early spring (as the leaves expand).

FRUITS: Fleshy pomes (pears) with gritty stone cells in the pulp, firm at first, juicy when ripe, **widest towards the tip, tapered to the base** (stalk), 2–12 cm long; seeds in leathery chambers in a core; fruits hang near branch tips when ripe in autumn.

HABITAT: Fields, fence lines, disturbed sites and woodland edges.

DISTRIBUTION: Introduced from Eurasia; occasionally grows wild in southern Ontario.

CRABAPPLE WOOD has been used to make tool handles, spear and harpoon shafts and even some of the working parts in gristmills. Interesting patterns and colours in the wood are exploited in carvings and furniture. Crabapple wood has also been used as firewood. • This slow-growing, short-lived tree is sometimes cultivated for its showy flowers, spicy fragrance and dense growth form. Although it produces only small fruit, wild crabapple is very hardy, so the trunks are used as stocks for grafting more productive but less hardy apple varieties. • Wild crabapple fruits are edible but sour, so they are usually cooked and sweetened to reduce their tartness. The small apples are rich in pectin and make excellent jelly; they are often mixed with other fruits that are low in pectin, to improve jelling. They also give a special scent to preserves. Wild crabapple cider is delicious. • Native peoples stored these crabapples to use through the winter, and they made syrup or cider from leftover apples in spring. • Grosbeaks, white-tailed deer and skunks feed on the fruits. Many songbirds nest and roost in the trees, sheltering in the dense, leafy branches.

Photo, centre left: *M. coronaria* cultivar

ALSO CALLED: Sweet crabapple, American crabapple, garland-tree • *Pyrus coronaria*, *Malus glabrata*

FRENCH NAMES: Pommier odorant, pommettier, pommier coronaire, pommier sauvage

SIZE AND SHAPE: Small trees or tall shrubs 6–10 m tall, often forming thickets; crowns broad, irregular.

TRUNKS: Straight, 15–30 cm in diameter; mature bark grey to reddish-brown, scaly; wood hard, strong, flexible.

BRANCHES: Spreading, with **thorn-like spur-shoots;** twigs red-brown with flaky greyish skin, hairy at first; **buds bright red, hairy,** 2–4 mm long (3–5 mm at twig tips), flat-lying.

LEAVES: Alternate, simple, deciduous; blades shiny bright green above, paler beneath, **essentially hairless,** ovate to long-triangular, 3–10 cm long, rounded or notched at the base, **coarsely toothed at the tip to almost lobed at the base, folded lengthwise in bud.**

FLOWERS: Showy, delicate, fragrant, pink fading to white, 2–3 cm across, bisexual; **sepals hairless on the outer surface; anthers pinkish,** numerous; flowers in **clusters of 2–3 on leafy dwarf shoots** in late **May–June** (after the leaves expand).

FRUITS: Green to yellowish-green, **waxy pomes (apples), 2.5–3.5 cm across;** remain hard, mature by September–October and may persist through winter.

HABITAT: Along roadsides and fence lines, and in the understorey of deciduous woodlands.

MANY CULTIVARS of Siberian crabapple and other domestic crabapples have been developed. These small trees are widely planted as ornamentals for their spectacular, lightly fragrant flowers, attractive fruit and dense branches. The flowers may be single or double (with extra petals) and may have red, purple, pink or white petals. The abundant fruits often remain on the tree well into winter, providing food for birds. Fruits of white-flowered crabapples are said to be more brightly coloured than those of pink-flowered cultivars. Types with different leaf colours, ranging from green to bronze to deep wine red, are also available for landscaping. Most have a broad crown, but weeping and columnar forms have also been developed. • Siberian crabapple has been crossed with some apple species to produce hardier cultivars. • Crabapple fruits look tasty, but they are usually too tart and seedy for eating raw. They do, however, make lovely, deep red jelly, with a rich apple flavour and fragrance. • This small, hardy tree can live more than 100 years. Bud production for next year's blooms begins in early summer, so any pruning should be done soon after the tree finishes flowering in spring. • The specific epithet, *baccata*, means 'bearing berries.'

ALSO CALLED: Flowering crabapple • *Pyrus baccata*

FRENCH NAME: Pommier de Sibérie

SIZE AND SHAPE: Small, wide trees 6–10 m tall; crowns broadly domed.

TRUNKS: Short; wood hard, reddish-brown.

BRANCHES: Spreading; **twigs hairless**.

LEAVES: Alternate, simple, deciduous; blades lustrous green above, paler beneath, hairless when mature, 3–8 cm long, relatively narrow, pointed at the tip, rounded to wedge-shaped at the base, finely toothed; stalks hairless; leaf scars with 3 vein scars; leaves yellow in autumn.

FLOWERS: White, 2.5–3.5 cm across, bisexual; petals relatively narrow and widely spaced; sepals long and slender, hairless when mature, soon shed; anthers yellow; ovary single; flowers appear in showy, few-flowered clusters in April–May (as the leaves expand).

FRUITS: **Yellow or red pomes (apples) about 1 cm long, without tiny persistent sepals at the tip,** hairless when young; fruits hang on long, slender stalks, mature in autumn.

HABITAT: Fields, thickets, clearings and railways.

DISTRIBUTION: Introduced from Siberia and northern China; occasionally grows wild in southern Ontario.

Common Apple *Malus pumila*

Rose Family

APPLE WOOD is solid and fine-grained. It has been used to make furniture, bowls, tools and carvings. It also makes excellent firewood, and its sawdust is used for smoking meat. • Thousands of cultivars have been developed from the common apple and from Siberian crabapple (p. 155). Apple trees are usually propagated by grafting cuttings, because trees grown from seed often produce inferior fruit. The common apple was first cultivated in Greece, and by 1000 AD, at least 30 different varieties had been developed. • Apples are probably the most popular fruit in North America. They are delicious raw, stewed and baked. All apples are rich in pectin, so they make excellent jellies. They are also excellent sources of vitamin C, potassium, sodium and phosphorus. The skin is the most nutritious part. • **Caution:** The small seeds contain toxic compounds that can prove fatal in large quantities. • Some wild apple trees grow from seeds dispersed by birds and small mammals, but most probably originate from cores discarded by people. • The taxonomy of the common apple is confusing. Most of the scientific synonyms listed below are currently used in some European and/or North American floras. *M. sylvestris* now more commonly refers to the European crabapple.

ALSO CALLED: Wild apple, paradise apple • *M. sylvestris, M. domestica, M. communis, Pyrus pumila, P. malus*

FRENCH NAMES: Pommier sauvage d'Europe, pommier commun, pommier nain

SIZE AND SHAPE: Small, widely spreading trees, up to 15 m tall; crowns low, broadly domed.

TRUNKS: Short; mature bark dark brownish-grey with flaky plates; wood red-brown, hard.

BRANCHES: Spreading, **crooked,** with **stubby (not thorn-like) spur-shoots;** twigs and buds hairy.

LEAVES: Alternate, simple, deciduous; blades dark green above, **lightly to densely hairy beneath, untwisting** from bud, elliptic to ovate, 4–10 cm long, abruptly pointed, rounded at the base, edged with **fine, sharp teeth;** stalks hairy; leaves yellow in autumn.

FLOWERS: Showy, pink, fading white, 3 cm across, bisexual; **sepals hairy** on the outside; **anthers yellow,** numerous; flowers borne in small clusters on spur-shoots in spring (after the leaves expand).

FRUITS: Large (6–12 cm in diameter), green, yellow or red, juicy pomes **(apples),** indented at both ends, tipped with a cluster of tiny **persistent sepals;** seeds dark brown, shiny, in small leathery chambers in a core; apples mature and drop each autumn.

HABITAT: Along roadsides, in clearings and near the edges of woods.

DISTRIBUTION: Introduced from Eurasia; grows wild at scattered sites in southern Ontario north to eastern Lake Superior.

AMERICAN MOUNTAIN-ASH is a relatively slow-growing, short-lived tree that is sometimes cultivated for its attractive flowers, fruits and leaves. The moderately light, close-grained, weak wood has no commercial value. • The fruits (fresh or dried) contain iron and vitamin C. They are also acidic and rich in tannins, however, and should be eaten in moderation. Fruits gathered after the first frost are bittersweet and can be made into jelly, jam, marmalade or juice. Mountain-ash 'berries' have also been used to make wine and to flavour liqueurs. Some tribes dried the fruits and ground them into meal. • The fruits have mild laxative, diuretic, astringent and digestive effects, so they were sometimes eaten with hard-to-digest foods. The Algonquins prepared a mild stimulant by boiling American mountain-ash twigs, new white spruce twigs, wintergreen leaves and elderberry flowers. • Grouse, cedar waxwings, grosbeaks, thrushes, squirrels and bears feed on the fruits. • American mountain-ash could be confused with related species. The leaflets of showy mountain-ash (p. 158) are slightly wider, and its flowers appear about a week later. European mountain-ash (p. 159) has hair on its buds and leaf undersides.

ALSO CALLED: American rowan-tree, dogberry, catberry, pigberry, roundwood, rowanberry, service-tree • *Pyrus americana*

FRENCH NAMES: Sorbier d'Amérique, cormier, maska, maskouabina

SIZE AND SHAPE: Trees or shrubs 4–10 m tall; crowns open, **narrow, rounded.**

TRUNKS: Short, 10–20 cm in diameter; **young bark pale grey with horizontal pores** (lenticels), thin, smooth, fragrant; mature bark reddish-brown, slightly scaly; wood pale, soft.

BRANCHES: Spreading; twigs dark reddish-brown to grey, becoming **hairless;** buds dark, shiny, essentially **hairless, 1–1.3 cm long, gummy.**

LEAVES: Alternate, deciduous, **positioned on edge and arching; compound, pinnately divided into 11–17 leaflets;** leaflets dull green, paler beneath, thin, lance-shaped to narrowly oblong, **3–5 times as long as wide, taper-pointed, sharp-toothed, short-stalked,** 5–10 cm long, roughly paired; leaflets often drop before main stalk (rachis).

FLOWERS: White, tiny, bisexual; petals 5, widest above middle, 3–4 mm long; sepals 5, fused in bell-shaped calyxes; stamens 15–20, anthers yellow; flowers on hairless stalks in **showy, many-branched, flat-topped or rounded, 5–15 cm wide clusters** (corymbs) in June–July (after the leaves expand).

FRUITS: Bright orange-red, berry-like pomes (like tiny apples) with thin flesh, **4–6 mm across;** seeds shiny chestnut-brown, 1–2 per fruit; **fruits in branched clusters,** mature in August–September, **persist** through winter.

HABITAT: Moist, shady sites near swamps and lakes, on rocky hillsides and in thickets and coniferous forests.

157

SHOWY MOUNTAIN-ASH can be cultivated as an ornamental, but European mountain-ash (p. 159) is more widely used in landscaping. • Birds are the main dispersers of mountain-ashes. The fleshy fruits provide important winter food for many birds and small mammals, persisting on branches above the snow when other fruits are scarce. If both native and introduced mountain-ash species are available, birds apparently eat the fruit of the native species first. Rising populations of cedar waxwings in urban areas reflect the popularity of mountain-ashes in landscaping. Flocks of drunken birds are sometimes reported when the birds eat the small pomes after they have fermented. • The specific epithet, *decora,* 'handsome and comely,' refers to the showy fruits and flowers of this attractive tree. • Showy mountain-ash is so similar to American mountain-ash that it was once classified as a variety of that species. American mountain-ash is distinguished by its narrower leaflets and smaller fruits and flowers. Also, the flowers of American mountain-ash appear 10–12 days earlier. • At one time, Fernald and other taxonomists included the genera *Sorbus* and *Malus* in the genus *Pyrus.*

ALSO CALLED: Northern mountain-ash, dogberry, northern-ash dogberry, northern-ash, showy northern-ash • *Pyrus decora*

FRENCH NAMES: Sorbier décoratif, sorbier plaisant, sorbier des montagnes

SIZE AND SHAPE: Small trees or tall shrubs to 10 m tall; crowns short, rounded.

TRUNKS: Straight, 10–30 cm in diameter; **young bark light greyish-green to golden-brown with conspicuous, horizontal pores** (lenticels), thin, smooth; mature bark becoming slightly scaly; wood pale brown, close-grained, moderately light, soft, weak.

BRANCHES: Coarse, ascending; twigs reddish-brown to greyish, **thin-skinned,** hairless; buds dark reddish-brown, gummy, 1–1.4 cm long, with **hairy-edged inner scales.**

LEAVES: Alternate, deciduous, **horizontal,** 10–25 cm long; **compound, pinnately divided into 13–17 leaflets** sub-opposite on a central stalk (rachis); **leaflets bluish-green, paler beneath, firm,** hairless with age, **oblong to oblong-elliptic, 2–3 times longer than wide,** blunt or **abruptly short-pointed, finely sharp-toothed,** 3–8 cm long; leaflets often drop before rachis.

FLOWERS: White, tiny, bisexual; petals 5, round, 4–5 mm long; sepals 5, tiny; stamens 15–20, anthers yellow; flowers numerous, on short, stout, hairy stalks in **dense, 6–15 cm wide, many-branched clusters** (corymbs) in June–July (after the leaves expand).

FRUITS: Shiny, orange-red, berry-like pomes (like small apples), thick-fleshed, **8–12 mm across;** seeds 1–2 per fruit, shiny, dark; fruits hang in **showy clusters** in August–September, persist over winter.

HABITAT: Rocky shores of lakes and streams.

THIS FAST-GROWING ORNAMENTAL is widely planted in gardens and parks and along streets in Ontario. • The wood of European mountain-ash is relatively hard. It has been used for tool handles, spinning wheels and other wooden products. • Birds frequently carry mountain-ash seeds to new sites, and the trees can become pests in natural habitats near our towns and cities. • In Scandinavia, the bitter-tasting fruits were used, fresh or dried, to flavour sauces and game (especially fowl). The vitamin C–rich 'berries' can be used to make delicious jellies. They have also been used in herbal remedies for diarrhea, hemorrhoids, scurvy and other ailments. • Scottish Highlanders planted this tree beside their homes for protection from witchcraft. • The generic name, *Sorbus,* was the classical Latin name for European mountain-ashes. The specific epithet, *aucuparia,* means 'I catch birds' and refers to the bird-attracting fruits. European bird catchers often planted this tree to lure prey. The alternative common name 'rowan-tree' comes from an old Scandinavian word meaning 'red,' in reference to the brilliant red fruits. • European mountain-ash is distinguished from native mountain-ashes by its hairier young twigs, its downy-white, non-sticky buds and its smaller, hairier leaves.

ALSO CALLED: Rowan-tree, dogberry

FRENCH NAME: Sorbier des oiseleurs

SIZE AND SHAPE: Trees or tall shrubs up to 15 m tall; crowns open, rounded.

TRUNKS: Short, up to about 50 cm in diameter; **young bark shiny grey-brown with elongated, horizontal pores** (lenticels), thin, smooth; mature bark scaly; wood pale brown, fine-grained, hard.

BRANCHES: Coarse, spreading; twigs greyish, shiny, **hairy when young;** buds dark purple, **white-woolly,** 9–12 mm long, **not gummy.**

LEAVES: Alternate, deciduous; **compound, pinnately divided into 9–17 sub-opposite leaflets** on a central stalk (rachis); leaflets green above, whitish and **hairy beneath, short-pointed** or blunt, **coarsely sharp-toothed** (except near the base), 3–5 cm long; leaflets often drop before rachis.

FLOWERS: White, tiny, bisexual; petals 5, round, 4–5 mm long; sepals tiny, 5; stamens 15–20, anthers yellow; flowers numerous, on **hairy stalks** in **erect, flat-topped, 10–15 cm wide, many-branched clusters** (corymbs) in May–June (after the leaves expand).

FRUITS: Orange-red, berry-like pomes (like tiny apples), fleshy, **1–1.2 cm across;** seeds shiny, dark brown, 3–4 mm long, 1–2 per fruit; fruits hang in round-topped clusters, mature in September, persist through winter.

HABITAT: Widespread along roadsides, fence lines and streams and in woods and wetlands.

DISTRIBUTION: Introduced from Europe; grows wild in southern Ontario north to Ottawa.

THIS ATTRACTIVE SMALL TREE was introduced to North America for its showy flowers. It is one of the most common trees in Great Britain, where countless kilometres of oneseed hawthorn were planted in the 17th and 18th centuries to produce tough, thorny, livestock-proof hedges. • The trunks are usually small, but the wood is hard and strong. Hawthorn wood is used for carving and lathe work. It has also been used to make toothpicks, awls, pins and fish hooks. • Most people find the sweet-fetid scent of hawthorn flowers unpleasant. Many insects, however, find it delightful and are tempted to feed on the pollen and nectar, cross-pollinating the flowers in the process. • Hawthorn species are notoriously difficult to tell apart, but oneseed hawthorn is quite distinctive. It is the only species in Ontario with leaves cut over halfway to the midvein, and the only one with single styles and single nutlets. However, oneseed hawthorn occasionally hybridizes with dotted hawthorn (p. 163), producing offspring with intermediate characteristics. • *Crataegus* was the traditional Latin name for hawthorn, derived from the Greek word *kratos*, 'strength,' in reference to the strong, hard wood. The specific epithet, *monogyna*, means 'with a single pistil or gynoecium' and refers to the single-seeded fruits.

ALSO CALLED: English hawthorn, maythorn

FRENCH NAME: Aubépine monogyne

SIZE AND SHAPE: Trees or shrubs up to 8–10 m tall; crowns broadly domed.

TRUNKS: Crooked, sometimes clumped, up to 30 cm in diameter; mature bark dark grey to brownish, slightly scaly; wood heavy, hard.

BRANCHES: Many, crooked, spreading; twigs lustrous; **thorns shiny, grey, straight, 1–2 cm long, in leaf axils and at the tips of 3–8 cm branchlets; buds round,** dark brown, often 2–3 together (1 producing a thorn).

LEAVES: Alternate, simple, deciduous; blades dark green, paler beneath, firm, triangular to broadly ovate, 1.5–5 cm long, **cut over halfway to the midvein** into 3–7 lobes tipped with irregular sharp teeth; leaves often persist into late autumn.

FLOWERS: Rose-coloured (cultivars dark red to white), unpleasant-smelling, 8–15 mm across, bisexual; petals 5; sepals 5, bases fused in a tube; flowers in **branched, flat-topped clusters** (corymbs) on dwarf shoots, in May–June.

FRUITS: **Bright red haws** (pomes, like small apples), thin-fleshed, rounded to ellipsoidal, 5–8 mm wide, tipped with sepals and **1 protruding style; seeds within bony nutlets, 1 per fruit;** fruits mature September–October, **often persist** through winter.

HABITAT: Open, often disturbed sites in clearings and open woodlands and along roadsides and fence lines, especially on calcium-rich soils.

DISTRIBUTION: Introduced from Europe and western Asia; often grows wild in southern Ontario north to Ottawa.

BLACK HAWTHORN is a mainly western species that is widespread from Alaska to California and east to Saskatchewan. However, it is also found in Ontario in a disjunct population in the northern Great Lakes region. • The tasty-looking haws are edible but not very juicy. • Eye scratches from hawthorn thorns can be very dangerous and may even cause blindness. • Hawthorns are mainly dispersed by fruit-eating animals. The fleshy fruits provide food for many birds and small mammals. Cedar waxwings and ruffed grouse are especially fond of the haws and can gather these fruits throughout the winter, when most berries are covered by snow. Small mammals such as mice and voles usually wait to gather fallen haws from the ground. Hawthorn twigs and leaves (especially those of species with relatively few thorns, such as black hawthorn) also provide food for browsing animals such as white-tailed deer and mule deer. • Dense tangles of thorny branches make ideal nesting sites for birds. • The specific epithet honours David Douglas (1798–1834) a Royal Horticultural Society collector best known for his work in the Pacific Northwest.

ALSO CALLED: Western hawthorn

FRENCH NAME: Aubépine noire

SIZE AND SHAPE: Trees or shrubs to 10 m tall, often forming thickets; crowns broad.

TRUNKS: Crooked, sometimes clumped; mature bark grey-brown, scaly; wood heavy, hard.

BRANCHES: Spreading, **sometimes thornless;** twigs lustrous, hairless; **thorns scattered,** stout, **1–2.5 cm long,** straight or slightly curved; buds dark brown, **rounded.**

LEAVES: Alternate, simple, deciduous; blades dark green, paler beneath, glossy and hairless when mature, ovate to broadly elliptic, mostly **2–4 cm long and 1.5–3 cm wide** (sometimes up to 8 cm by 4 cm), edged with **coarse, gland-tipped teeth** and usually with **5–9 shallow, irregular lobes above midleaf.**

FLOWERS: White to pinkish, with an unpleasant odour, 1–1.3 cm across, bisexual; petals 5, soon shed; sepals 5, bases fused, tips silky-hairy and bent backwards; anthers 10–20, white or pink; flowers in branched, **flat-topped clusters (corymbs) of 5–12** on dwarf shoots, in June.

FRUITS: Dark reddish-purple to purplish-black haws (pomes, like small apples), succulent, short-ovoid, 8–10 mm wide, tipped with tiny sepals and 5 protruding styles; seeds within bony nutlets, 3–5 per fruit; fruits mature in September, **often persist** through winter.

HABITAT: Open, often disturbed sites around clearings and on lakeshores, streambanks, cliffs and rocky ridges.

THIS HIGHLY VARIABLE SPECIES has been variously classified and re-classified over the years. • Cockspur hawthorn is a fast-growing, short-lived tree that readily invades cleared land, but because it requires high light levels, it is soon shaded out when other trees become established. • The specific epithet, *crus-galli*, comes from the Latin *crus*, 'shin or leg,' and *gallus*, 'cock,' alluding to the sharp thorns that resemble rooster spurs. • The leaves described below are typical of flowering or fruiting shoots and are usually more than twice as long as wide. Leaves on vegetative shoots can be very different. Often they are elliptic to oblong and widest near the middle. Also, leaves on vegetative shoots may be somewhat lobed and can grow to twice the size of those on flowering shoots, reaching 5–9 cm in length and 3–8 cm in width. Such variability between vegetative and flowering branches is common in hawthorns. In some cases, the range of variation on a single tree or within a single population exceeds that between species. The larger leaves on short (flowering) shoots are usually the most useful for identifying hawthorns to species.

ALSO CALLED: Cockspur thorn • *C. bushii, C. fontanesiana, C. pyracanthoides, C. tenax*

FRENCH NAME: Aubépine ergot-de-coq

SIZE AND SHAPE: Trees or tall shrubs 6–10 m tall; crowns broadly domed or depressed.

TRUNKS: Sometimes clumped; mature bark grey-brown, slightly scaly; wood heavy, hard.

BRANCHES: Numerous, crooked, **stiff, wide-spreading, horizontal;** twigs hairless; **thorns many, 2–7 cm long,** straight or slightly curved; **buds rounded,** dark brown, often 2–3 together (1 producing a thorn).

LEAVES: Alternate, simple, deciduous; **blades glossy dark green above,** dull and paler below, **leathery, ovate, widest above the middle, with broad tips and wedge-shaped bases,** 3–5 cm long, sharp-toothed (at least above middle), **mostly unlobed;** stalks 3–12 mm long.

FLOWERS: White, unpleasant-smelling, 1–1.5 cm wide, bisexual; petals 5, soon shed; sepals 5, slender, bases fused; anthers about 10, white, pale yellow or pink; flowers many, in **loose, hairless, flat-topped clusters** (corymbs) on dwarf shoots, in May–June.

FRUITS: **Green to dull red haws** (pomes, like small apples), **often dark-dotted,** rather hard, with thin, dry flesh, **short-egg-shaped to almost round, often 5-sided, 8–10 mm wide,** tipped with sepals and protruding styles; seeds in bony nutlets, 1–2 (sometimes 3) per fruit; fruits mature in September–October, **often persist** through winter.

HABITAT: Open, often disturbed sites such as pastures and open woodlands, especially on dry, rocky ground.

THIS ABUNDANT NATIVE SPECIES is one of our more easily recognized hawthorns. Dotted hawthorn is often made conspicuous in winter by its numerous horizontal branches and pale grey branchlets. In autumn, the leathery, dull, broad-tipped leaves and pale-dotted red to yellow haws identify this species. The leaves are always longer than wide, though they can vary greatly on the same tree. Leaves on vegetative shoots are often more lobed and much wider-tipped than those on flowering shoots. Sometimes the leaves on vegetative shoots are almost fan-shaped and have notched (rather than pointed or blunt) tips. • Many hawthorns are planted as ornamentals for their showy flowers, and the attractive clusters of fruit can add colour to the winter landscape. When planted as a hedge, hawthorns can provide an impassable barrier of dense, thorny branches. However, these fast-growing trees can also become pests when they invade open areas such as pastures and parks. Long, sharp thorns are seldom appreciated along paths and fence lines and can be especially hazardous when unwanted trees must be removed. • The specific epithet, *punctata*, 'dotted,' refers to the pale dots that speckle the haws of this species.

ALSO CALLED: Whitehaw

FRENCH NAME: Aubépine ponctuée

SIZE AND SHAPE: Trees or shrubs to 8–10 m tall, often in thickets; crowns open, broad.

TRUNKS: Mostly single, with **branched thorns;** mature bark brownish-grey, fissured; wood hard.

BRANCHES: Stiff, stout, wide-spreading, with **short, 3–9-leaved side-shoots;** twigs lustrous, hairless; **thorns slender, 2–8 cm long, straight, slightly curved or branched; buds rounded,** often 2–3 together (1 producing a thorn).

LEAVES: Alternate, simple, deciduous; **blades dull green with impressed veins** above, paler and **slightly hairy beneath,** firm, elliptic-oblong to ovate, 2–8 cm long, **widest and sharply single- or double-toothed above midleaf, often unlobed,** bases tapered.

FLOWERS: White, unpleasant-smelling, 1–2 cm across, bisexual; petals 5, soon shed; sepals 5, densely grey-hairy, slender, with fused bases; anthers about 20, pink, red or yellow; flowers

many, in **loose, flat-topped clusters** (corymbs) on dwarf shoots, in May–June.

FRUITS: Dull red or orange-red, sometimes yellow (var. *aurea*), **pale-dotted haws** (pomes, like small apples), pear-shaped to **spherical** and **1–1.5 cm wide,** tipped with sepals and protruding styles, mellow-fleshed to scarcely succulent; seeds within bony nutlets, 3–5 per fruit; fruits mature in September–October, **often persist** through winter.

HABITAT: Open, rocky ground in clearings and on floodplains, especially on calcium-rich soils.

THE HAWS OF FLESHY HAWTHORN are succulent and juicy when ripe, but sometimes they remain hard and dry until late in the season. All hawthorn haws are edible, but flavour and fleshiness can vary greatly with the species, habitat and time of year. Although haws are rich in pectin, they are often very seedy, so usually they are combined with other fruit to make jams, jellies and compotes. Some tribes mixed the flesh of haws with dried meat to make pemmican. • The specific epithet, *succulenta,* means 'with juicy flesh.' • Fleshy hawthorn belongs to Series Macracanthae. According to ITIS (2000), the species for which this group is named, **C. macracantha**, is now included in *C. succulenta*. • Another species in the

Macracanthae, **pear hawthorn (C. calpodendron),** is very similar to fleshy hawthorn but is distinguished by its woolly to silky-hairy young twigs and its larger (5–9 cm long by 4–8 cm wide), more prominently hairy, dull yellowish-green leaves. Pear hawthorn is also a smaller tree (at most 3–4 m tall) with small (4–8 mm long), shiny orange-red, pear-shaped haws and few (if any), 3–4 cm long thorns. Pear hawthorn is common in southern Ontario. Its specific epithet, *calpodendron* or 'urn-tree,' refers to the shape of the fruit.

ALSO CALLED: Succulent hawthorn

FRENCH NAME: Aubépine succulente

SIZE AND SHAPE: Trees or shrubs up to 6–8 m tall; crowns broadly domed.

TRUNKS: Crooked, clumped; mature bark scaly; wood heavy, hard.

BRANCHES: Numerous, spreading; **twigs dark, lustrous, hairless** (or slightly hairy when young); **thorns glossy, blackish, strong,** 3–4.5 cm (sometimes to 8 cm) long; **buds rounded,** often 2–3 together (1 producing a thorn).

LEAVES: Alternate, simple, deciduous; **blades dark, lustrous green with impressed veins** above, paler and **finely hairy (at least on veins) beneath, firm, broadly elliptic to ovate or diamond-shaped,** 3–6 cm (sometimes to 8 cm) long, **finely sharp-toothed, shallowly 9–11-lobed above midleaf;** stalks usually **glandless, grooved and winged near the blade.**

FLOWERS: White, unpleasant-smelling, 1–1.8 cm across, bisexual; petals 5, soon shed; sepals 5, **glandular-toothed,** bases fused, tips bent backwards or shed; anthers 10–20, white, pale yellow or pink; flowers in branched, **flat-topped clusters** (corymbs) on dwarf shoots, in May–June.

FRUITS: **Glossy, bright red haws** (pomes, like small apples), tipped with persistent sepals and protruding styles, **round, 6–12 mm across;** seeds within bony nutlets, 2–3 per fruit; fruits mature in September–October, **often persist** through winter.

HABITAT: Dry, rocky sites in fields and along fence lines, roadsides and beaches.

MAP: Pale green, *C. succulenta;* dark green, *C. succulenta/C. calpodendron* overlap.

THE ROUND, RED HAWS of fireberry hawthorn are usually fleshy and mellow when ripe. • The specific epithet, *chrysocarpa,* from the Greek *chryso,* 'golden,' and *karpos,* 'fruit,' is not very appropriate, because the fruits are usually red. • Fireberry hawthorn is one of 4 Ontario species in Series Rotundifoliae, in addition to **Blanchard's hawthorn *(C. irrasa)*, Dodge's hawthorn *(C. dodgei* or *C. flavida)* and Margarett's hawthorn *(C. margarettiae* or *C. margaretta).*** All 4 species are shrubby and typically have small, round leaves with delicate, glandular stalks. They also have numerous, slender thorns, spherical fruits and clusters of a few small flowers that appear early in the year. • Members of Series Brainerdianae, represented by 3 rather rare species, are relatively uncommon in Ontario. **Brainerd hawthorn *(C. brainerdii)*,** also known as *aubépine de Brainerd,* has red, mellow haws. The toothed, lobed leaves are broad with wedge-shaped bases and abruptly pointed tips. Also, the nutlets in Brainerd hawthorn's haws have a shallow pit in the inner surface (not found in fireberry hawthorn stones). • *C. irrasa* is found east of Georgian Bay and west of Lake Superior. *C. dodgei, C. margarettiae* and *C. brainerdii* have restricted ranges in southern Ontario.

Bottom photos: *C. brainerdii*

ALSO CALLED: Round-leaved hawthorn • *C. aboriginum, C. brunetiana, C. faxonii, C. rotundifolia*

FRENCH NAME: Aubépine dorée

SIZE AND SHAPE: Trees or shrubs to 6 m tall, often forming thickets; crowns broad.

TRUNKS: Crooked, sometimes clumped; mature bark scaly; wood heavy, hard.

BRANCHES: Numerous, stout, usually thorny; twigs lustrous, smooth; **thorns shiny black, slender,** straight or slightly curved, 2–8 cm long; **buds round,** often 2–3 together (1 producing a thorn).

LEAVES: Alternate, simple, deciduous; blades usually dull yellowish-green, often with slightly impressed veins above, soon becoming hairless, firm, 2–9 cm long, **usually about as wide as long,** pointed to round-tipped, **edged to below midleaf with gland-tipped teeth and 7–13 shallow lobes;** stalks slender, **often with tiny glands** near the blade.

FLOWERS: White, unpleasant-smelling, 1–1.5 cm across, bisexual; petals 5, soon shed; sepals 5, edged with glands, fused at base; anthers about 10, white or pale yellow; flowers in flat-topped, branched clusters (corymbs) on dwarf shoots, in May–June.

FRUITS: Hairy, deep red (rarely yellow) haws (pomes, like small apples), tipped with tiny sepals and protruding styles, round, 8–10 mm wide; seeds within bony nutlets, 3–4 per fruit; fruits mature in August–October, **often persist** through winter.

HABITAT: Open, rocky or gravelly sites on streambanks and lakeshores and near swamps.

165

THE SPECIFIC EPITHET, *flabellata* or 'fan-shaped,' refers to the shape of the leaves. • It is easy to determine if a tree is a hawthorn, but it is much more difficult, and sometimes impossible, to identify the species. *Crataegus* is a large, complex genus with over 1000 'species' described from North America alone. However, many of these taxa are hybrids or poorly defined varieties. • It has been suggested that the evolutionary diversification of North American species began when hawthorns invaded areas cleared for agriculture by Native peoples, before the arrival of Europeans. These clearings opened new habitats where hawthorn species could spread and intermix, increasing the rate of evolution. • Fanleaf hawthorn belongs to Series Tenuifoliae but forms a link with Series Rotundifoliae through its affinities with fireberry hawthorn (p. 165). These 2 species occupy the same geographical region, and fanleaf hawthorn may have contributed genes to fireberry hawthorn. • A more widespread member of Series Tenuifoliae, **bigfruit hawthorn (C. macrosperma),** can be distinguished by its early spring flowering. Many taxonomists include it in the species *C. flabellata*.

Bottom photo: *C. macrosperma*

ALSO CALLED: New England hawthorn • *C. densiflora, C. grayana*

FRENCH NAME: Aubépine flabelliforme

SIZE AND SHAPE: Trees or shrubs 5–6 m tall, often in thickets; crowns broad.

TRUNKS: Crooked, clumped; mature bark scaly; wood heavy, hard.

BRANCHES: Numerous, stout; twigs lustrous, hairless, slender; **thorns numerous, slender, straight or slightly curved, 5–6 cm (sometimes 3–10 cm) long; buds rounded,** often 2–3 together (1 producing a thorn).

LEAVES: Alternate, simple, deciduous, **often**

bent backwards; blades hairless when mature, ovate to diamond-shaped or triangular (often nearly round on vegetative shoots), 3–5 cm (sometimes to 8 cm) long, tapered to a point, wedge-shaped or squared at the base, **edged with 7–13 pointed, sharply toothed lobes** (often with tips curved out or back).

FLOWERS: White, unpleasant-smelling, 1.5–1.8 cm across, bisexual; petals 5, soon shed; sepals 5, **slender, smooth-edged,** bases fused; anthers 10–20, pink; flowers numerous, in loose, **flat-topped clusters** (corymbs) on dwarf shoots, in May–June.

FRUITS: Crimson, thick-fleshed, juicy haws (pomes, like small apples), tipped with sepals and protruding styles, oblong to round, 8–12 mm across, sometimes slightly angled; seeds within bony nutlets, 3–5 per fruit; fruits mature in September–October, **often persist** in winter.

HABITAT: Open, often rocky, calcareous sites including clearings, pastures, streambanks and woodlands.

MAP: Pink, *C. macrosperma;* dark green, *C. flabellata/C. macrosperma* overlap.

POLYPLOIDY (the splitting of genetic material) and apomixis (producing seed without fertilization) have contributed to the expansion of the genus *Crataegus* and to a good deal of taxonomic confusion. Through apomixis, even sterile hybrids can produce large groups of genetically identical plants with relatively stable characteristics, and these groups may eventually be described as species. In the long term, this lack of genetic diversity could become a weakness, but meanwhile it allows one plant to produce hundreds or even millions of identical offspring. The common dandelion is a good example of an apomictic success story.

• Scarlet hawthorn belongs to Series Coccineae. Confusingly, the species for which the group was named, *C. coccinea,* has been variously reclassified as other species, e.g., **Fuller's hawthorn *(C. fulleriana),* Holmes' hawthorn *(C. holmesiana),*** scarlet hawthorn *(C. pedicellata),* and **Pringle's hawthorn *(C. pringlei),*** and as components of species in other series, e.g., fireberry hawthorn (p. 165). • The members of another series, Pruinosae, have pinkish to purplish or crimson, waxy-coated fruits tipped with prominent, elevated sepals. **Frosted hawthorn** or waxyfruit hawthorn *(C. pruinosa),* which gave rise to the series name, is identified by its leaves (>5 cm long, hairless, widest above the middle), anthers (20, white or pink) and sepals (smooth-edged).

Bottom photo: *C. pruinosa*

ALSO CALLED: *C. aulica, C. ellwangeriana*

FRENCH NAME: Aubépine écarlate

SIZE AND SHAPE: Trees or shrubs up to 10 m tall, highly variable; **crowns usually compact and conical.**

TRUNKS: Crooked, sometimes clumped; mature bark scaly; wood heavy, hard.

BRANCHES: Numerous, slender, spreading; twigs lustrous, hairless with age; **thorns smooth, shiny, stout, usually slightly curved, 2–6 cm long; buds rounded,** dark brown, often 2–3 together (1 producing a thorn).

LEAVES: Alternate, simple, deciduous; blades dark green and hairless above **(often rough-hairy when young), ovate to almost round, widest below midleaf,** 6–9 cm long, broad-based, edged with **sharp, double teeth and 7–11 shallow lobes;** stalks ⅓–⅘ as long as the blade, often glandular.

FLOWERS: White, with a sweet but unpleasant smell, 1.3–2 cm across, bisexual; petals 5, soon shed; sepals 5, **glandular-toothed,** fused into a tube at the base; anthers 10–20; flowers numerous, in branched, **slender-stalked, flat-topped clusters** (corymbs) on dwarf shoots, in May–June.

FRUITS: Bright red, thick-fleshed, often juicy haws (pomes, like small apples), tipped with tiny persistent sepals and protruding styles, **spherical,** 1–1.4 cm across; seeds within bony nutlets, 3–5 per fruit; fruits mature in autumn, **often persist** through winter.

HABITAT: Open, often disturbed sites such as pastures, fence lines and streambanks.

MAP: Pale green, *C. pedicellata;* dark green, *C. pedicellata/C. pruinosa* overlap.

167

MANY PARTS OF HAWTHORN TREES have been used in medicine. Dried leaves or flowers have been administered in capsules, teas and tinctures for treating heart and circulatory problems. Studies have shown that hawthorn dilates blood vessels, thereby improving circulation, increasing oxygen supply to the heart and stabilizing blood pressure. Hawthorn may also strengthen the heart by making it pump harder. Extracts have been used to treat moderate congestive heart failure, heart arrhythmia and mild angina, but more often hawthorn is recommended for preventing future heart problems. Some studies suggest that hawthorn may be effective in controlling or even lowering cholesterol, triglyceride and blood sugar levels. High doses also slow the central nervous system, and extracts have been used as a sedative for treating insomnia. • The specific epithet, *mollis,* means 'soft' and probably refers to the soft-hairy leaves, flower clusters and fruits of this species. • Ontario's smaller (4–6 m tall) member of Series Molles, **Quebec hawthorn *(C. submollis,*** also called *C. champlainensis)*, resembles downy hawthorn but is readily distinguished by its flowers (with 10 anthers) and its pear-shaped fruits.

ALSO CALLED: Red hawthorn

FRENCH NAME: Aubépine duveteuse

SIZE AND SHAPE: Trees or shrubs up to 8–10 m tall, often forming thickets; crowns broad.

TRUNKS: Crooked; mature bark brownish-grey, slightly scaly; wood heavy, hard.

BRANCHES: Numerous, slender, wide-spreading; twigs reddish-brown and silky-hairy when young, smooth and grey with age; **thorns few,** reddish-brown, **straight, slender, 2–6 cm long; buds rounded,** often 2–3 together (1 producing a thorn).

LEAVES: Alternate, simple, deciduous; blades densely **short-hairy above and woolly beneath when young,** dark green, hairless above and slightly hairy beneath when mature, **widest at or below midleaf,** 4–8 cm long and almost as wide, sharply double-toothed or with 9–11 **sharp-toothed lobes.**

FLOWERS: White, unpleasant-smelling, 2–2.5 cm across, bisexual; petals 5, soon shed; sepals 5, **woolly, glandular-toothed,** fused at the base; **anthers 20, white or pale yellow;** flowers in **showy, hairy-branched, flat-topped clusters** (corymbs) on dwarf shoots, in May–June.

FRUITS: Bright red haws (pomes, like small apples), usually thick-fleshed and mellow, **hairy** (at least near the ends), tipped with sepals and protruding styles, **round,** 1–1.2 cm across; seeds in bony nutlets, usually 5 per fruit; fruits mature in autumn, **often persist** through winter.

HABITAT: Fence lines, roadsides and open woods, especially on calcareous soils.

MAP: Pale green, *C. mollis;* pink, *C. submollis.*

THE FRUITS of downy serviceberry are rather dry and flavourless, but Cree people used them to make a pudding said to be almost as good as plum pudding. • Squirrels, chipmunks, skunks, raccoons, black bears and at least 40 species of birds eat and disperse the fruits. Deer browse on the twigs and leaves. • 'Serviceberry' is a contraction of an earlier name, 'sarvissberry,' from 'sarviss,' a transformation of *Sorbus* (mountain-ash). 'Downy' refers to the silvery-hairy young leaves of this species. The inclusion of 'shad' in some common names alludes to the shad fish migration, which coincides with the blooming of this shrub. • It is easy to identify the genus *Amelanchier*, but identifying the species is much more difficult and sometimes impossible. Taxonomic problems stem from a combination of hybridization, polyploidy (splitting of genetic material) and apomixis (producing seed without fertilization). For example, serviceberries often produce fertile triploid offspring, i.e., plants with three sets of chromosomes. Most serviceberries hybridize freely and produce relatively fertile intermediate offspring. Even the most distinctive species can blend together in a continuous series of shrubs with intergrading characteristics. • Only two of Ontario's serviceberries are described in this guide. Most species never reach tree size.

ALSO CALLED: Downy juneberry, Allegheny serviceberry, apple shadbush, common serviceberry, shadblow

FRENCH NAME: Amélanchier arborescent

SIZE AND SHAPE: Trees or shrubs to 12 m tall; crowns irregular, narrow.

TRUNKS: Usually **clumped; bark bluish-grey, thin, smooth;** wood heavy, hard.

BRANCHES: Slender; twigs purplish when young, ridged lengthwise below leaf scars; buds slender, **twisted, pointed, 8–12 mm long,** approximately 5-scaled.

LEAVES: Alternate, simple, deciduous; **blades densely whitish-woolly beneath and folded when young,** dark green and hairless above when mature, paler beneath with a **few hairs on the veins,** thin, 3–8 cm long, sharp-tipped, with **about 25 regular, sharp teeth and fewer than 12 prominent veins per side; stalks finely hairy,** slender, 1–2.5 cm long.

FLOWERS: **White,** bisexual; petals 5, strap-like, 8–15 mm long; sepals 5, in bell-shaped calyxes; flowers on silky-hairy stalks in axils of slender, reddish, silky-hairy bracts, forming **showy, branched clusters** (racemes) at branch tips, in April–May **(as the leaves begin to expand).**

FRUITS: **Dark reddish-purple, berry-like but dry pomes** (like tiny apples), 6–10 mm across; tipped with persistent sepals; **lowermost stalks about 1.2 cm long;** seeds hard, 5–10 per pome; fruits ripen and drop in June–July.

HABITAT: Dry sites in fields, woodlands and clearings and on rocky or sandy bluffs.

SERVICEBERRIES seldom grow large enough to produce wood of commercial importance, but their hard, heavy trunks have been used to make tool handles, walking sticks and other small articles. • The sweet, juicy fruits are edible and rich in iron and copper. They can be eaten fresh from the tree; served with milk and sugar; added to pancakes, muffins and pies; or made into jellies, jams and preserves. Native peoples dried the small pomes like raisins or mashed and dried them in cakes. Often the dried fruits were mixed with meat and fat to form pemmican, a lightweight, high-energy food that could support winter travellers for long periods if the diet was supplemented with vitamin C (usually in the form of rose hips or spruce tea) to prevent scurvy. • The twigs have a faint bitter-almond flavour. • This hardy, attractive shrub, with its showy flower clusters and its edible, bird-attracting fruits, is often planted in gardens and parks. • The name *laevis* means 'smooth,' in reference to the hairless leaves and flower clusters of this species. • Smooth serviceberry is very similar to downy serviceberry (p. 169) and is sometimes considered a variety of that species. Often the two grow together.

ALSO CALLED: Smooth juneberry, Allegheny serviceberry

FRENCH NAME: Amélanchier glabre

SIZE AND SHAPE: Trees or shrubs 2–10 m tall; crowns irregular, narrow.

TRUNKS: Often clumped; **bark thin, smooth, grey,** with dark vertical lines; wood heavy, hard.

BRANCHES: Slender; twigs purplish, hairless, ridged lengthwise below leaf scars; **buds narrowly egg-shaped, pointed, 8–12 mm long, twisted,** approximately 5-scaled.

LEAVES: Alternate, simple, deciduous; **blades coppery-red, hairless and folded when young,** dark green when mature, paler beneath, essentially hairless, thin, **oval to elliptic,** 3–8 cm long, abruptly pointed, with about **25 sharp teeth and 10 or fewer veins per side;** stalks slender, 1–3 cm long, **hairless.**

FLOWERS: White, bisexual; petals 5, strap-like, 1–2 cm long; sepals 5, in a bell-shaped calyx, 3–4 mm long, bent backwards; **flowers on hairless, 1–3 cm long stalks** in axils of slender, ephemeral bracts, forming **showy, elongated, drooping clusters** (racemes), in April–May **(when leaves are at least half grown).**

FRUITS: Dark **reddish-purple to black, berry-like, fleshy and juicy pomes** (like tiny apples), 6–10 mm wide, tipped with sepals; **lowermost stalks 2.5–4.5 cm long;** seeds hard, 5–10 per pome; fruits ripen and drop in July–August.

HABITAT: Coniferous or mixed woodlands, clearings, thickets; along fence lines and roadsides.

THIS ATTRACTIVE TREE is thought to be extirpated in Ontario and in Canada. The only natural populations were probably those discovered by John Macoun at Canada's southernmost point, Pelee Island, in 1892. That population has since disappeared, but redbud was recently re-introduced to the island. The natural range of redbud is difficult to determine because it has been so widely planted and frequently escapes cultivation. • This flowering tree is a lovely ornamental, but it is hardy only as far north as Toronto and in sheltered sites near Lake Huron. It is especially attractive beside evergreens. Redbud grows rapidly under good conditions and begins to flower at about 5 years of age. Once mature, it blooms almost every year, and in cool weather, the spring flower display can continue for 3 weeks. • Boiled in water, redbud twigs produce a yellow dye. • The generic name, *Cercis*, comes from the Greek *kerkis*, 'shuttlecock,' which was thought to describe the shape of the pods. • Until recently, *Cercis* was considered a member of the pea family (Fabaceae or Leguminosae). It is now placed in the cassia family (Caesalpiniaceae).

ALSO CALLED: Judas-tree, eastern redbud

FRENCH NAMES: Gainier rouge, arbre de Judée, bouton rouge, gainier du Canada

SIZE AND SHAPE: Small trees 4–8 m tall; crowns low, spreading.

TRUNKS: Short, straight, up to 30 cm in diameter; young bark greyish, smooth; mature bark reddish-brown, scaly; wood dark brown, hard, weak.

BRANCHES: Horizontal to ascending; twigs reddish-brown, slender, zigzagged, with 3 lengthwise ridges from each leaf scar; leaf buds dark reddish-brown, small, 5–6-scaled, sometimes with a tiny secondary bud at the base; flower buds rounded, clustered, stalked.

LEAVES: Alternate, simple, deciduous; blades bluish-green above, paler beneath, **broadly heart-shaped,** thin, 7–12 cm long, with **5–9 prominent veins radiating from the stalk; stalks swollen near the blade;** leaves warm yellow in autumn.

FLOWERS: **Deep to pale pink, pea-like, showy,** 1 cm long, bisexual; anthers 10, attached at the middle, splitting lengthwise; flowers on 1 cm stalks in **abundant, 4–8-flowered, tassel-like clusters along branches** (not on new twigs) and **sometimes on trunks,** in May (before the leaves expand).

FRUITS: **Reddish-brown, flat, thin pods** (legumes), tapered at both ends, 5–10 cm long; seeds 10–12 per pod, shiny brown, flattened, 6–8 mm across; pods hang in small clusters, mature in autumn and persist into winter.

HABITAT: Moist forests, often near streams.

THIS TREE IS RARE in Ontario and Canada. Although honey-locust grows wild in southern regions, it has also been widely planted and often escapes cultivation, so its native range is unclear. • The hard, heavy wood is easily polished but fairly brittle. It has been used for fence posts, furniture and occasionally lumber. The long, hard thorns were sometimes made into nails and pins. • Honey-locust pods have been used to make beer. They contain a sweetish substance that tastes like a mixture of castor oil and honey, hence the 'honey' in the name. • The sweet flowers attract many bees. White-tailed deer, rabbits, squirrels and quail eat the seeds and the sweet pulp of the pods. Cattle also eat the seeds, pods and tender young plants. • Gardeners often prune young trees to form protective thorny hedges. Honey-locust is also considered an excellent lawn tree because the delicate foliage casts light shade. Cuttings from male-flowered branches grow into trees with pollen flowers only, so they do not produce fruit. Cultivars of a thornless variety **(thornless honey-locust, G. triacanthos var. inermis)** boast straight trunks and spreading canopies and are common in plantings along city streets.

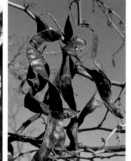

ALSO CALLED: Thorny-locust, sweet-locust, tree-thorned acacia

FRENCH NAMES: Févier épineux, carouge à miel, févier à trois épines, févier d'Amérique

SIZE AND SHAPE: Trees 15–30 m tall; crowns broad, open; roots deep, spreading.

TRUNKS: Usually short, 60–100 cm in diameter, with long (to 30 cm), branched thorns; young bark brownish, smooth, with horizontal pores (lenticels); mature bark furrowed, scaly-ridged; wood reddish-brown, hard, heavy, resistant to decay.

BRANCHES: With **reddish, smooth, forked thorns;** twigs of 2 types: long, greenish- to reddish-brown, zigzagged shoots, and very short leaf- and flower-bearing shoots; buds small, absent at twig tips.

LEAVES: Alternate, deciduous, 15–30 cm long; **compound, once or twice pinnately divided,** with **18–30 leaflets but no tip leaflet;** twice-compound leaves have 4–7 pairs of branches on the main stalk (rachis); leaflets dark green above, paler beneath, oblong to lance-shaped, 2.5–5 cm long; leaves yellow in autumn.

FLOWERS: Greenish-white, about 5 mm across, 5-petalled; unisexual (occasionally some bisexual) with male and female flowers on same tree; male flowers in dense, 5–7 cm long clusters (racemes); female flowers few, in loose, 7–9 cm long clusters; flowering in May–June.

FRUITS: Brownish, **leathery, flattened, spirally twisted pods** (legumes), **15–40 cm long;** seeds bean-like, hard, about 2 cm apart in pods; pods mature by autumn, drop over winter without opening.

HABITAT: Open sites in moist, rich lowlands.

NATURAL POPULATIONS of this tree are rare in our province and in Canada. Most discovered in or before 1950 have not been found since.

• Kentucky coffee-tree is too rare to have commercial value, but the moderately heavy, decay-resistant wood has been used in cabinets, fence posts, railway ties and general construction.

• This species has by far the largest leaves of any native tree in Canada. However, one can easily mistake the leaf branches or the many small leaflets for individual leaves. This tree is often used in landscaping well beyond its natural range because it transplants easily and can tolerate urban conditions. • Animals seldom eat the bitter seeds and pods, but early settlers roasted the seeds to make a coffee substitute. Some tribes ate the roasted seeds like nuts.

• The raw seeds are **poisonous.** Roasting is said to destroy their toxins, but given their bitterness and potential toxicity, eating the seeds is not recommended. • Cattle have become sick after drinking water contaminated with the leaves or fruits of these trees. • *Gymnocladus*, from the Greek *gymnos*, 'naked' and *klodos*, 'branch,' refers to the relatively late emergence of the leaves in spring and the early leaf drop each autumn.

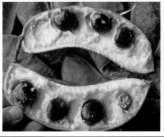

ALSO CALLED: Coffeenut

FRENCH NAMES: Chicot févier, café du Kentucky, caféier du Kentucky, chicot dioïque, chicot du Canada, gros févier, gymnocladier dioïque

SIZE AND SHAPE: Trees 15–25 m tall; crowns narrow.

TRUNKS: Straight, 40–60 cm in diameter; mature bark dark grey, hard, with thin ridges of outcurled scale edges; wood reddish-brown, hard.

BRANCHES: Widely spaced; **twigs coarse,** greyish-brown; buds dark brown, silky-hairy, 6–9 mm long, **in groups of 2–3 above leaf scars, absent at twig tips.**

LEAVES: Alternate, early-deciduous; compound, **twice pinnately divided, with 3–7 pairs of branches (no terminal branches or tip leaflets) on a sturdy 30–90 cm long central stalk** (rachis) that is easily mistaken for a slender twig; leaflets bluish-green, ovate, 4–6 cm long, pointed, short-stalked, seldom opposite, usually about 70; leaf scars large, heart-shaped.

FLOWERS: Greenish-white, soft-hairy, 1.5–2 cm across, 5-petalled; unisexual, usually with male and female flowers on separate trees; anthers 10, attached at the middle, splitting lengthwise; flowers in open, many-branched, 6–20 cm long clusters (panicles), in May–June (as the leaves expand).

FRUITS: Dark reddish-brown pods (legumes), **leathery, becoming woody, flattened but thick, 8–25 cm long;** seeds few, dark brown, hard, slightly flattened, 1–2 cm across, embedded in sticky pulp; pods hang on stout, 2–3 cm long stalks, mature in autumn and **persist through winter.**

HABITAT: Moist woods with deep, rich soil.

THE DECAY-RESISTANT WOOD of black locust was once used for railway ties, fence posts, stakes and pilings and was exported to England for shipbuilding. Unfortunately, locust borer beetles *(Megacyllene robiniae)* often spoil the wood. Although it has been used as firewood, black locust tends to flare and throw sparks. • This species was introduced to Europe from North America in the early 1600s and is now naturalized across the continent. • Cattle and humans have been poisoned by the **toxic** inner bark and leaves. Some tribes used the poisonous wood in arrows. Although the seeds are toxic to humans, many animals (e.g., rabbits, squirrels, pheasants, mourning doves) eat them with impunity. • Like most members of the pea family, black locust has root nodules containing nitrogen-fixing bacteria. Black locust has been used to reforest waste areas (e.g., mine spoils) where few other trees could survive. Its root suckers produce dense colonies that help prevent erosion. The strong root networks have even been used to support dikes. • **Clammy locust *(R. viscosa)*** is another ornamental that may occasionally escape cultivation in Ontario. Unlike black locust, it has pink, odourless flowers and sticky twigs, leaf stalks and pods.

ALSO CALLED: False acacia, common locust, white locust, yellow locust

FRENCH NAMES: Robinier faux-acacia, acacia blanc, acacia commun, faux-acacia, robinier

SIZE AND SHAPE: Trees 9–15 m tall; crowns open, irregular; roots wide-creeping.

TRUNKS: Irregular, 30–60 cm in diameter; mature bark dark brown, deeply furrowed, scaly; wood yellowish-green, hard, heavy.

BRANCHES: Brittle, short; **twigs spiny,** reddish-brown, slender, **zigzagged; spines paired at each bud or leaf base/scar,** about 1 cm long, largest on vigorous shoots; buds tiny, clustered (usually 3–4), embedded under leaf stalk bases.

LEAVES: Alternate, deciduous, 20–35 cm long; compound, **pinnately divided** into **7–19 leaflets (with a terminal leaflet)** in pairs along a 20–30 cm long stalk; leaflets dull green, oval, 2–5 cm long; leaf scars 3-cornered, with 3 vein scars.

FLOWERS: White with a yellow blotch on the upper petals, fragrant, pea-like, 1.5–2.5 cm long, bisexual; **flowers hang in loose, showy, 10–14 cm long clusters** near shoot tips in early summer (about 1 month after the leaves expand).

FRUITS: Reddish-brown to black, flattened, thin-walled, hairless pods (legumes), **7–10 cm long; seeds dark, pea-like, hard,** 3–5 mm long, 4–8 per pod; fruits clustered, persist through winter.

HABITAT: Fence lines, roadsides, pastures and moist, open woodlands.

DISTRIBUTION: Introduced from the eastern U.S.; aggressively invades native vegetation in southern Ontario north to the Ottawa district, especially on sandy soils.

WITH ITS STRIKING FORM, showy fruit clusters and brilliant autumn foliage, staghorn sumac is sometimes planted as an ornamental. However, its spreading, suckering roots can be troublesome. • The wood is sometimes used for decorative finishing and novelty items. • The tannin-rich fruit, bark and leaves were used to tan hides. The leaves and fruits were also boiled to make black ink, and the dried leaves were an ingredient in smoking mixtures. The milky sap has been used as a treatment for warts. • The juicy fruits can be eaten as a trail nibble or gathered in larger quantities to make jelly. They can also be crushed and/or boiled to make a lemonade-like drink. They should not be boiled for too long or consumed in large quantities, because they contain tannic acid. • Sumac thickets provide food and cover for many mammals and birds, including deer, moose, rabbits, grouse and pheasants. • The fuzzy, widely spreading branches look like velvet-covered deer antlers, hence the name 'staghorn.' • Staghorn sumac could be confused with **smooth sumac *(R. glabra)***, but smooth sumac has hairless leaves and twigs. These 2 species often cross-pollinate to produce **pulvinate sumac *(Rhus* x *pulvinata)*.**

Bottom photo: *R. glabra*

ALSO CALLED: Velvet sumac, sumac vinegar-tree • *R. hirta*

FRENCH NAMES: Sumac vinaigrier, sumac amarante, vinaigrier sumac

SIZE AND SHAPE: Small trees or shrubs up to 6 m tall, usually **forming thickets;** crowns flat-topped; roots shallow, spreading, suckering.

TRUNKS: Short, forked, 5–10 cm in diameter; young bark dark yellowish-brown, thin, with prominent pores (lenticels); mature bark scaly; wood orange-green, soft, brittle.

BRANCHES: Few, wide-spreading; **twigs dark velvety-hairy,** stout, exuding **milky juice** when broken; **pith yellowish-brown, large;** buds densely hairy, without scales, 5–7 mm across, absent at branch tips.

LEAVES: **Alternate,** deciduous; compound, **pinnately divided into 11–31 leaflets;** central stalks reddish, hairy, 30–50 cm long; leaflets dark green above, paler and finely hairy beneath, lance-shaped, 7.5–13 cm long, slender-pointed, sharp-toothed, stalkless; leaf scars almost encircle the buds; leaves scarlet, orange or purplish in autumn.

FLOWERS: Yellowish-green, tiny; usually unisexual with male and female flowers on separate trees; petals 5; **stamens 5;** flowers borne in **dense, erect, 13–25 cm long, cone-shaped clusters** (panicles) at branch tips, in late June–July (after the leaves expand).

FRUITS: **Reddish, fuzzy** drupes 3–5 mm long, **in dense, erect, cone-shaped clusters** at branch tips; seeds single, in small stones; fruits mature July–August, **persist through winter.**

HABITAT: Open, often disturbed sites, typically on dry rocky or sandy soil.

MAP: Pale green, *R. typhina*; pink, *R. glabra*; dark green, overlap.

IT IS VERY IMPORTANT to recognize poison-sumac because most people develop severe skin reactions from contact with it. Those who have gathered sprays of the beautiful white fruits and dark glossy leaves for decorations have paid dearly for their mistake. **Caution:** If you touch this plant, wash your hands thoroughly with soap and warm water to remove the toxic oil. Never use oil-based salves or liniments on your skin because they can dissolve and spread the toxin. • The allergenic oil in all parts of this shrub can be picked up directly from the plant or indirectly from contaminated pets, clothing or other items. Smoke from burning plants also carries the oil and can cause severe reactions of skin, eyes and mucous membranes in the nose, mouth and throat. • Game birds and many songbirds eat the 'berries' with impunity and disperse the seeds. • Poison-sumac is distinguished from true sumacs (p. 175), mountain-ashes (pp. 157–159) and **elderberry** shrubs **(*Sambucus* spp.)** by its smooth-edged (not toothed) leaves. Ashes (pp. 204–209) and **common prickly-ash (*Zanthoxylum americanum*)** shrubs may have toothless leaves, but ash leaves are opposite (not alternate), and common prickly-ash has thorny branches. Poison-sumac's persistent fruits facilitate year-round identification.

ALSO CALLED: Poison-sumach, swamp-sumac, poison-dogwood, poison-elderberry, poison-elder, poison-oak • *Rhus vernix*

FRENCH NAMES: Sumac à vernis, sumac lustré, arbre du vernis, bois-chandelle

SIZE AND SHAPE: Small trees or tall shrubs 3–5 m tall; crowns small, rounded.

TRUNKS: Slender, often branched from bases, 6–8 cm in diameter; bark grey, smooth, thin; wood moderately soft, weak.

BRANCHES: Moderately stout; twigs slender, drooping, dark green and hairy to mottled brownish-yellow and hairless, dotted with pores (lenticels); damaged twigs exude milky sap; buds purplish-brown, hairy, several-scaled, conical, **1–1.9 cm long at branch tips,** smaller below.

LEAVES: Alternate, deciduous; compound, **pinnately divided into 7–13 leaflets,** often crowded in umbrella-like clusters at branch tips; central stalks 15–30 cm long; leaflets dark lustrous green, whitened beneath, **essentially hairless,** oblong to elliptic or ovate, 3–8 cm long, **short-stalked,** pointed, **smooth-edged** (sometimes wavy); leaf scars shield-shaped.

FLOWERS: Yellowish-green, tiny; unisexual with male and female flowers on separate plants; petals 5; **stamens 5;** flowers in elongated, nodding clusters (raceme-like panicles) up to 20 cm long from leaf axils, in June to early July (after the leaves expand).

FRUITS: Glossy, **whitish, pearl-like drupes,** dry, 4–6 mm across, in loose, arching to hanging clusters; seeds single, within stones; fruits mature July–August, persist through winter.

HABITAT: Open, **swampy** woodlands and bog edges, often with tamarack (p. 57).

JESUIT MISSIONARIES brought tree-of-heaven to England from China in 1751, and it was introduced to North America in 1874. • This hardy, smog-tolerant tree is widely planted as an ornamental. It grows rapidly (up to 2–3 m per season) and thrives in even the poorest, driest soils, adding green to city landscapes and producing oxygen in return. Unfortunately, the leaves and male flowers have an unpleasant odour and the pollen can cause severe hay fever, so female trees are usually preferred. Also, the spreading roots can damage wells and drainage systems, and the wood is so brittle that snow, wind and even moderately heavy storms can bring down dozens of trees. • Escaped trees often take over clearings, producing impenetrable thickets from root suckers. Once established, the thickets are hard to eliminate, so many people regard tree-of-heaven as a troublesome weed. • This species is featured in Betty Smith's *A Tree Grows in Brooklyn*, a story about a young girl inspired by a tree's determination to survive. • Tree-of-heaven has very bitter bark, wood and seeds. The small glands on the leaf lobes give off an unpleasant odour when rubbed, hence the alternative name 'stinking-ash.'

ALSO CALLED: Copal tree, ailanthus, Chinese-sumac, stinking-ash • *A. glandulosa*

FRENCH NAMES: Ailante glanduleux, faux-vernis du Japon, frêne puant

SIZE AND SHAPE: Trees 15–25 m tall; crowns broad, rounded; roots spreading.

TRUNKS: Often clumped, 30–75 cm in diameter; young bark greenish-grey; mature bark grey, thin, with irregular vertical lines; wood soft, weak.

BRANCHES: Few, fragile; **twigs stout,** yellowish- to reddish-brown, with **prominent leaf scars and pores** (lenticels); buds downy, hemispherical, 2–4-scaled, **absent at branch tips.**

LEAVES: Alternate, deciduous, ill-smelling; compound, **pinnately divided into 11–41 leaflets; central stalks 25–75 cm long,** with swollen bases; leaflets dark glossy green, paler beneath, **5–15 cm long, with a gland-tipped lobe (sometimes 2) near the base,** slender-pointed, **stalked.**

FLOWERS: Yellowish-green, 5 mm across, 5-parted, unpleasant-smelling (especially males); unisexual with male and female flowers on separate trees (occasionally bisexual); flowers in **erect, pyramidal, 10–30 cm long clusters** (panicles) at branch tips in late spring (after the leaves expand).

FRUITS: Pale reddish- to yellowish-brown, **winged nutlets** (samaras), 3–5 cm long, with a **seedcase at the centre of a flat, spirally twisted wing;** seeds single; **fruits hang in dense clusters,** mature in late summer, persist into winter.

HABITAT: Open, often disturbed sites such as empty lots and old fields.

DISTRIBUTION: Introduced from northern China; grows wild in southern Ontario, often in urban centres.

COMMON HOP-TREE IS RARE in Canada. Many populations grow in protected areas, but some are threatened by waterfront development. • This short-lived, slow-growing species is sometimes planted as an ornamental or hedge for its bright, shiny leaves and unusual clusters of persistent, buff-coloured fruits. Common hop-tree is hardy beyond its natural range and can grow as far north as Lake Superior. This tree is fairly shade-tolerant, but it flowers only in full sunlight. • The close-grained wood is fairly strong, but the trunks are too small for commercial use. • In earlier days, when bad-tasting medicines were considered best, hop-tree juice was sometimes given as a substitute for quinine. The fruits have been used in beer as a substitute for hops (*Humulus* spp.), hence the name 'hop-tree.' • The flowers smell like rotting flesh and attract carrion flies, which carry pollen from one tree to the next. The fruits are seldom used by wildlife, but the trees can provide shelter for birds in otherwise open areas. • *Ptelea* was the Greek name for elm. It was transferred to the hop-tree genus by Linnaeus because of the resemblance of the fruit to that of elms.

ALSO CALLED: Wafer-ash, stinking-ash, three-leaved hop-tree • *P. angustifolia*

FRENCH NAMES: Ptéléa trifolié, bois puant, orme de Samarie, orme de Samarie à trois folioles

SIZE AND SHAPE: Small trees or tall shrubs 4–5 m tall; crowns irregular, rounded.

TRUNKS: Short, 8–15 cm in diameter; **young bark shiny reddish-brown, with prominent pores** (lenticels); mature bark greyish, rough, scaly; wood yellowish-brown, heavy, hard.

BRANCHES: Numerous, twisted, short; twigs yellowish- to **reddish-brown** with prominent pores (lenticels), **foul-smelling when bruised;** pith large, white; **buds woolly, rounded, tiny,** sunken under leaf-stalk bases, absent at branch tips.

LEAVES: **Alternate,** deciduous; compound, **divided into 3 leaflets; leaflets dark glossy green** above, paler beneath, **speckled with tiny, translucent glands** (visible in front of strong light), ovate to elliptic, 5–10 cm long, sharp-pointed with wedge-shaped bases, smooth-edged or faintly toothed; leaf stalks 7–15 cm long; leaf scars horseshoe-shaped around buds.

FLOWERS: **Greenish-white,** foul-smelling, 4–5-parted; unisexual with male and female flowers on separate trees (occasionally bisexual); petals hairy, 4–7 mm long; flowers in 4–8 cm wide, **repeatedly branched clusters** (cymes) at branch tips, in mid-June (after the leaves expand).

FRUITS: Buff-coloured, **winged nutlets** (samaras) 2–2.5 cm across, **with 2 seedcases surrounded by a flat, circular, net-veined wing; fruits hang in dense, stalked clusters,** mature in late summer, persist through winter.

HABITAT: Sandy soil in and around woodlands and along shorelines.

AMERICAN BASSWOOD is one of our softest, lightest hardwoods, valued for use in hand carving and turnery. It has also been used for interior trim, veneer, plywood, cabinets, furniture, musical instruments, measuring sticks and pulp and paper. The odourless wood makes excellent food containers. • Native peoples and settlers soaked the inner bark in water to separate its tough fibres, which were then used to make ropes, nets, mats, shoes, clothing and thread. • Some tribes carved ritual masks on living trees, then split the masks away to hollow and dry the inside. If the tree survived, the mask was believed to have supernatural powers. • A hot bath with basswood (linden) flowers, followed by a cup of linden-flower tea, is said to soothe cold symptoms and enhance sleep. The flowers are also used in beauty products. • This fast-growing, moderately long-lived tree is a popular ornamental because of its fragrant flowers, large leaves, excellent response to pruning and deep, spreading roots that make it wind-firm. • Easily damaged by fire and heavily browsed by rabbits (its primary pest), American basswood often resprouts as clumps. • In forestry, *Tilia* species are called 'basswoods'; in horticulture, 'lindens'; and in England, 'lime-trees.'

ALSO CALLED: American linden, whitewood, bee-tree, bast-tree, lime-tree, lime, spoonwood • *T. glabra*

FRENCH NAMES: Tilleul d'Amérique, bois blanc

SIZE AND SHAPE: Trees 18–22 m tall; crowns regular, rounded; roots deep, wide-spreading.

TRUNKS: Straight, 40–80 cm in diameter; young bark pale, smooth; mature bark dark greyish-brown with blocky, narrow, flat-topped ridges; inner bark fibrous; wood light, soft, uniform.

BRANCHES: Spreading and upcurved to ascending and arching; twigs yellowish-brown, hairless, zigzagged; **buds plump, asymmetrical, 2–3-scaled,** hairless, 5–7 mm long, in 2 rows, absent at twig tips.

LEAVES: Alternate, simple, deciduous; blades dull green, paler beneath with hairy vein axils, **heart-shaped, asymmetrical at bases,** abruptly slender-pointed, 12–15 cm long, palmately veined, edged with coarse, **sharp, gland-tipped teeth;** stalks almost half as long as the blades; leaf scars semi-oval, raised, with 5–10 vein scars.

FLOWERS: Creamy-yellowish, 1.1–1.3 cm across, fragrant, bisexual; petals 5; sepals 5; flowers hang in loose, branched clusters (cymes) on slender stalks **from the lower midvein of prominent 10–12.5 cm long, strap-like bracts,** borne in axils of new leaves in July (6–8 weeks after the leaves expand).

FRUITS: Brown-woolly, round, nut-like capsules, 6–8 mm across, 1-seeded; fruits hang in **long-stalked clusters on strap-like bracts,** mature in September–October, persist through winter.

HABITAT: Cool, moist, rich woods, often near water and mixed with other hardwoods.

THIS HARDY TREE tolerates urban conditions well, and it has been planted since ancient times as an ornamental for its fragrant flowers, dense, deep green, neatly textured canopy and bright yellow autumn leaves. • In Saxon times, littleleaf linden was the dominant tree of many forests in England and Wales. Today, it is widely planted in North America, but in Europe the **common lime *(Tilia* x *europaea*—a hybrid of *T. cordata* and another European species, *T. platyphyllos*, largeleaf lime)** is preferred for landscaping. • The fine-textured, easily worked wood is ideal for carving and turning. Many of the intricate carvings of the famous English artist Grinling Gibbons (1648–1721) were made with this wood. Because linden wood does not warp, it is used for drawing boards and for the sounding boards and keys of pianos and organs. • The dried flowers are sometimes sold in health stores. They are used to make medicinal teas for stimulating sweating, enhancing resistance to infection and inducing sedation. • This shapely tree can become burred, sprouty and heavily branched with age. Some trees in English parks are more than 350 years old. • The specific epithet, *cordata* or 'heart-shaped,' refers to the leaves.

ALSO CALLED: Small-leaved European linden, small-leaved lime

FRENCH NAME: Tilleul à petites feuilles

SIZE AND SHAPE: Trees 12–15 m tall; crowns pyramidal to round; roots deep, spreading.

TRUNKS: Straight, 40–80 cm in diameter; young bark pale, smooth; mature bark dark greyish-brown, with blocky ridges; wood light, soft, even-grained.

BRANCHES: Arching (typically) to spreading; twigs reddish-brown, soon hairless, zigzagged; **buds plump, asymmetrical, 2-scaled,** greenish-red, in 2 rows, absent at twig tips.

LEAVES: Alternate, simple, deciduous; blades dark shiny green, paler beneath with rusty-hairy vein axils, **heart-shaped to nearly round,** only slightly asymmetrical, **3.5–8 cm long,** edged with coarse, **sharp, gland-tipped teeth;** stalks hairless; leaf scars semi-oval, with 5–10 vein scars; leaves pale yellow to tan in autumn.

FLOWERS: Greenish-yellow, fragrant, star-shaped, 1–1.2 cm across, bisexual; petals 5; sepals 5; flowers spreading to erect in branched, 5–8-flowered, **4 cm wide clusters** (cymes) on slender stalks **from midveins of 3.5–8 cm long, strap-like bracts,** in June–July (after the leaves expand).

FRUITS: Greyish to pale yellow, rusty-hairy, nut-like capsules, faintly ribbed (if at all), about 5 mm long, 1-seeded, thin-shelled; capsules **hang in clusters from strap-like bracts,** mature in autumn, persist through winter.

HABITAT: Disturbed, open sites.

DISTRIBUTION: Introduced from Europe; occasionally grows wild in southern Ontario.

RUSSIAN-OLIVE is an attractive, silver-leaved shrub or small tree that is often planted as an ornamental. It is hardy enough to grow in all but the northernmost parts of Ontario, and it resists drought, tolerates city smoke and grows on salty soil. Occasionally, it can become a pest when it sends up suckers from spreading roots. Russian-olive commonly naturalizes in western Canada but escapes much less frequently in the east.

• Although the fruits are rather mealy, they are sweet and edible. In the Far East, they were used to make a type of sweet sherbet. • The flowers have an unusual, heavy fragrance that some people find nauseating. • Another introduced species, **autumn-olive** *(E. umbellata),* also called umbellate oleaster, Japanese silverberry and Asiatic oleaster, is distinguished by the mixture of brown and silvery scales on its leaves and twigs; by the relatively long tube formed by its petals (longer than the sepals); and by its long-stalked red fruits. In recent years, autumn-olive has become a serious competitive invader in parts of southernmost Ontario, especially in areas with nutrient-poor, sandy soils. • Without flowers or fruits, Russian-olive could be confused with willows, but willows lack silvery scales on their leaves, have 3 vein scars in their leaf scars and have 1-scaled buds.

ALSO CALLED: Oleaster

FRENCH NAME: Olivier de Bohême

SIZE AND SHAPE: Small, slender trees or shrubs up to 10 m tall; crowns dense, low.

TRUNKS: Often crooked or leaning; bark greyish-brown, thin, fissured, **shredding in strips.**

BRANCHES: Usually **spiny; twigs densely silvery with tiny scales,** some reduced to leafless, spine-forming shoots; buds small, ovoid, several-scaled.

LEAVES: **Alternate,** in small clusters, simple, deciduous; **blades dull silvery-green above and beneath** with tiny scales and star-shaped hairs, leathery, **narrowly oblong to lance-shaped, pointed, 3–8 cm long, 3–8 times as long as wide;** leaf scars with 1 dash-like vein scar.

FLOWERS: **Yellow inside, silvery-scaly outside,** fragrant, bisexual or unisexual, **bell-shaped,** about **1 cm long,** with a short, tubular nectary around the style; petals lacking, sepals 4; flowers short-stalked, forming clusters of 1–3 at the base of new growth, in June–July.

FRUITS: **Yellow to brownish, silvery-scaled, mealy, drupe-like 'berries'** (enlarged hypanthium bases), elliptic-oblong, **1–2 cm long,** tipped with sepals; each contains a small, dry, smooth, 7–8 mm nutlet (achene) that encloses a single seed; fruits mature in autumn.

HABITAT: Moist sites, usually on salty to alkaline soils.

DISTRIBUTION: Introduced from Eurasia; grows wild in southern Ontario.

BLACK TUPELO is rare in Canada and is our only native species of *Nyssa*. This attractive shade tree is often planted as an ornamental for its interesting form, abundant, bird-attracting blue fruits and decorative leaves (shiny dark green in summer; golden to brilliant scarlet in autumn). Black tupelo is hardy as far north as Ottawa and Georgian Bay, well north of its native range. • This tree rarely reaches commercial size in Canada. In the past, its strong wood found many uses, especially when resistance to wear was important. Unusual items included pipes in a salt factory, hatters' blocks, pistol grips and even rollers for glass. Today the wood is considered suitable for making furniture (mostly hidden frames), panelling, boxes and crates. • The fruits are too sour for human tastes, but they are an important food source for many animals. Foxes, wood ducks, wild turkeys, robins, pileated woodpeckers, brown thrashers, northern mockingbirds, thrushes, northern flickers and European starlings all eat the oil-rich drupes. White-tailed deer and beavers eat the twigs and leaves, and the flowers are an excellent source of nectar for bees. • The name *sylvatica* means 'of the woods.'

ALSO CALLED: Blackgum, sourgum, pepperidge

FRENCH NAMES: Nyssa sylvestre, gommier noire, nyssa des forêts, tupélo de montagne

SIZE AND SHAPE: Trees up to 20 m tall; crowns broadly elongated, flat-topped.

TRUNKS: Straight, 10–30 cm in diameter; mature bark dark grey, with thick, irregular, blocky segments; wood fine-grained, hard, heavy.

BRANCHES: Crooked, horizontal; twigs reddish-brown with greyish skin, long and slender or short and dwarfed; **pith with hard, greenish**

crossbars (in long-section); buds reddish-brown, hairy-tipped, **pointing outwards.**

LEAVES: Alternate, clustered at shoot tips, simple, deciduous; **blades dark shiny green,** whitened beneath, tough, 5–12 cm long, **shape variable, generally widest above midleaf, abruptly pointed, tapered to a wedge-shaped base, with slightly wavy edges** (rarely irregularly coarse-toothed); stalks reddish; leaves golden to scarlet in autumn.

FLOWERS: Greenish-white, inconspicuous, tiny; unisexual (sometimes a few bisexual) with male and female flowers on separate trees; stalkless (female) or short-stalked (male) flowers in compact clusters (umbels) that are on 1–4 cm long, hairy stalks, in June (after the leaves expand).

FRUITS: Blue-black, plum-like drupes, 1–1.5 cm long, with thin, oily flesh around a stone; seeds single within indistinctly 10–12-grooved stones; fruits stalkless, in **clusters of 1–3 on 3–6 cm long stalks;** mature in autumn.

HABITAT: Usually wet, lowland sites; sometimes in uplands with a shallow water table.

GLOSSY BUCKTHORN was introduced to our continent primarily as an ornamental. The cultivar 'Columnaris' (tallhedge buckthorn) is popular in hedges and windbreaks. Glossy buckthorn is hardy as far north as North Bay, and it has become a serious, aggressive invader of some wetlands. • The hard wood has been used for making shoe lasts, nails and veneers. Its charcoal was once highly prized for making gunpowder. • Buckthorns were long ago credited with protective power against witchcraft, demons, poisons and headaches, but glossy buckthorn's true value, as a laxative, was not recognized until the 1300s. It might have been overlooked earlier because violent purgatives were then fashionable, whereas buckthorn is relatively mild. Today, herbalists recommend a tea of glossy buckthorn bark as a laxative. In Europe, the bark is often included in commercial laxatives. • The fruits mature over several weeks, so green, red and black fruits can occur at the same time. Unripe 'berries' produce a green dye, and the bark gives a yellow dye. • Birds eat glossy buckthorn fruits, which are slightly **poisonous** to humans (usually causing vomiting). • European buckthorn (p. 184) is distinguished by its spine-tipped branches, sub-opposite, finely toothed leaves and deeply grooved 'seeds' (stones).

ALSO CALLED: European alder-buckthorn, European-alder, columnar buckthorn, fen buckthorn, arrow-wood, black-dogwood • *Rhamnus frangula*

FRENCH NAME: Nerprun bourdaine

SIZE AND SHAPE: Small trees or shrubs to 6 m tall; crowns rounded.

TRUNKS: Short; bark thin, with conspicuous, pale, elongated pores (lenticels); wood fine-grained.

BRANCHES: Rather stout; twigs brown to grey, mottled with lenticels, minutely hairy, brittle; **buds lacking scales.**

LEAVES: **Mostly alternate,** simple, deciduous; blades glossy green, with **5–10 conspicuous, parallel veins per side,** elliptic to ovate and widest above midleaf, 5–8 cm long, 3–5 cm wide, abruptly pointed, **smooth-edged** or slightly wavy-edged; stalks stout, to 2 cm long, with slender, ephemeral stipules.

FLOWERS: **Greenish-yellow, less than 6 mm across, bisexual;** petals 5, 1–1.4 mm long, with notched tips; sepals 5, with fused bases; flowers on slender, unequal, 3–10 mm stalks, in 1–6-flowered clusters (umbels) in lower leaf axils, in June (after the leaves expand).

FRUITS: **Green to red to purplish-black, berry-like drupes,** about 7 mm across; seeds single within **smooth, nutlet-like stones,** 2–3 stones per fruit; fruits hang in clusters, mature in August–September.

HABITAT: Moist, shady sites in woods and ravines and around bogs.

DISTRIBUTION: Introduced from Eurasia and North Africa; grows wild in many parts of southern Ontario, mainly near cities.

BUCKTHORNS cannot be categorized neatly as alternate- or opposite-leaved. Most have alternate leaves, but European buckthorn is more or less opposite-leaved. • This small tree's hardiness, spiny branches, insect resistance and responsiveness to pruning have made it a popular hedge plant. European buckthorn escaped from cultivation many years ago in Ontario and has been widely dispersed by birds. It is now an aggressive invader that is so common it often appears indigenous. • The extremely unpleasant-tasting fruits are somewhat **poisonous** for humans and have a strong laxative effect. In 1650, European buckthorn syrup (which contained cinnamon, nutmeg and aniseed to cut the bitter flavour of the fruits) was included in the British pharmacopoeia. In the 1800s, British children were given buckthorn syrup laced with ginger and sugar as a laxative. Buckthorn fruits are still recommended as a laxative and are listed in the U.S. National Formulary. • In the 1600s, poultices of buckthorn leaves were recommended for staunching bleeding wounds. The bruised leaves were applied as a cure for warts. • European buckthorn retains green leaves late in the year. In autumn, such introduced species often stand out in sharp contrast to native plants, which shed their leaves promptly each fall.

ALSO CALLED: Common buckthorn, purging buckthorn, European waythorn, Hart's thorn, Carolina buckthorn

FRENCH NAME: Nerprun cathartique

SIZE AND SHAPE: Small trees or shrubs to 6 m tall; crowns rounded.

TRUNKS: Short; bark greyish-brown with elongated pores (lenticels), thin, smooth, peeling in curly-edged sheets; wood fine-grained.

BRANCHES: Often **spine-tipped;** twigs rigid, of 2 types: long, smooth, rather angled shoots, and short, warty shoots with crowded leaf scars and/or thorn-like tips; **buds scaly,** blackish, flat-lying.

LEAVES: Mostly opposite, simple, late-deciduous; blades dark green, hairless, with **3–5 conspicuous, strongly upcurved veins per side, minutely blunt-toothed,** broadly ovate to elliptic, 3–8 cm long, with **tips abruptly pointed, slightly folded and often curved back;** stalks hairy, grooved.

FLOWERS: Greenish-yellow, less than 6 mm across; functionally unisexual with male and female flowers on separate plants; petals 4, lance-shaped, 1–1.3 mm long (male flowers) or 0.6 mm long (female); sepals 4, fused; flowers on thread-like, unequal stalks in compact clusters (umbels) from leaf axils, in June (as the leaves expand).

FRUITS: Green to red to purplish-black, berry-like drupes, 5–6 mm across; seeds single within **grooved, nutlet-like stones,** usually 4 stones per fruit; fruits in dense clusters, mature in August–September.

HABITAT: Moist to dry pastures, clearings, woodlands and roadsides.

DISTRIBUTION: Introduced from Europe; grows wild in much of southern Ontario.

DOGWOODS typically have opposite leaves, but this species is an exception to the rule. • The strong wood has no commercial value, but it was once sought after for building seed and grist mills. Because the wood resists abrasion and withstands friction, it was used to make bearings and parts for mills. • The roots, mixed with vinegar, yield a light to dark brown dye. • Alternate-leaf dogwood and its cultivars are popular ornamental shrubs because of their profuse spring flowers, scarlet autumn leaves and purple, bird-attracting fruits. Also, these small trees have an unusual shape owing to their distinct layers of horizontal branches, giving rise to the alternative name 'pagoda dogwood.' Alternate-leaf dogwood is hardy as far north as Lake Superior and North Bay. It is not prone to serious diseases, but it is sometimes damaged by dogwood borer and other insect pests. • The dry, bitter fruits are not edible by human standards, but they provide food for grouse, pheasants, wild turkeys and squirrels. White-tailed deer browse on the twigs and leaves. • The name *alternifolia* refers to the alternate leaves.

ALSO CALLED: Pagoda dogwood, green osier, blue dogwood, pagoda-tree

FRENCH NAMES: Cornouiller à feuilles alternes, cornouiller alternifolié

SIZE AND SHAPE: Small trees or large, straggly shrubs 4–6 m tall; crowns flat, layered.

TRUNKS: Short, 5–10 cm in diameter; young bark greenish- to reddish-brown, thin, smooth; mature bark shallow-ridged; wood heavy, hard, fine-grained.

BRANCHES: Almost horizontal with upcurved tips, **in tiers;** twigs shiny reddish-green to purplish, with pores (lenticels) and often with **1–2 side-branches longer than the central shoot;** buds shiny chestnut-brown, with 2 loose outer scales.

LEAVES: Alternate (sometimes semi-opposite on short shoots), **clustered at branch tips,** simple, deciduous; blades green and hairless above, greyish and minutely hairy beneath, oval, with **4–5 parallel side-veins arched towards the tip,** 4–13 cm long, tapered to a point, **smooth- or slightly wavy-edged;** stalks 8–60 mm long; **leaves turn red** in autumn.

FLOWERS: White or cream-coloured, small, 4-parted, bisexual; numerous, on jointed stalks **in irregular, 5–10 cm wide, rounded to flat-topped clusters** (cymes), in June (after the leaves expand).

FRUITS: Dark blue to bluish-black, berry-like drupes, about 6 mm across; seeds single within egg-shaped stones; **fruits on short, red stalks,** mature July–August.

HABITAT: Open woodlands and slope bases near water, on rich soils.

185

THIS FAST-GROWING, SHORT-LIVED TREE is popular in southern parks and gardens. With its beautiful spring flowers, showy, bird-attracting fruits and red autumn leaves, eastern flowering dogwood is one of our finest native ornamental trees, but its delicate flower buds are not frost hardy. Sadly, dogwood anthracnose *(Discula destructiva)* is rapidly eradicating eastern flowering dogwood in southern Ontario and elsewhere. • The hard, strong wood has been used for golf-club heads, tool handles, rolling pins, weaving shuttles, spindles, small wheel hubs, barrel hoops and engravers' blocks. • Some tribes used the roots to make a scarlet dye for colouring porcupine quills and eagle feathers. The bark also yields a red dye. • Dried, ground bark was used as a quinine substitute for treating fevers. A bark decoction was used to treat mouth problems, and the fibrous twigs were used as chewing sticks (early toothbrushes), said to whiten teeth. • The drupes are not poisonous but are bitterly inedible when raw. Occasionally they have been mashed, seeded and mixed with other fruits in jams and jellies. • Many birds and small mammals eat the bitter fruits.

ALSO CALLED: Arrow-wood, bitter red-cherry, common dogwood, white cornel, dogtree, Florida dogwood, great-flowered dogwood, Virginia dogwood

FRENCH NAMES: Cornouiller fleuri, bois de flèche, bois-bouton, cornouiller à grandes fleurs, cornouiller de Floride, cornouiller à fleurs

SIZE AND SHAPE: Small trees or tall shrubs 3–10 m tall; crowns bushy, spreading.

TRUNKS: Short, 10–20 cm in diameter; mature bark dark reddish-brown, deeply checked with 4-sided scales; wood white, heavy and fine-grained.

BRANCHES: Spreading in more or less horizontal tiers; twigs greenish to reddish with white hairs and pores (lenticels); flower buds stalked, dome-shaped, at twig tips.

LEAVES: **Opposite, usually 2–4 at branch tips,** simple, deciduous; blades green above, greyish-green beneath, elliptic to oval, with **parallel veins arched towards the tip,** 5–15 cm long, narrow-pointed, **slightly wavy-edged;** leaves bronze to scarlet in autumn.

FLOWERS: Yellowish, tiny, 4-parted, bisexual, forming small, **dense 20–30-flowered clusters at the centre of 4 white or pinkish, petal-like bracts** (each 2–5 cm long and tipped with a reddish notch); **pseudanthia (flowers plus bracts) resemble single, showy, 5–10 cm wide flowers** at branch tips; appear in late May (before the leaves expand).

FRUITS: **Shiny, red, berry-like drupes** 1–1.5 cm long, tipped with persistent sepals, with thin, mealy flesh around a stone; seeds single within stones; **fruits in stalked, dense clusters of 3–6 or more,** undeveloped fruits often present; mature August–September.

HABITAT: In and around wet or sandy woodlands and ravines.

EASTERN WAHOO is too small to be commercially important. It is sometimes planted for its attractive autumn leaves and fruits, but European species of *Euonymus* are more popular for landscaping. • Eastern wahoo bark was used in folk medicine for many years as a tonic, laxative, diuretic and expectorant. Some American tribes boiled the bark to make medicinal teas for treating problems of the uterus or eyes, and for applying to facial sores. Various extracts, syrups and medicinal teas have been used over the years for treating fevers, upset stomachs, constipation, lung ailments, liver congestion and heart problems. Dried root bark was taken to relieve dropsy (fluid retention). The seed oil was used to induce vomiting and evacuation of the bowels, and the whole fruits were said to increase urine flow. In 1917, bark and root extracts were reported to affect the heart much like digitalis, and wahoo soon became a popular heart medicine. By 1921 this species was dropped as an official drug plant, although it remained on the U.S. Formulary until 1947. • **Caution:** The fruits, seeds and bark of this tree are considered poisonous. The bright-coloured fruits can attract children. • Many species of birds eat and disperse the seeds.

ALSO CALLED: Burning-bush euonymus, spindle-tree • *E. atropurpurea*

FRENCH NAME: Fusain pourpre

SIZE AND SHAPE: Small trees or shrubs 4.5–6 m tall; crowns rounded; roots spreading.

TRUNKS: Straight, often short or clumped; bark greenish-grey, often streaked reddish-brown, thin; wood nearly white, hard, dense.

BRANCHES: Spreading; twigs greenish, smooth, **somewhat 4-sided;** buds green, reddish-tinged, 6-scaled, 2–4 mm long, **pointed, flat-lying.**

LEAVES: Opposite, simple, deciduous; blades light green and hairless above, paler and **sparsely hairy beneath,** oblong-ovate to ovate or elliptic, 5–13 cm long and 2.5–5 cm wide, **abruptly pointed, finely sharp-toothed;** stalks about 1 cm long; leaves red in autumn.

FLOWERS: Purplish-maroon, 6–8 mm across, bisexual, usually 4-parted; petals 4, wide-spreading; sepals 4, fused at the base; flowers borne on slender stalks in branched, 2–4 cm wide, 5–18-flowered clusters (cymes) on 2–5 cm long stalks from leaf axils, in June–July (after the leaves expand).

FRUITS: Prominently 4-lobed capsules, pink to red or purplish when mature, 1–1.4 cm wide, **splitting open across the bottom;** seeds 4, each **enclosed in a fleshy, bright red aril;** fruits hang on slender stalks, mature in September, **empty capsules persist** into winter.

HABITAT: Low, moist sites such as damp woods and streamside thickets.

187

THE DENSE, HARD WOOD of this species was once favoured by carvers. It has also been used to make toothpicks, spindles, skewers, pipe stems and high-quality, easily erased art charcoal. Tanners valued the bark for preparing fine leather for gloves. • The bark, leaves and fruits of European spindle-tree have provided herbalists and drug manufacturers with a strong laxative. Unfortunately, the medicine is rather too effective, causing drastic purging and pain in the colon. The U.S. Food and Drug Administration classifies this tree as dangerous. • European spindle-tree is planted as an ornamental for its red autumn leaves and fruits. • *Euonymus,* meaning 'well-reputed' or 'famous,' was euphemistically bestowed in recognition of the plants' toxicity. • **Winged burning-bush** or *fusain ailé* **(E. alatus)** is an Asian species that is used in horticulture and occasionally grows wild in southern Ontario. It is readily distinguished by the 2–4 conspicuous corky wings on its twigs and by its stalkless leaves, which turn bright red in autumn. • The native *Euonymus,* eastern wahoo (p. 187), is easily identified by its hairy lower leaf surfaces, bright red arils and maroon flowers.

ALSO CALLED: European euonymus, skewer-wood, prickwood

FRENCH NAME: Fusain d'Europe

SIZE AND SHAPE: Small trees or tall shrubs up to 6 m tall; crowns rounded; roots spreading.

TRUNKS: Straight, often short or clumped; bark greenish-grey, often reddish-streaked, thin; wood hard, dense.

BRANCHES: Spreading; twigs greenish, smooth, **somewhat 4-sided; buds loosely 6-scaled, 2–4 mm long, plump, not flat-lying,** present at twig tips.

LEAVES: Opposite, simple, deciduous; **blades hairless,** green above, paler beneath, oblong-ovate to lance-shaped or elliptic, 5–12 cm long, **abruptly pointed, finely toothed;** stalks less than 2.5 cm long; **leaves red in autumn.**

FLOWERS: Greenish to yellowish-white, about 6 mm across, bisexual, usually 4-parted; petals 4, wide-spreading; sepals 4, fused at the base; flowers on slender stalks in loose, branched, 3–7-flowered clusters (cymes) on 2–5 cm long stalks from leaf axils, in June (after the leaves expand).

FRUITS: Prominently 4-lobed capsules, red or purplish when mature, 1–1.4 cm wide, **splitting open across the bottom;** seeds 4, each **enclosed in a fleshy, orange aril;** fruits hang on slender stalks, mature in September, **empty capsules persist.**

HABITAT: Low, moist sites on shores, in and around woods, in waste places and along roads.

DISTRIBUTION: Introduced from Europe; occasionally grows wild near urban centres in southern Ontario.

ALTHOUGH NOT WIDELY GROWN in Ontario, this shade-tolerant native shrub has been cultivated since 1640 for its attractive dark green leaves, lightly fragrant flower clusters and distinctive, persistent fruits. The hanging clusters of unusual papery pods attract attention through much of the year. The pods, along with the striped greenish branches, add interest in winter when the shrubs are leafless, and loose seeds in the pods rattle in the breeze. Children sometimes like to crush the pods to hear them pop. • The spreading roots send up suckers that may form thickets in open areas. In gardens, this tendency can cause problems when shoots appear in unwanted places. Otherwise, this attractive shrub is relatively maintenance free. It transplants easily and can be grown from cuttings or seeds. • The genus name, *Staphylea,* is derived from the Greek *staphyle,* 'bunch of grapes,' in reference to the hanging clusters of flowers. The specific epithet, *trifolia,* describes the 3-parted leaves. • When fruits and flowers are absent, American bladdernut may be confused with common hop-tree (p. 178). However, these two species are easily distinguished by examining their leaves and branches, which are opposite in bladdernuts and alternate in hop-trees.

ALSO CALLED: Tall bladdernut

FRENCH NAME: Staphylier à trois folioles

SIZE AND SHAPE: Trees or shrubs to 5 m tall; crowns rounded; roots spreading.

TRUNKS: Often clumped; young bark smooth, green, often with mottled stripes; mature bark grey to brown, becoming slightly ridged with pale, longitudinal stripes.

BRANCHES: Erect, rather stiff; twigs stout, greenish, almost ringed at nodes, somewhat striped; buds egg-shaped, 2–4-scaled.

LEAVES: Opposite; compound, divided into **3 leaflets;** leaflets dark green and smooth above, paler and sparsely hairy beneath, 4–10 cm long, pointed, finely sawtoothed; tip leaflet long-stalked, side leaflets essentially stalkless; main leaf stalk at least 10 cm long, with slender, ephemeral bracts at the base (2 stipules) and at the top (2 stipules below each leaflet); leaves green to pale yellow in autumn.

FLOWERS: Greenish-white, narrowly bell-shaped, 8–9 mm long, bisexual, 5-parted; sepals nearly as long as the petals; **flowers in nodding, branched, 4–10 cm long clusters (racemes) at branch tips,** in May (just before the leaves expand fully).

FRUITS: Inflated, thin-walled, veiny capsules with 3 pointed lobes, green to yellowish-brown, 3–6 cm long, opening near tips; seeds yellow-brown, bony, 1–4 per chamber, **rattling in ripe capsules;** fruits hang on slender stalks, mature in late summer, persist into winter.

HABITAT: Moist, often rocky woods, floodplains and hillsides; sometimes wooded sand dunes.

Horsechestnut *Aesculus hippocastanum* Horsechestnut Family

HORSECHESTNUT is a hardy, moderately fast-growing tree often planted as an ornamental. It lives about 80–100 years and can tolerate urban conditions, but its broad, domed canopy requires considerable space. • Horsechestnut is the 'spreading chestnut tree' that Henry Wadsworth Longfellow wrote about. The large, sweeping branches tipped with showy, erect flower clusters suggest enormous candelabras.

• The fruits and seeds have been used for centuries to treat colds, whooping cough, fever, rheumatism, backache, nerve pain and sunburn. Today, horsechestnut-seed preparations are sold in Europe and the U.S. for reducing inflammation and pain associated with varicose veins, ulcers, hemorrhoids and phlebitis.

• **Caution:** The seeds, leaves and bark contain aesculin, a toxic alkaloid that can cause vomiting, stupor, twitching and even paralysis. Some sources report that horsechestnuts have been used as horse fodder, but most say these fruits are poisonous to livestock. • Horsechestnut trees produce good seed crops almost every year. The large, inedible fruits are largely shunned by wildlife, although squirrels occasionally eat the embryo stalks in the seeds.

• The name 'horsechestnut' reflects the similarity between these seeds and the edible seeds of chestnuts (*Castanea* spp., p. 92). Be careful never to confuse the two.

FRENCH NAMES: Marronnier d'Inde, faux-marron, marronnier commun

SIZE AND SHAPE: Trees 12–25 m tall; crowns broad, rounded.

TRUNKS: Short, 30–150 cm in diameter; young bark dark grey-brown, smooth; mature bark fissured, scaly; wood pale, light, close-grained.

BRANCHES: Ascending, then downcurved and finally upcurved at tips; **twigs stout, with an unpleasant odour when bruised;** buds dark brown, **sticky, 2–4 cm long at twig tips,** smaller and paired below.

LEAVES: Opposite, deciduous; compound, **palmately divided into 5–9 (usually 7) stalkless leaflets at the tip of a long stalk;** leaflets yellowish-green, widest above midleaf, 10–25 cm long; leaf scars large, horseshoe-shaped.

FLOWERS: White to cream-coloured, red- and yellow-spotted, bell-shaped, 2–3 cm long; unisexual and bisexual flowers in each cluster; **petals 5, unequal;** flowers in **showy, erect, 20–30 cm long, cone-shaped clusters (panicles) at tips of branches** in spring (after the leaves expand).

FRUITS: Green to brown, spiny, leathery, round capsules, 5–6 cm across, splitting lengthwise into 3 segments; **seeds up to 5 cm across, 1–2 (rarely 3) per capsule,** smooth, **satin-shiny, brown with a rough, pale end;** fruits hang in clusters, drop in autumn.

HABITAT: Disturbed sites along fences and in woodlands.

DISTRIBUTION: Introduced from southeastern Europe; occasional escape in southern Ontario.

OHIO BUCKEYE is Canada's only indigenous *Aesculus* species. It is occasionally planted as an ornamental shade tree, and adventive trees are known from several areas (usually on floodplains). The first native specimens were discovered only recently, in 1982, when a population of large trees was confirmed on Walpole Island at the northern end of Lake St. Clair. • The weak, uniform wood is easy to carve and resists splitting, so it is ideal for making artificial limbs. It has also been used to make troughs for collecting maple syrup and as a source of paper pulp. Ohio buckeye was once a valuable timber tree in the U.S., but because of its increasing rarity, it now has little commercial importance. • Most parts of this tree, including the large seeds, contain the **toxic** alkaloid aesculin. Perhaps because of its toxicity, Ohio buckeye is relatively disease- and insect-free, and its fruits are seldom harvested by wildlife. However, squirrels sometimes eat the soft, young 'nuts.' • The name 'buckeye' refers to the seeds, which somewhat resemble the eyes of deer. • Horsechestnut (p. 190) is readily distinguished by its larger (10–25 cm), more numerous (usually 7), abruptly pointed leaflets and its sticky winter buds.

ALSO CALLED: Fetid buckeye

FRENCH NAME: Marronnier glabre

SIZE AND SHAPE: Trees 9–15 m tall; crowns broad.

TRUNKS: Straight, up to 50 cm in diameter; young bark grey, smooth; mature bark dark brown, with thick, scaly plates; wood pale, light, close-grained.

BRANCHES: Spreading to drooping, upcurved at tips; **twigs stout,** reddish-brown, with orange pores (lenticels), unpleasant-smelling when bruised; **buds 1.5–1.8 cm long at twig tips,** reddish, powdery-coated, smaller and paired below.

LEAVES: **Opposite,** deciduous; compound, **palmately divided into 5–7 (usually 5) stalkless leaflets at the tip of a long stalk;** leaflets bright or yellowish green above, paler and hairy beneath, lance-shaped, **widest above midleaf,** 6–15 cm long, unevenly sharp-toothed; leaf scars large, horseshoe-shaped; leaves yellow to orange in autumn.

FLOWERS: **Pale greenish-yellow,** narrowly bell-shaped, 1.5–3.5 cm long; unisexual and bisexual flowers in each cluster; **petals 4, unequal; stamens 7, often twice as long as the petals; flowers in showy, erect, 10–15 cm long, cone-shaped clusters (panicles) at branch tips,** in May (after the leaves expand).

FRUITS: **Yellowish-green, spiny, leathery capsules 2.5–5 cm across,** splitting lengthwise into 3 segments; **seeds satin-shiny, dark reddish-brown with a rough, pale end, 2–3.5 cm across, 1–3 per capsule;** fruits drop in September–October.

HABITAT: Rich, well-drained sites, especially on floodplains.

Key to the Maples (Genus *Acer*, Family Aceraceae)

1a Leaves compound, divided into 3–5 leaflets .... ***A. negundo*, Manitoba maple** (p. 201)
1b Leaves simple **2**

2a Leaves deeply 3–5-lobed, otherwise smooth-edged or with a few coarse teeth, notches rounded ... **3**
2b Leaves variously lobed, edged with many sharp teeth, notches pointed at the base and often toothed almost to the base **5**

3a Flower petals conspicuous; flowers borne on ascending, hairless stalks in elongated, stalked clusters; keys with wings spreading at almost 180°; leaf juice milky
.... ***A. platanoides*, Norway maple** (p. 195)
3b Flowers lacking petals, hanging on slender, hairy stalks in tassel-like clusters; keys with wings spreading at less than 120°, often almost parallel; leaf juice clear **4**

4a Leaves mostly 3-lobed with drooping edges, smooth- or wavy-edged or with a few irregular coarse teeth, green or brownish and more or less hairy beneath .... ***A. nigrum*, black maple** (p. 194)
4b Leaves mostly 5-lobed with flat (not drooping) edges, edged with regular, coarse, pointed teeth, pale and essentially hairless beneath .... ***A. saccharum*, sugar maple** (p. 193)

5a Leaves deeply cut into 5 coarsely toothed, relatively narrow lobes, with lobe bases usually narrower than the upper lobe **6**
5b Leaves more shallowly cut into 3–5 parallel-sided to broadly triangular lobes, edged with regular, coarse to fine teeth **7**

6a Flower petals conspicuous; flowers borne in elongated, stalked clusters, appearing after the leaves unfold; keys mature in mid- to late summer, wings spread at <30°; leaves with coarse single teeth
.... ***A. pseudoplatanus*, sycamore maple** (p. 195)
6b Flowers lacking petals, hanging on slender stalks in tassel-like clusters, appearing long before the leaves; keys mature in spring, wings spread at about 90°; leaves with many double teeth
.... ***A. saccharinum*, silver maple** (p. 196)

7a Leaves narrowly triangular, longer than wide, with 2 small basal lobes and a large, coarsely toothed central lobe .... ***A. ginnala*, Amur maple** (p. 199)
7b Leaves more rounded, usually about as wide as long, with 3 large lobes above midleaf and sometimes 2 smaller basal lobes **8**

8a Buds 6–10-scaled; main lobe at leaf tip with roughly parallel sides; flowers in compact, tassel-like clusters, appearing before the leaves; keys mature in spring ... ***A. rubrum*, red maple** (p. 197)
8b Buds 2-scaled; main lobe at leaf tip triangular, gradually tapered from the base; flowers in elongated, branched clusters, appearing after the leaves; keys mature in summer **9**

9a Young trunks greyish, not striped; leaves edged with coarse (2–3 per cm), single teeth; flowers in erect, many-branched clusters .... ***A. spicatum*, mountain maple** (p. 198)
9b Young trunks green with pale stripes; leaves edged with fine (7–12 per cm), double teeth; flowers hanging, in simple, elongated clusters .... ***A. pensylvanicum*, striped maple** (p. 200)

SUGAR MAPLE is Canada's national tree, as represented by the 'maple leaf' on our flag.
• The fine-grained, durable wood polishes well and sometimes has a beautiful wavy or speckled appearance. It is highly valued for flooring, furniture, veneer, panelling, plywood, sports articles, musical instruments, tool handles, spindles, cutting blocks and other items that require hard wood. In the past, the wood was used for plows, wagons and early wooden railway rails. • Settlers used potash-rich maple ashes as fertilizer. The ashes have also been used in soap and in pottery glazes. • 'Sugaring-off' was an important part of pioneer culture. Sap was gathered in pails each spring and boiled over wood fires to produce maple syrup or sugar. The sap contains 2–6% sugar, so 30–40 L produces 1 L of syrup. Today, vacuum plastic tubing carries sap from trees to processing sites, where oil- or gas-powered evaporators reduce it to syrup in a multimillion-dollar industry. • Severe declines in Canada's sugar bushes in the 1980s were caused by a combination of drought, extremely cold winters, severe defoliation and acid rain.

ALSO CALLED: Rock maple, hard maple, bird's-eye maple, curly maple, head maple, sugartree, sweet maple • *A. saccharaphorum*

FRENCH NAMES: Érable à sucre, érable sucrier, érable dur, érable franc, érable du Canada, érable piqué, érable moiré, érable ondé

SIZE AND SHAPE: Trees 20–35 m tall; crowns rounded, narrow; roots wide-spreading.

TRUNKS: Straight, 50–150 cm in diameter; mature bark grey, irregularly ridged, sometimes scaly; wood light yellowish-brown, hard, heavy.

BRANCHES: Sturdy; twigs shiny reddish-brown, hairless, straight; buds brown, faintly hairy, **sharply pointed, with 12–16 paired scales,** 6–12 mm long at twig tips, smaller and paired below.

LEAVES: Opposite, simple, deciduous; blades deep yellowish-green above, paler and hairless beneath, 8–20 cm long, with **5 palmate lobes** (occasionally 3) separated by rounded notches, edged with a **few irregular, blunt-pointed teeth;** stalks 4–8 cm long; leaves yellow to bright red in autumn.

FLOWERS: Greenish-yellow, small; functionally unisexual, often with male and female flowers in mixed clusters on same tree; petals absent; sepals 5; **flowers hang on slender, hairy, 3–7 cm long stalks** in tassel-like clusters (umbels) at or near branch tips, in spring **(before the leaves expand).**

FRUITS: Green to brown **pairs of winged keys** (samaras), **U-shaped, with spreading to almost parallel wings shorter than the slender stalks;** keys 2–4 cm long; seedcases plump; fruits hang in clusters, drop in autumn.

HABITAT: Deep, rich soils in fairly dry woods, especially in calcareous regions.

BLACK MAPLE has strong, straight-grained, uniformly textured wood that is sold as 'hard maple.' Like sugar maple wood, it is used for furniture, fixtures, farm tools, spindles, veneer, plywood, flooring, dies and cutting blocks. • The sap from black maple trees can be collected and used to make syrup and sugar. • Like sugar maple, black maple has shade-tolerant saplings that can survive for many years in the forest understorey until new openings provide the light necessary for them to shoot up quickly and take their place in the canopy. • Black maple and sugar maple (p. 193) hybridize frequently, producing offspring with intermediate characteristics. Some taxonomists classify black maple as a variety of sugar maple. These trees are usually distinguished by their leaves and bark. Sugar maple leaves are flat, deep yellow-green and hairless, and their central lobes are rather square, with parallel sides. Black maple leaves are drooping and deep green with velvety lower surfaces, and their central lobes tend to taper from the base. Sugar maple bark is greyish with loose-edged plates, whereas black maple bark is blackish-grey and more deeply furrowed.

ALSO CALLED: Black sugar maple, hard maple, rock maple • *A. saccharum* var. *nigrum*

FRENCH NAME: Érable noir

SIZE AND SHAPE: Trees 20–30 m tall; crowns open, rounded.

TRUNKS: Straight, 50–150 cm in diameter; mature bark blackish-grey, with long, irregular, vertical ridges, sometimes scaly; wood pale yellowish-brown, heavy, hard.

BRANCHES: Stout; twigs dull reddish-brown, stout, straight; buds dark greyish-brown, hairy, with paired scales, 3–5 mm long at twig tips, smaller and paired below.

LEAVES: **Opposite,** simple, deciduous, appearing **wilted;** blades dark green above, **densely brownish velvety beneath,** 10–15 cm long, **with 3 palmate lobes** (sometimes 5 indistinct lobes) separated by **open, shallow notches,** edged with a **few irregular, blunt-pointed teeth;** stalks hairy; leaves yellow to brownish-yellow (seldom red) in autumn.

FLOWERS: Yellowish, small; unisexual with male and female flowers mixed or in separate clusters on the same tree; petals absent; sepals 5; **flowers hang on slender, hairy, 1.8–5 cm long stalks,** in tassel-like clusters (umbels) at or near branch tips, in spring **(before the leaves expand).**

FRUITS: Green to brown **pairs of winged keys** (samaras), **U-shaped with spreading to almost parallel wings about as long as the slender, hairy stalks;** keys about 3 cm long; seedcases plump; fruits hang in clusters, drop in autumn.

HABITAT: Moist, fertile sites in bottomlands and on floodplains.

THIS POPULAR ORNAMENTAL shade tree can grow in polluted urban sites with compacted, nutrient-poor soils. It is more resistant than native maples to insects and fungal diseases. Norway maple usually produces abundant seed, and it is becoming an aggressive invader of natural vegetation in some regions. • Many cultivars of this beautiful, hardy species have been developed. The cultivar 'Schwedleri' (Schwedler maple), with its purplish-red spring leaves and bright orange-red to purple autumn foliage, has been planted in North America for over a century. 'Crimson King' boasts rich maroon leaves and is also very popular. Norway maple keeps its leaves about 2 weeks longer than native maples in the autumn. • Norway maple could be confused with sugar maple, but Norway maple's dark green (rather than yellow-green) leaves have 5–7 (rather than 3–5), bristle-tipped (rather than blunt-pointed) lobes and turn only yellow (never red or orange) in autumn. • Another European introduction, **sycamore maple** or *érable sycomore (A. pseudoplatanus)*, is also widely planted in southern Ontario, but it rarely if ever escapes. It is distinguished by its thicker, more wrinkled leaves, with white-hairy veins and numerous coarse teeth.

FRENCH NAMES: Érable de Norvège, érable plane, érable platanoïde

SIZE AND SHAPE: Trees 18–21 m tall; crowns dense, rounded, broad.

TRUNKS: Straight; bark very dark grey, with regular low, intersecting ridges, not scaly; wood pale, straight-grained, uniformly textured.

BRANCHES: Ascending to spreading; twigs stout, straight, purplish-tinged to reddish, hairless, with prominent pores (lenticels) and **milky juice;** buds purplish to reddish, plump, blunt, with **6–8 fleshy, paired scales, 3–4 mm long at twig tips,** smaller and paired below.

LEAVES: **Opposite,** simple, deciduous, with **milky juice;** blades dark green, hairless, 8–16 cm long, 10–18 cm wide, with **5–7 palmate lobes** plus a few large, bristle-tipped teeth; stalks long; leaves yellow in autumn.

FLOWERS: Greenish-yellow, about 1 cm across, bisexual or male; petals 5; sepals 5; flowers in **erect, rounded clusters (corymbs) at branch tips,** in April–May **(as the leaves expand).**

FRUITS: Green to brown **pairs of winged keys** (samaras), with wings spreading at almost 180°; keys 3.5–5 cm long; seedcases flat; **fruits hang on slender stalks in clusters,** mature in autumn, often persist through winter.

HABITAT: Roadsides, vacant lots, hedgerows and thickets.

DISTRIBUTION: Introduced from Europe; naturalized in many parts of southern Ontario.

A. pseudoplatanus   *A. platanoides*

195

SILVER MAPLE has straight-grained, rather brittle wood that is usually used where strength is not important, e.g., for inexpensive furniture, veneer, boxes, crates and pulp. • Although not as showy as most maples in autumn, this handsome, fast-growing, hardy tree is widely planted as an ornamental. However, silver maple requires considerable space and usually produces abundant seed and leaf fall each year. Also, its brittle limbs break easily and its roots can spread aggressively to clog sewer pipes. • Several cultivars with deeply divided leaves have been developed and are propagated from cuttings. 'Laciniatum,' or 'Wieri' (cut-leaf silver maple), is especially popular. • Silver maple sap is only half as sweet as that of sugar maple (p. 193), but with patient boiling it yields a delicious pale syrup. • When felled, silver maple sends up vigorous shoots from dormant buds in the stump. Also, fallen branches can sprout roots and grow into new trees. • Many birds and small mammals (e.g., grosbeaks, squirrels) eat the abundant seeds. Silver maple trees commonly have hollow trunks that provide dens for squirrels, raccoons and other mammals; nesting cavities for wood ducks and other birds; and hideouts for small children.

ALSO CALLED: Soft maple, white maple, river maple

FRENCH NAMES: Érable argenté, érable blanc, plaine blanche, érable a fruits cotonneaux, plaine de France, plane blanche

SIZE AND SHAPE: Trees 20–30 m tall; crowns rounded, open; roots spreading, shallow.

TRUNKS: Short in open sites, 50–100 cm in diameter; young bark grey, smooth; **mature bark grey, often shaggy** with thin strips that peel from both ends; wood pale, hard, heavy.

BRANCHES: Sharply ascending then arching downward to upturned tips; twigs shiny, hairless,

unpleasant-smelling when broken; buds shiny, reddish, blunt, with 6–10 paired scales; flower buds plump, ringing the twigs.

LEAVES: Opposite, simple, deciduous; blades light green, **silvery-white beneath,** 8–15 cm long, with **5–7 palmate lobes separated by deep, concavely narrowed notches, irregularly coarse-toothed;** stalks 7.5–10 cm long; leaves pale yellow to brown in October.

FLOWERS: Greenish-yellow or reddish, tiny; unisexual with male and female flowers in separate clusters on same or separate trees; petals absent; sepals 5; flowers in dense, almost stalkless clusters (umbels) in late winter **(long before the leaves expand).**

FRUITS: Yellowish-green to brownish **pairs of winged keys** (samaras) with **wings spreading at 90°,** often only 1 per pair maturing; **keys 4–7 cm long;** seedcases ribbed; **fruits hang on slender stalks in clusters,** drop singly in late May to early June (as the leaves expand fully).

HABITAT: Moist to wet sites near streams, swamps and lakes.

RED MAPLE'S straight-grained, uniform wood has been used for pulp and for making crates, furniture, cabinets, veneer and flooring. • Pennsylvanian colonists made a dark red ink by boiling the bark, which also yields brown or black dyes with different mordants. • This attractive, red-tinged tree is widely planted as an ornamental. Several cultivars have been developed that endure urban conditions. • Although red maple sap is only half as sweet as that of sugar maple (p. 193), it can be used to make syrup. • Red maple is one of the first trees to flower each spring. It grows quickly and usually lives 75–100 years. • This widespread, variable species is very similar to silver maple (p. 196), especially when leafless, and the 2 species often cross-pollinate to produce a hybrid known as **Freeman's maple *(Acer x freemanii)*.** The leaves of Freeman's maple turn blotchy red and yellow in autumn, and their notches are narrower than those of red maple but wider than those of silver maple. The keys of Freeman's maple are similarly intermediate (2.5–4 cm long). This hybrid is a widespread, frequently overlooked tree of swamp forests in southern Ontario. Reports of silver maple from north of its usual range may actually indicate Freeman's maple.

Photo, bottom left: *A. rubrum,* male flowers
Bottom right: *A. x freemanii*

ALSO CALLED: Scarlet maple, soft maple, swamp maple, curled maple

FRENCH NAMES: Érable rouge, érable tendre, plaine rouge, plane rouge

SIZE AND SHAPE: Trees 20–25 m tall; crowns long, rounded; roots shallow, wide-spreading.

TRUNKS: Short on open sites, 40–130 cm in diameter; young bark light grey, smooth; mature bark dark greyish-brown, scaly, with thin plates that peel from both ends; wood pale brown, heavy, hard.

BRANCHES: Ascending; twigs shiny, reddish, hairless, not unpleasant-smelling; buds shiny, reddish, hairless, usually with 8 paired scales, blunt, 3–4 mm at twig tips, smaller and paired below; flower buds usually ring dwarf twigs.

LEAVES: Opposite, simple, deciduous; blades light green, whitish beneath, 5–15 cm long, with **3–5 palmate lobes separated by shallow, sharp notches, irregularly double-toothed;** stalks 5–10 cm long; leaves bright red in August–September.

FLOWERS: Reddish, short-stalked, about **3 mm** across; unisexual, usually with male and female flowers on separate branches on the same tree; petals 5; sepals 5; **flowers in tassel-like clusters (umbels),** in late winter **(long before the leaves expand).**

FRUITS: Red, reddish-brown or yellow **pairs of winged keys** (samaras) with **wings spreading at 50–60°,** slender-stalked; **keys 1.5–2.5 cm long; fruits hang in clusters,** mature and drop singly in late May to early June (4–6 weeks after flowering).

HABITAT: Cool, moist sites by swamps, streams and springs; sometimes on drier upland sites.

MOUNTAIN MAPLE is Canada's smallest and most northerly maple. Although it has no commercial value, it is sometimes cultivated for its colourful leaves and fruits. • Some tribes boiled the young twigs with a pinch of alum and used the solution to soothe eyes irritated by smoke. • Mountain maple is very important for preventing erosion on streambanks and steep slopes. When spreading branches become buried in leaf litter, they put down roots and send up new shoots. This process (layering) can produce impenetrable thickets on recently cleared land. • Moose and deer eagerly seek new mountain maple growth. • Without flowers or fruits, this species might be confused with some of the viburnums. Mapleleaf viburnum (p. 214) is a similar shrub distinguished by its downy twigs and resin-dotted lower leaf surfaces. Highbush cranberry (p. 214) has small, club-shaped glands on its leaf stalks near the blade. These viburnums have relatively short-stalked leaves (often with slender stipules) with more sparingly toothed blades than mountain maple. • Leafless maples could be confused with dogwoods, but the fruits (keys) and finely hairy twigs identify them as maples.

ALSO CALLED: Dwarf maple, moose maple, low-moose maple, whitewood, whiterod, white maple

FRENCH NAMES: Érable à épis, plaine bâtarde, fouéreux, plaine bleue, plane bâtarde

SIZE AND SHAPE: Small trees or tall shrubs 3–5 m tall; crowns uneven; roots shallow.

TRUNKS: Crooked, often clumped, 7–20 cm in diameter; bark greenish-grey to reddish, thin, smooth or finely grooved; wood pale, soft, weak.

BRANCHES: Slender, ascending, few; **twigs velvety,** minutely grey-hairy, **yellowish-green** to purplish-grey or pink; buds grey-hairy, 2-scaled, stalked, single at twig tips, paired below.

LEAVES: Opposite, simple, deciduous; blades deep yellowish-green, whitish-hairy beneath, 5–12 cm long, **irregularly saw-toothed,** with **3 prominent lobes** above midleaf and **sometimes 2 small lower lobes,** lobes separated by **wedge-shaped notches;** stalks usually longer than blades, reddish; leaves red, yellow or brown in autumn.

FLOWERS: Pale yellowish-green, 6 mm across; bisexual and unisexual, with all 3 flower types often present on the same tree; petals 5; sepals 5; flowers in groups of 2–4 along a central stalk, forming **erect, 6–10 cm long, branched clusters** (panicles), in late May–June (after the leaves expand).

FRUITS: Scarlet to yellow or pinkish-brown pairs of keys (samaras) with wings diverging at 90° or less; keys 1.8–2 cm long; **seedcases indented on one side; fruits hang in slender clusters,** mature in July–August, often persist into winter.

HABITAT: Moist mixed woods, thickets, swamps and rocky ravines.

THIS POPULAR ORNAMENTAL tree is widely planted for its fragrant flowers, showy reddish keys and spectacular autumn foliage. Amur maple is one of the few maples with perfumed flowers and one of the best trees for fall colour. It makes a good patio shade tree and can be planted in groups to form borders, hedges, screens and backgrounds. Tree form, leaf characteristics and fruit colour are all highly variable, so selection of desirable cultivars would seem appropriate, but few have been developed. • Amur maple is adapted to northern areas with relatively cool summers, and it tolerates dry conditions and partial shade. It even thrives in tubs along the streets of Montreal. This hardy tree requires little maintenance, though occasionally weedy seedlings can be a problem. • Although Amur maple is usually shrubby, it can withstand heavy pruning and is often shaped into a tree form. Maples should not be pruned until the leaves are fully expanded, because the heavy flow of spring sap causes excessive 'bleeding' if trees are pruned too early. • The name *ginnala* is derived from the vernacular name for this species in its native range in eastern Asia.

FRENCH NAME: Érable ginnala

SIZE AND SHAPE: Small trees or tall shrubs 4–6 m tall; crowns rounded, shrubby and uneven when young; roots shallow.

TRUNKS: Usually clumped, sometimes pruned to a single stem; bark dark grey, scaly, fissured; wood pale, light, soft, weak.

BRANCHES: Slender, often wand-like and arching; twigs slender, yellowish-brown, hairless, somewhat angled; buds reddish-brown to tan, with hairy-tipped scales.

LEAVES: Opposite, simple, deciduous; blades deep glossy green, paler beneath, essentially **hairless with age,** 3–10 cm long, narrowly triangular, 3-lobed (rarely undivided or 5-lobed) with **2 short basal lobes and a large central lobe, notches wedge-shaped,** edges irregularly **double sharp-toothed;** stalks slender, 3–4 cm long; leaves brilliant red (sometimes yellow or orange) in autumn.

FLOWERS: Pale yellow to creamy white, fragrant, 5 mm long; petals 5, inconspicuous; sepals 5; **flowers in drooping clusters** (corymbs) at branch tips, in May–June (as the leaves expand).

FRUITS: Scarlet or pinkish-brown pairs of dry keys (samaras) with **inner edges of wings almost parallel;** keys 2–2.5 cm long, hairless; **fruits hang in clusters,** mature in July–August, often persist into winter.

HABITAT: Roadsides, fence lines and other open, disturbed sites.

DISTRIBUTION: Introduced from Manchuria and Japan; widely planted and escaped in southern Ontario.

STRIPED MAPLE'S soft, weak wood has no commercial value, but it is sometimes used as firewood. • This shade-tolerant tree lives about 100 years. It is planted as an ornamental in North America and Europe for its beautiful leaves (the largest of any Ontario maple) and attractive winter bark. • Sometimes a tree will produce only male flowers one year and only female flowers the next. • Beavers and hares eat the bark of this tree, and the keys provide food for songbirds, grouse and small mammals (mainly rodents). This shrub is a favourite food of deer and moose, hence the alternative name 'moosewood.' In fact, the word 'moose' originated from the Algonquian word *mousou*, or 'twig-eater.' • In winter, shrubby striped maples could be confused with American bladdernut (p. 189). Bladdernut also has striped bark and opposite branching, but its leaves are compound (trifoliate) and its fruits are 3-lobed, inflated capsules. Some of the viburnums with opposite, 3-lobed leaves, such as highbush cranberry and mapleleaf viburnum (p. 214), may also resemble striped maple, but viburnum bark is not striped and viburnum fruits are berry-like drupes.

ALSO CALLED: Moosewood, moose maple, whistlewood, goosefoot maple

FRENCH NAMES: Érable de Pennsylvanie, bois barré, bois noir, bois d'orignal, érable strié, érable barré

SIZE AND SHAPE: Trees or shrubs 4–10 m tall; crowns uneven; roots spreading, shallow.

TRUNKS: Short, 7–20 cm in diameter; **young bark green with conspicuous, whitish vertical stripes;** mature bark greenish-brown with darkened stripes; wood pale, light.

BRANCHES: Ascending, arching; twigs shiny, reddish-brown, hairless, rather stout; **buds** hairless, 2-scaled, stalked, 1 cm long at twig tips, smaller and paired below.

LEAVES: Opposite, simple, deciduous; blades yellowish-green, hairless, **10–18 cm long,** tipped with 3 palmate, shallow, slender-pointed lobes (sometimes unlobed with rapid growth), **finely double-toothed;** stalks 2.5–8 cm long; leaves yellow in autumn.

FLOWERS: Bright greenish-yellow, bell-shaped, 6 mm across; unisexual (rarely bisexual) with male and female flowers in separate clusters on the same or separate trees; petals 5; sepals 5; flowers on slender stalks along a central axis, forming **drooping, 3–10 cm long clusters** (racemes), in late May–June (after the leaves expand).

FRUITS: Greenish **pairs of winged keys** (samaras) with **wings spreading at 90–120°;** keys 2.5–3 cm long; **seedcases indented on one side; fruits hang on short stalks from a central axis in elongated clusters** at branch tips, mature in late July–August, drop in autumn.

HABITAT: Cool, moist, **shady** woodlands.

MANITOBA MAPLE trunks are usually too small and irregular to provide lumber, but the close-grained wood has been used occasionally for crates, boxes, paper pulp and firewood. • When sugar was scarce, Prairie settlers sometimes tapped this tree to make maple syrup, but Manitoba maple is the least productive maple for this purpose. • This hardy, fast-growing tree can survive dry and extremely cold conditions, so it is widely planted as a shade and shelterbelt tree. Unfortunately, its weak, spreading branches are easily broken by wet snow, ice and wind. Manitoba maple is shade-intolerant, growing rapidly for the first 15–20 years and living about 60–75 years. • The abundant seeds of female trees can be a nuisance in gardens, but they do provide important winter food for mice, squirrels and seed-eating birds such as evening grosbeaks. • The box-elder bug *(Boisea trivittata)* is a widespread pest that can occur in large numbers in urban areas where Manitoba maple is common. • Manitoba maple could be mistaken for an ash, but ash trees usually have more numerous (5–9), smooth-edged or regularly toothed leaflets. Also, ash leaf scars are well separated (not meeting); ash keys are single with symmetrical wings; and ash seedcases are smooth.

ALSO CALLED: Western box-elder, ashleaf maple

FRENCH NAMES: Érable à feuilles composées, érable négundo, érable à Giguère, érable à feuille de frêne, érable du Manitoba, frêne à fruits de érable, plane à Giguère, plane négundo

SIZE AND SHAPE: Trees 8–20 m tall; crowns uneven; roots mostly shallow.

TRUNKS: Usually short, 30–75 cm in diameter; young bark light greyish-brown, smooth; mature bark darker greyish-brown, narrow-ridged; wood nearly white, soft.

BRANCHES: Spreading, crooked; twigs brown to greenish-purple, smooth, shiny or **waxy-powdered; buds finely white-hairy**, blunt, with 4–6 paired scales, 3–8 mm long at twig tips, flat-lying or hidden by leaf-stalk bases below.

LEAVES: Opposite, deciduous; compound, **pinnately divided into 3–5 leaflets** (sometimes 7–9 with rapid growth); leaflets yellowish-green, **5–12 cm long, irregularly coarse-toothed or shallow-lobed; leaf scars meeting around twigs;** leaves yellow in autumn.

FLOWERS: Pale yellowish-green, tiny; unisexual with male and female flowers on separate trees; petals absent; sepals 5; male flowers hang in loose bundles (umbels); female flowers short-stalked along a central axis in nodding clusters (racemes); flowers appear in spring (as or before the leaves expand).

FRUITS: Green to pale brown **pairs of winged keys** (samaras) with **wings usually spreading at less than 45°;** keys 3–5 cm long; **seedcases wrinkled,** elongated; **fruits hang in elongated clusters,** mature in autumn, persist into winter.

HABITAT: Open, often disturbed sites, usually near water or on floodplains.

Key to Genera in the Olive Family (Oleaceae)

1a Leaves pinnately divided into leaflets; flowers unisexual, without petals or sepals, in small, inconspicuous clusters; fruits slender, long-winged keys . . . . . ***Fraxinus,* ash** (key to species, below)

1b Leaves simple, heart-shaped; flowers bisexual, 4-lobed, trumpet-shaped, in showy white to deep purple clusters; fruits woody capsules . . . . ***Syringa,* lilac** (p. 203)

Key to the Ashes (Genus *Fraxinus*)

1a Leaflets smooth-edged (sometimes with a few faint, irregular, blunt teeth); keys with cylindrical seedcases winged on the upper part only (not to the base) **2**

1b Leaflets regularly (sometimes faintly) toothed above the middle; keys various **3**

2a Wings extending about ⅓ of the way down the seedcases; leaflets 6–15 cm long, with lower leaf surfaces pale green, essentially hairless and dulled by many minute bumps
. . . . ***F. americana,* white ash** (p. 204)

2b Wings extending over halfway down the seedcases; leaflets 12–25 cm long, with lower leaf surfaces pale yellowish-green, soft-hairy and lacking minute bumps
. . . . ***F. profunda,* pumpkin ash** (p. 206)

3a Leaves divided into 5–9 leaflets, distinctly paler beneath; seedcases cylindrical, winged on the upper part only (not to the base), tapered to the base; calyx visible at the base of each key; uppermost side-buds close against the branch-tip bud . . . . . ***F. pennsylvanica,* red ash** (p. 205)

3b Leaves divided into 7–13 leaflets, green above and below; seedcases flattened, winged to the blunt base; calyx minute, not visible on each key; uppermost side-buds clearly separated from the branch-tip bud **4**

4a Twigs 4-sided, with 4 corky ridges; bark soft and velvety; leaflets stalked
. . . . ***F. quadrangulata,* blue ash** (p. 209)

4b Twigs round; bark firm and hard; leaflets stalkless **5**

5a Leaflets rusty-woolly at the point of attachment to the central stalk but otherwise hairless; seed wings often twisted . . . . ***F. nigra,* black ash** (p. 207)

5b Leaflets hairy beneath along the midveins but not rusty-woolly at the base; seed wings flat
. . . . ***F. excelsior,* European ash** (p. 208)

Fraxinus americana, white ash   *Fraxinus excelsior,* European ash

THIS TOUGH IMMIGRANT is probably the most commonly planted flowering shrub in Canada. Hundreds of cultivars have been developed. The world's largest lilac collection—close to 800 varieties—is housed at the Royal Botanical Gardens in Hamilton. • Lilacs bloom about 2 weeks in spring, but hot weather shortens the flowering period and hot sun may fade the flowers. • The fragrance of lilac bouquets can fill a room. To make bouquets last longer, cut flowers just as they are starting to open and bash the woody stem ends with a hammer or immerse them in boiling water for a few seconds. Most such bouquets will last 7–10 days. • Lilac flowers can be eaten raw in fruit salads, crystallized with a coating of beaten egg whites and sugar or added to the batter for fritters. • North America's oldest lilacs, in New Hampshire and Michigan, are close to 300 years old. Their trunks are more than 50 cm in diameter and have an unusual, pronounced twist. • The generic name, *Syringa*, is derived from the Greek *syrinx*, 'pipe,' in reference to the hollow stems. The specific epithet, *vulgaris*, means 'common' or 'of the common people.'

FRENCH NAME: Lilas commun

SIZE AND SHAPE: Shrubby trees or tall shrubs **2–5 m tall;** crowns rounded; roots spreading, often sending up suckers and forming thickets.

TRUNKS: Usually clumped, small; bark flaky.

BRANCHES: Numerous; twigs olive-green, round, stiff, soon hairless; buds green or brown, hairless, broadly egg-shaped, with 3–5 pairs of scales, usually paired at twig tips.

LEAVES: Opposite, simple, deciduous; blades dull dark green, paler beneath, **ovate to heart-shaped, 5–12 cm long,** pointed, with squared or notched bases, smooth-edged; stalks slender, 2–3 cm long; leaf scars with 1 horizontal vein scar.

FLOWERS: Purple, pink or white, fragrant, about 1 cm across, bisexual; **petals 4,** widely spreading, bases fused in a 1 cm long tube; sepals 4, fused at the base, glandular-hairy; stamens 2; flowers **in dense, conical, 10–20 cm long, usually paired clusters** (panicles) at tips of last year's branches, in May (as the leaves expand).

FRUITS: Green to brown, **leathery to woody,** hairless, flattened, **pointed capsules,** 1–1.5 cm long; seeds 4 per capsule; fruits persist through winter.

HABITAT: Roadsides, waste places and abandoned farmsteads, especially on calcareous soils.

DISTRIBUTION: Introduced from southeastern Europe; grows wild in Ontario north to Ottawa; sometimes an aggressive weed.

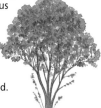

WHITE ASH is Ontario's most common ash species. It is the main source of commercial ash, a tough, shock-resistant wood highly valued for hockey sticks, baseball bats and tennis rackets. It is also used for tool handles, boats, barrels, casks, ladders and furniture veneer. In earlier days, ploughing implements and airplane and automobile frames were made of ash wood. White ash also makes excellent fuel, comparable to oak and hickory. • Some tribes used the bark to produce a yellow dye. • Ash leaf juice has been recommended for soothing mosquito bites and bee stings. • The colourful autumn leaves, slender, graceful shape and neatly patterned bark make white ash an attractive ornamental. • Many white ash populations have undergone a progressive dieback called 'ash yellows,' probably triggered by climate-induced stresses that left trees more susceptible to insects or disease. Wood ducks, quail, wild turkeys, grouse and songbirds (e.g., finches, grosbeaks) feed on the seeds. • *Fraxinus* is derived from the Greek *phraxis*, 'hedges,' because European ashes were often used in hedges. 'White' refers to the silvery to pale grey leaf undersurfaces, twigs and bark.

ALSO CALLED: American ash, Canadian white ash

FRENCH NAMES: Frêne blanc, frêne d'Amérique, frêne blanc d'Amérique, frêne franc

SIZE AND SHAPE: Trees 5–20 m tall; crowns pyramidal; roots usually deep.

TRUNKS: Straight, long, 50–100 cm in diameter; mature bark greyish, with **thin intersecting ridges in regular diamond patterns;** wood light brown, straight-grained, heavy.

BRANCHES: Ascending to spreading; **twigs hairless,** shiny, developing a waxy, greyish skin, stout; buds reddish-brown with a soft, granular surface, 2–6-scaled; **tip buds broadly pyramidal** and 5–14 mm long, flanked by a smaller bud on each side.

LEAVES: Opposite, deciduous, 20–40 cm long; compound, **pinnately divided into 5–9 (usually 7) similar leaflets;** leaflets dark green, paler beneath, essentially hairless, ovate to oblong, 6–15 cm long, on 5–15 mm stalks, abruptly sharp-pointed, **smooth-edged or with a few rounded teeth; leaves yellow or bronze-purple** in autumn, leaflets shed singly.

FLOWERS: Purplish to yellowish, tiny; unisexual with male and female flowers on separate trees; petals absent; sepals minute; flowers in compact clusters along twigs, in May (before the leaves expand).

FRUITS: Pale green to yellowish, **slender, winged nutlets** (samaras), 2.5–5 cm long, **with a long wing enclosing the upper 1/3 of each cylindrical seedcase;** seeds single; **fruits hang in long clusters,** mature in autumn, persist into winter.

HABITAT: Upland sites with rocky to deep, well-drained soils.

THE TOUGH WOOD of red ash is not as strong as that of white ash, but it is marketed under the same name and has been used for canoe paddles, baseball bats, tennis rackets, snowshoe frames, tool handles and picture frames. • Red ash bark produces a red dye, and the wood ashes are a source of potash. • A fast-growing, hardy tree, red ash is often planted as an ornamental (especially in the west), but it can become invasive in urban landscapes. • The abundant seeds provide important autumn and winter food for quail, wild turkeys, cardinals and finches, as well as for squirrels and other rodents. • It is fairly easy to identify a tree as an ash but much more difficult to determine which species. In Canada, ashes with hairy twigs are red ash or the rare pumpkin ash (p. 206). White ash (p. 204) is distinguished from red ash by its hairless twigs and leaves and its grey, regularly diamond-patterned bark. • Red ash is Canada's most widely distributed and variable ash. The variety *F. pennsylvanica* var. *subintegerrima* is called **green ash** or *frêne vert.* Green ash has essentially hairless leaves, twigs and flower/fruit stalks. This variety is the most common ash on the Prairies.

ALSO CALLED: Rim ash, soft ash

FRENCH NAMES: Frêne rouge, frêne de Pennsylvanie, frêne pubescent, frêne de rivage, frêne de savane

SIZE AND SHAPE: Shrubby to tall trees 10–15 m tall, variable; crowns rounded.

TRUNKS: Straight, 30–50 cm in diameter; bark greyish-brown, often reddish-tinged, flaky, with **irregular, shallow ridges in diamond-shaped patterns;** wood light greyish-brown, straight-grained.

BRANCHES: Ascending to spreading; **twigs often hairy;** buds reddish-brown, hairy, 4–6-scaled, **pyramidal and 3–8 mm long at branch tips with a smaller bud on each side.**

LEAVES: Opposite, deciduous, 23–35 cm long; compound, **pinnately divided into 5–9 (usually 7) leaflets; central stalks hairy; leaflets hairy,** yellowish-green, pale beneath, oval, 8–15 cm long, taper-pointed, **shallow-toothed above the middle,** borne on **short, narrowly winged stalks;** leaf scars semicircular; leaves yellowish-brown in autumn, leaflets shed singly.

FLOWERS: Purplish to yellowish, tiny; unisexual with male and female flowers on separate trees; petals absent; sepals minute; **flowers on densely hairy stalks** in many-flowered, compact clusters along twigs, in early spring (before the leaves expand).

FRUITS: Pale green to yellowish, **slender, winged nutlets** (samaras), 3–6 cm long, **with a long wing enclosing the upper 1/2 or more of each cylindrical seedcase,** wings often with notched tips; seeds single; **fruits hang in long clusters,** mature in autumn, persist into winter.

HABITAT: Moist to wet soils on open floodplains and swamps, with other hardwoods.

Pumpkin Ash *Fraxinus profunda*

PUMPKIN ASH is native to the eastern U.S. and was only recently discovered in Canada. • The wood of all ash species except black ash (p. 207) is sold as 'white ash.' Pumpkin ash has no commercial value because of its scarcity. Although the wood is inferior to that of white ash (p. 204), it has been used for crates, railway ties, veneer, pulp and fuel. • Ash samaras are dispersed by wind and water. The seeds require exposure to cool, moist conditions for several months before they germinate. • Many small birds and mammals eat the seeds, and white-tailed deer browse on the twigs and leaves. Pumpkin ash snags provide nest sites and dens for hollow-dwelling birds and small mammals. • Gall gnats sometimes cause the male flowers of ash trees to develop abnormally into galls, which stay on the trees for several months. • The specific epithet, *profunda,* means 'deep' or 'profound' and refers to the swampy habitat of this species. • The leaves and fruits of pumpkin ash are distinctly larger than those of Ontario's other ashes. The leaves can grow 45 cm long, with leaflets up to 25 cm long. The samaras average 5.5 cm in length and 9 mm in width.

ALSO CALLED: *F. tomentosa*

FRENCH NAME: Frêne pubescent

SIZE AND SHAPE: Trees up to 30 m tall; crowns narrow, oval; roots spreading, shallow.

TRUNKS: Straight, single, usually buttressed; mature bark greyish, with **thin intersecting ridges in regular diamond patterns;** wood greyish-brown, straight-grained, hard.

BRANCHES: Straight; **twigs downy,** greyish-brown, stout; **buds broadly pyramidal at branch tips;** bud scales paired, soft, granular-textured.

LEAVES: **Opposite,** deciduous, **20–45 cm long;** compound, **pinnately divided into 5–9 (usually 7) similar leaflets;** central stalks woolly; leaflets dark green above, **paler yellowish-green and soft-hairy beneath, 12–25 cm long,** lance-shaped to elliptic, taper-pointed, often unequal at the base, **smooth-edged** (or nearly so), **on wingless, 8–15 mm long stalks;** leaf scars broadly U-shaped.

FLOWERS: Tiny; unisexual with male and female flowers on **separate trees;** petals absent; sepals 1–4 mm long; flowers in compact, many-flowered clusters, in early spring (before the leaves expand).

FRUITS: Pale green to yellowish, **winged nutlets** (samaras), single, slender, often widest above the middle, **4–8 cm long,** with **tiny sepal remnants at the base** and a **wing extending over halfway down each thick, cylindrical seedcase,** wings round or notched at the tip; seeds single; **fruits hang in long clusters,** mature in autumn, persist into winter.

HABITAT: Low, open, wet sites.

BLACK ASH wood is much softer and heavier than that of white ash, but it has been used for interior trim, furniture, cabinets and veneer. The wood is also very flexible and can be permanently bent, so it was favoured for snowshoe frames and canoe ribs. When soaked and pounded, the logs separate readily along their annual rings into thin sheets. Long strips from these sheets were used for making barrel hoops and for weaving baskets and chair seats. • The wood ashes are rich in potash. • This shade-intolerant, moisture-loving tree can tolerate standing water for many weeks. Usually it grows in mixed stands with other moisture-loving trees such as black spruce, eastern white-cedar and silver maple. • Black ash produces good seed crops at intervals of up to 7 years. Fallen seeds lie dormant for a season before germinating. • Hanging on branches through winter or buried under snow, the seeds provide important food for wild turkeys, grouse and small mammals. White-tailed deer and moose often browse new growth heavily. • This tree is easily recognized in winter by its soft, pale grey bark and blue-black buds. • Black ash is a small, rare tree in Newfoundland, the only ash native to that province.

ALSO CALLED: Swamp ash, hoop ash, basket ash, brown ash, water ash

FRENCH NAMES: Frêne noir, frêne gras, frêne à feuilles de sureau, frêne de grève

SIZE AND SHAPE: Trees 10–20 m tall; crowns narrow, open; roots shallow, spreading.

TRUNKS: Slender, often bent, 30–50 cm in diameter; young bark light grey, **soft, corky-ridged,** easily rubbed off; mature bark scaly; wood greyish-brown, straight-grained.

BRANCHES: Coarse, ascending; **twigs stout, soon dull grey, hairless; buds blackish-brown, pointed,** 6-scaled; **tip bud pyramidal, 4–10 mm long, slightly above 2 smaller side-buds.**

LEAVES: Opposite, deciduous; 22–45 cm long; compound, **pinnately divided into 7–11 similar leaflets;** leaflets dark green, **hairless (except for reddish-brown fuzz at the bases),** elongated-ovate, 7–14 cm long, slender-pointed, **finely sharp-toothed, stalkless;** leaf scars large, rounded; leaves reddish-brown in autumn, shed as whole leaves.

FLOWERS: Purplish, tiny; mostly bisexual, sometimes unisexual, with 1, 2 or 3 flower types on a single tree; petals absent; sepals minute; stamens 2; flowers on hairless stalks in compact clusters along twigs and at branch tips, in early spring (before the leaves expand).

FRUITS: Pale green to yellowish, **winged, slender nutlets** (samaras) 2.5–4 cm long, **with broad, often twisted wings encircling seedcases;** wings with round or notched tips; seeds single; **fruits hang in long clusters,** mature in late summer, persist into winter.

HABITAT: Open, cool, wet sites in **swampy** woodlands and along shores.

THIS FAST-GROWING, ATTRACTIVE TREE and its many cultivars have seen wide use in landscaping. • In Europe, the hard, strong wood of this important forest tree has been used since ancient times for countless items, from spears and bows to furniture and interior trim. When seasoned, European ash wood bends well, and when steamed, it can be pressed into different forms, lending it to uses in joists, railway carriages, wagons, airplanes, axe handles, ladders and oars. • The astringent bark was used for tanning nets and for making bitter tonics that were taken to stop menstruation, remove obstructions from the liver and spleen and relieve rheumatism and arthritis. The wood ashes were said to cure scabby and leprous heads, and the leaves were taken as a laxative. Ash keys had a reputation as a remedy for flatulence, so they were preserved with salt and vinegar and used as a pickle or as a caper substitute. • When pastures were poor, the green autumn leaves were fed to sheep and cattle, though this feed turned cow's milk rank. • European ash and black ash (p. 207) have similar leaves, fruits and twigs, but European ash has firm, cracked, non-scaly bark.

ALSO CALLED: Weeping ash

FRENCH NAMES: Frêne commun, frêne élevé, grand frêne

SIZE AND SHAPE: Trees 20–25 m tall; crowns rounded to broadly spreading, dense; roots shallow, spreading.

TRUNKS: Straight; young bark light grey, smooth; mature bark dark grey, ridged; wood light-coloured, straight-grained, heavy, tough and elastic.

BRANCHES: Coarse, ascending to spreading; twigs greenish-grey to **greyish-brown, hairless, stout; buds coal-black, hairy; branch tip bud pyramidal, usually adjacent to 2 smaller side-buds.**

LEAVES: Opposite, deciduous, **20–35 cm long;** compound, **pinnately divided into 7–13 similar** leaflets; leaflets dark green above, paler beneath, **hairy on lower midveins only, 5–14 cm** long, slender-pointed, **finely sharp-toothed, stalkless;** leaf scars large, rounded, not notched; leaves green until shed in autumn.

FLOWERS: Purplish to yellow or greenish, tiny; bisexual or unisexual with male and female flowers on separate trees; petals absent; sepals minute; stamens 2; flowers in compact clusters along twigs and at branch tips, in May (before the leaves expand).

FRUITS: Pale green or yellowish to brown, **slender, winged nutlets (samaras) with a broad wing encircling each seedcase,** 2.5–4 cm long, wings short-pointed to slightly notched at the tips; seeds single; **fruits hang in clusters,** mature in late summer, persist into winter.

HABITAT: Roadsides and fence lines.

DISTRIBUTION: Introduced from Europe and Asia Minor; only occasionally escaped in southern Ontario, e.g., on the Niagara Peninsula.

BLUE ASH is becoming increasingly rare in Ontario and in Canada. COSEWIC (2000) has designated it a threatened species. Land clearing, pasturing, mining in rock quarries and viticulture all pose threats. • The wood is durable, though somewhat brittle, and it has been sold as white ash. It is now of no commercial value because of the tree's scarcity, but it was once used in sporting goods, agricultural tools, furniture, flooring and interior trim. • Blue ash is sometimes planted as an ornamental shade tree. It grows quickly and can live 125–150 years. • The name *quadrangulata* means '4-angled' and refers to the 4 corky ridges on the twigs. This characteristic distinguishes blue ash from all other ashes. Another unique feature is the sticky sap from the inner bark, which turns blue when exposed to air, hence the common name. To produce a blue dye, the bark is chopped into pieces and steeped in boiling water, which is then boiled down to concentrate the colour. • The unusual scaly bark of blue ash is also distinctive. On older trees, the loose, hanging plates bring to mind the bark of shagbark hickory (p. 86).

FRENCH NAMES: Frêne bleu, frêne anguleux, frêne quadrangulaire

SIZE AND SHAPE: Trees 10–20 m tall; crowns narrow, rounded, often irregular.

TRUNKS: Straight, slender, 15–25 cm in diameter; mature bark greyish, shaggy with loose scaly plates; **inner bark blue when exposed to air;** wood yellowish-brown, coarse-grained, hard, heavy.

BRANCHES: Spreading, stout; **twigs conspicuously 4-sided, with 4 corky ridges;** buds dark brown, hairy, 6-scaled, 6–8 mm long; branch tip bud **slightly flattened, with a smaller bud on each side.**

LEAVES: Opposite, deciduous, **20–40 cm long;** compound, **pinnately divided into 5–11 similar leaflets;** leaflets dark yellowish-green, paler beneath, hairy in main vein axils or hairless, lance-shaped, 8–14 cm long, taper-pointed, with asymmetrical bases, short-stalked, coarsely toothed; leaf scars oval to crescent-shaped.

FLOWERS: Purplish, tiny, **bisexual;** petals absent; sepals minute, soon shed; flowers on hairless stalks in compact, many-flowered clusters, in early spring (before the leaves expand).

FRUITS: Green to yellowish, **winged nutlets** (samaras), **with a broad, often twisted wing enclosing each flattened seedcase, oblong-lance-shaped,** 2.5–4 cm long, wings with rounded or (usually) notched tips, **bases lacking sepal remnants;** seeds single; **fruits hang in loose clusters,** mature in autumn, persist through winter.

HABITAT: Scattered on floodplains, along sandy beaches and on limestone outcrops.

CATALPAS ARE CULTIVATED for their showy flowers and large, tropical-looking leaves. They respond well to pruning and can be shaped into small, dense, round trees that do not flower. Unfortunately, the weak branches often break during storms. Catalpas are hardy as far north as Ottawa and Georgian Bay. • Catalpa wood is weak and light but slow to rot in soil. In the U.S., this fast-growing tree is often grown in dense plantations to produce fence posts and telephone poles. Catalpa wood is also used occasionally in inexpensive furniture. • Northern catalpa flowers at about 15 years of age and produces large seed crops every 2–3 years. Insects pollinate the beautiful flowers, producing conspicuous seed pods that are of little value to wildlife. • The name *Catalpa* was first used by tribes in Carolina; *speciosa* means 'beautiful' or 'showy.' • **Southern catalpa** or *catalpa commun* **(C. bignonioides)**, from the southeastern U.S., is also planted in Ontario. However, it is less hardy and less likely to escape. Southern catalpa is a smaller tree (to 15 m), with smaller (3–5 mm wide), more numerous flowers and short-pointed leaves that have an unpleasant odour when crushed.

Photo, bottom right: *C. bignonioides*

ALSO CALLED: Catawba, cigar-tree, hardy catalpa, Indian bean-tree, western catalpa

FRENCH NAMES: Catalpa à feuilles cordées, catalpa remarquable, catalpa du Nord

SIZE AND SHAPE: Trees 10–30 m tall; crowns narrow to broad, rounded.

TRUNKS: Straight, 20–40 cm in diameter; mature bark dark reddish-brown with large, irregular, thick scales; wood light brown, soft, coarse-grained.

BRANCHES: Stout; twigs stout, blunt-tipped; buds 6-scaled, 2–5 mm long, absent at branch tips.

LEAVES: Opposite or whorled, simple, deciduous; **blades yellowish-green** above, paler and soft-hairy beneath, **heart-shaped, slender-pointed, 10–30 cm long,** usually smooth-edged; stalks 10–16 cm long; leaf scars rounded, with a ring of vein scars; leaves blackened by first frost.

FLOWERS: **White with yellow stripes and purple spots, bell-shaped, 2-lipped, showy, 5–7 cm across,** bisexual; petals fused in a tube with 5 spreading, frilly lobes; sepals greenish-purple, fused, irregularly split; **flowers in erect, few-flowered clusters (panicles) up to 20 cm long** at branch tips, in midsummer (after the leaves expand).

FRUITS: **Green to dark brown, cylindrical capsules 25–60 cm long,** splitting open lengthwise; seeds numerous, **flat, 2.5 cm long, with 2 blunt, hair-tipped, papery wings;** fruits hang in clusters of 1–3, mature in autumn, **persist through winter.**

HABITAT: Roadsides, fence lines, forest edges and fields.

DISTRIBUTION: Introduced from the Mississippi Valley; may grow wild in southern Ontario.

Key to the Viburnums (Genus *Viburnum*, Family Caprifoliaceae)

1a Leaves maple leaf–like, with 3 palmate lobes and palmate veins **2**
1b Leaves ovate, not lobed, regularly saw-toothed **3**

2a Leaf stalks with club-shaped glands just below the blade; stipules thick-tipped
. . . . **V. trilobum, highbush cranberry** (p. 214)
2b Leaf stalks with saucer-like glands just below the blade; stipules bristle-like
. . . . **V. opulus var. opulus, European highbush cranberry** (p. 214)

3a Flower and fruit clusters stalkless, with branches arising directly from the leaf axils; some leaf
stalks grooved and winged; plant often large (to 10 m tall) and tree-like
. . . . **V. lentago, nannyberry** (p. 212)
3b Flower and fruit clusters with branches arising from the tip of a slender stalk; leaf stalks not
grooved and winged; plant usually small (less than 4 m tall) and shrubby **4**

4a Lower leaf surfaces with tiny star-shaped hairs (at least when young); winter buds naked; stones
3-grooved . . . . **V. lantana, wayfaring-tree** (p. 213)
4b Lower leaf surfaces lacking tiny star-shaped hairs, sometimes with minute red-brown scales; winter
buds with 2 outer scales; stones not grooved . . . . **V. nudum, witherod** (p. 212)

Viburnum trilobum, highbush cranberry

THIS HARDY, FAST-GROWING SHRUB is often planted as an ornamental for its showy, fragrant flowers, attractive fruits and reddish winter twigs. It takes pruning well and can be shaped into a handsome hedge, but its root suckers can be a problem in small gardens. Nannyberry sometimes forms thickets from root sprouts. • The flesh of the fruit is edible and has a sweet raisin- or date-like flavour. The 'berries' can be eaten straight from the branch as a nibble, or cooked and seeded to make jams and jellies. Often the sweet pulp is mixed with tart fruits in fruit stews and sauces. • The fruits provide food for wild turkeys, ruffed grouse, sharp-tailed grouse, pheasants and many songbirds, which in turn disperse the seeds. • The names *Viburnum* (from the Latin *viere*, 'to link') and *lentago* (from the Latin *lentus*, 'pliant') both refer to the supple twigs. • Nannyberry could be confused with the closely related **witherod** or *alisier* **(V. nudum)**, also known as *V. cassinoides*, possumhaw, wild raisin and *bleuets sains*, a similar small tree or large shrub that reaches 4–5 m in height. Witherod is distinguished by its smooth- to wavy-edged or irregularly blunt-toothed (not sharp-toothed) leaves, its stalked flower clusters and its golden to yellowish buds.

ALSO CALLED: Sweet viburnum, blackhaw, wild raisin, sheepberry

FRENCH NAMES: Viorne lentago, alissier, bleuets sains, viorne flexible, bourdaine, viorne alisier, viorne à manchettes

SIZE AND SHAPE: Small trees or shrubs 4–7 m tall; crowns open, irregular; roots spreading.

TRUNKS: Slender, crooked, 10–20 cm in diameter; mature bark greyish-brown, with small, irregular scales; wood dark reddish-brown, hard, heavy, fine-grained.

BRANCHES: Few, arching, stout, tough; twigs becoming purplish-brown, slender, smooth, **unpleasant-smelling** when bruised; buds brownish-grey, **granular, lacking scales,** with 2 immature leaves visible, slender, bulbous-based and 2–3 cm long at branch tips, smaller below.

LEAVES: Opposite, simple, deciduous, with an **unpleasant odour** when bruised; **blades hairless,** deep yellowish-green, slightly paler and speckled with **brown dots beneath, ovate to oval, 5–10 cm long, abruptly sharp-pointed,** edged with fine, sharp, incurved teeth; **stalks grooved, usually winged** with a narrow, irregular extension of the blade.

FLOWERS: Creamy-white, pleasant-smelling, 4–8 mm across, 5-parted, bisexual; numerous, in **round-topped, stalkless, wide-branching clusters (cymes) 5–10 cm across,** at branch tips in late May–early June (as the leaves expand).

FRUITS: Bluish-black, berry-like drupes with a whitish bloom, 8–12 mm long, thin-fleshed, with a black, flattened stone; seeds single within stones; **fruits in open, branched clusters,** mature and drop in August–September.

HABITAT: Wet, rich sites near water, along forest edges, by roadsides and in thickets.

MAP: Pale green, *V. lentago*; pink, *V. nudum*; dark green, overlap.

THE VERY HARD WOOD of the wayfaring-tree has been fashioned into mouthpieces for tobacco pipes. The flexible young branches were used as switches for driving livestock and as ties for binding kindling in the days before string. • This shrub is widely planted as an ornamental for its showy flowers (lasting about 2 weeks), attractive foliage (deep green in summer, purplish-red to scarlet in autumn) and attractive fruits (initially pinkish-white and becoming rose, red, purple and finally black). It is a tough, low-maintenance plant that resists most insects and diseases, tolerates dry soils and spreads readily via seeds and suckers. • The juicy 'berries' attract many songbirds. Although the fruits are so astringent as to be inedible raw, they make wonderful jams and jellies. The fruit clusters, preserved by immersion in glycerine and boiling water, add colour to dried flower arrangements. Mature fruits were once used to make ink. • The distinctive, dense, star-shaped hairs on the lower leaf surfaces help to protect the leaves from insects and disease and to conserve moisture in dry environments. • The name wayfaring-tree arose because of this shrub's commonness along lanes and byways in southern England.

ALSO CALLED: Wayfaring viburnum

FRENCH NAME: Viorne mancienne

SIZE AND SHAPE: Small trees or large shrubs up to 4 m tall; crowns dense and rounded; roots spreading.

TRUNKS: Slender, usually clumped; mature bark greyish-brown, scaly.

BRANCHES: Wide-spreading, tough, thick; **twigs yellowish-grey with dense star-shaped hairs; buds greyish,** with yellowish-white hairs, **lacking scales,** with **1–2 pairs of immature leaves visible;** flower buds large, wider than long, surrounded by 2 young leaves.

LEAVES: Opposite, simple, deciduous; blades dull dark green above, **greyish with dense star-shaped hairs beneath, 5–12 cm long,** prominently veined, appearing wrinkled and leathery, **ovate, short-pointed to blunt-tipped,** rounded to slightly notched at the base, sharp-toothed; stalks 1–3 cm long, hairy; leaves deep red in autumn.

FLOWERS: Creamy-white, sweet-smelling, 5-parted, 6–10 mm across, bisexual; numerous, **in short-stalked, flat-topped, 5–10 cm wide clusters (cymes) with star-shaped hairs,** borne at branch tips in May–June.

FRUITS: Coral-red to black, berry-like drupes, slightly flattened, 8–10 mm long, fleshy, with a **flattened stone bearing 3 grooves on one side;** seeds single within stones; **fruits in flat-topped clusters,** mature August–September.

HABITAT: Roadsides and fence lines, especially on calcareous soils.

DISTRIBUTION: Introduced from Europe and western Asia; escaped in southern Ontario.

HIGHBUSH CRANBERRY fruits are boiled and strained to make jellies and jams. The fruits smell a bit like dirty socks, but their flavour isn't bad. Lemon or orange zest helps eliminate the odour. • The 'berries' make an excellent winter-survival food because they remain above the snow and are sweeter after freezing. Birds often eat them when other foods are gone. • The bark has been used to treat menstrual pains, stomach cramps, aching muscles, asthma, hysteria and convulsions. It was sometimes given to women to stop contractions and prevent abortion. • **European highbush cranberry** or *viorne obier* **(*V. opulus* var. *opulus*),** also called Guelder-rose, is a European introduction that frequently escapes cultivation in southern Ontario. It is very similar to highbush cranberry and is distinguished by its bristle-like leaf stipules and by the saucer-like glands at the tops of its leaf stalks. The popular cultivar 'Sterile,' or 'Roseum' (snowball), has very showy balls of enlarged flowers, all sterile. • Two other Ontario viburnums have 3-lobed leaves, but both are less than 2 m tall and have less conspicuous flower clusters without showy sterile flowers. **Mapleleaf viburnum *(V. acerifolium)*** has downy and resin-dotted lower leaf surfaces and blue fruits. **Squashberry *(V. edule)*** has shallowly lobed leaves without stipules.

ALSO CALLED: American cranberrybush, cranberry viburnum • *V. opulus* var. *americanum,* *V. opulus* ssp. *trilobum*

FRENCH NAME: Viorne trilobeé

SIZE AND SHAPE: Tall shrubs or small trees up to 4 m tall; crowns open, irregular; roots spreading.

TRUNKS: Upright; mature bark greyish.

BRANCHES: Few, arching; twigs grey, hairless; buds paired at branch tips, reddish, with 2 fused scales.

LEAVES: Opposite, simple, deciduous; blades dark green and hairless above, paler and smooth or thinly hairy beneath, **maple leaf–like,** 5–11 cm long and wide, **deeply cut into 3 spreading, pointed lobes** (lobes sometimes poorly developed on leaves near branch tips), sparsely coarse-toothed to smooth-edged; **stalks grooved, with 1–6 club-shaped glands at the top** (near the blade) and 2 slender, thick-tipped stipules at the base.

FLOWERS: White, 5-parted, bisexual, of 2 types: **small, fertile flowers at the cluster centre, and large (1.5–2.5 cm wide), flat, sterile flowers around the outer edge;** flowers numerous, in **flat-topped, wide-branching, 5–15 cm wide clusters** (cymes) on 2–5 cm stalks at branch tips, in late June–July (after the leaves expand).

FRUITS: Juicy, red to orange, berry-like drupes, 8–10 mm across; seeds single, within a flat-tened stone; **fruits hang in branched clusters,** mature in August–September, often persist into winter.

HABITAT: Moist, rich sites near water and in cool woodlands and thickets.

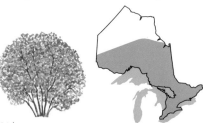

About the Author

An avid naturalist since childhood, Linda Kershaw focused on botany at the University of Waterloo, earning her master's degree in 1976. Since then she has worked as a consultant and researcher in northwestern Canada and as an author and editor in Edmonton, while pursuing two favourite pastimes—photography and illustrating. Linda hopes that her books will help people to appreciate the beauty and fascinating history of plants and to recognize the intrinsic value of nature's rich mosaic.

Author photo: Peter Kershaw

Photo Credits

Photos are by Linda Kershaw, except the following:

George Argus: 137b, 137c
Wasyl Bakowsky: 22, 25b, 26c, 49a, 51, 60b, 64b, 68a, 69a, 89, 91b, 98b, 121c, 157b, 158b, 171a, 176a, 182b, 182c, 183b, 207b
Bill Crins: 63b, 118, 151a, 157a, 166b, 167b, 170a
Don Doucette: 11
Tamara Eder: 18, 93b, 191c
Mary Gartshore: 81a, 85a, 85b, 169a, 206a, 206b, 206c
Erich Haber: 53c, 54b, 55b, 57a, 58b, 61c, 62a, 77a, 88a, 92a, 100b, 103b, 105c, 106b, 107b, 124c, 136a, 143b, 156a, 184a, 185c, 190c, 195c, 198b, 204b
Alex Inselberg: 4
Dawn Loewen: 67c
Glen Lumis: 1, 28b, 29a, 30a, 30b, 30c, 68c, 71a, 71c, 77b, 88b, 95c, 97a, 99b, 106c, 107c, 144a, 146a, 146c, 158a, 170c, 172c, 173b, 181a, 183a, 184b, 185b, 186b, 190b, 193c, 194c, 197b, 199b, 200a, 200c, 202a, 212b, 212c, 213a, 213b
Tim Matheson: 15, 16, 20, 143a, 196b
Allison Penko: 17
Jim Pojar: 112a
Robert Ritchie: 13, 14, 23, 49b, 154b, 169c, 193b, 200b
Anna Roberts: 130, 138b
Royal Botanical Gardens: 63c, 87b, 87c, 109a, 109b, 109c, 151b, 151c, 154c, 182a, 209c
Don Sutherland: 67a, 92c, 154a
John Worrall: 112b

Appendix • Arboreta in Ontario

BARRIE
Centennial Arboretum, Barrie Horticultural Society

BRAMPTON
J.A. Carol Arboretum

BRIGHTON
Cedar Valley Botanical Gardens, Garden Club of London

ETOBICOKE
Centennial Conservatory, Etobicoke Parks and Recreation

GUELPH
Edna and Frank C. Miller English Garden, University of Guelph
Lord and Burnham Conservatory, University of Guelph
University of Guelph Arboretum

HAMILTON
Royal Botanical Gardens

KAKABEKA FALLS
Plum Grove Arboretum

KINGSTON
Lemoine Point Gardens

LONDON
Civic Gardens Complex
Sherwood Fox Arboretum, University of Western Ontario

MILLER LAKE
Larkwistle Garden

MISSISSAUGA
Erindale College Arboretum
Mississauga Public Garden

NEW LISKEARD
Becky Hughes Arboretum, New Liskeard College of Agriculture

NIAGARA FALLS
Niagara Parks Botanical Gardens

OAKVILLE
Appleby College

OTTAWA
Dominion Arboretum, Central Experimental Farm

REXDALE
Humber Arboretum

RIDGETOWN
J.J. Neilson Arboretum, Ridgetown College of Agricultural Technology

SAULT STE. MARIE
Canadian Forestry Service Arboretum, Botanical Society of Sault Ste. Marie

SEBRINGVILLE
Brickman Botanical Garden

ST. CATHARINES
Niagara College Arboretum and Greenhouse
Walker Botanic Garden

SUDBURY
Laurentian University Arboretum

THUNDER BAY
Centennial Conservatory, Thunder Bay Parks and Recreation
International Friendship Garden, Thunder Bay Parks Division
Lakehead University Arboretum

TORONTO
Allan Gardens, Toronto Parks and Recreation
Metropolitan Toronto Zoo
University of Toronto Botany Greenhouse, St. George Campus

WATERLOO
University of Waterloo Botanical Garden
University of Waterloo Greenhouse

WINDSOR
Fogolar Furlan Botanic Garden

Dominion Arboretum, Ottawa

Herbaria in Ontario • Appendix

CHALK RIVER
Petawawa National Forestry Institute Herbarium (PFES)*

GUELPH
Guelph University Herbarium (OAC)

HAMILTON
McMaster University Herbarium (MCM)
Royal Botanical Gardens Herbarium (HAM)

KINGSTON
Fowler Herbarium (QK), Queen's University

LONDON
Western Ontario University Herbarium (UWO)

MAPLE
Southern Research Station Herbarium (MFB)

MISSISSAUGA
Erindale College Herbarium (TRTE)

NIAGARA FALLS
Niagara School of Horticulture Herbarium (NFO)

NORTH YORK
York University Herbarium (YUTO)

OTTAWA
Canadian Forest Service Herbarium (OTF)
Carleton University Herbarium (CCO)
Eastern Cereal and Oilseed Research Centre Vascular Plant Herbarium (DAO), Central Experimental Farm
National Herbarium of Canada (CAN), Canadian Museum of Nature
Ottawa University Herbarium (OTT)

PETERBOROUGH
Trent University Herbarium (TUP)

SAULT STE. MARIE
Abitibi Paper Company Herbarium (AWL)
Great Lakes Forestry Centre Herbarium (SSMF)

SUDBURY
Laurentian University Herbarium (SLU)

THUNDER BAY
Lakehead University Herbarium (LKHD)

TORONTO
Royal Ontario Museum Vascular Plant Herbarium (TRT)
Scarborough College Herbarium (TRTS)

WATERLOO
Waterloo University Herbarium (WAT)
Wilfred Laurier University Herbarium (WLU)

WAWA
Lake Superior Provincial Park Herbarium (LSP)

WHITNEY
Algonquin Provincial Park Visitor Centre Herbarium (APM)

WINDSOR
Windsor University Herbarium (WOCB)

* The 2- to 4-letter code after each name is the internationally accepted designation for that herbarium, as recorded in the Index Herbariorum.

A mounted and labelled herbarium specimen

Glossary

Page numbers indicate where terms are illustrated.

achene: a small, thin-walled, dry fruit containing a single seed (p. 222)

acorn: the hard, dry nut of oaks, with a single, large seed and a scaly, cup-like base (p. 222)

adventive: introduced but only locally established in the wild, if at all; compare 'naturalized'

adventitious: growing from unusual places, e.g., roots growing from stems

aggregate fruit: a fruit produced by two or more pistils of a single flower, sometimes appearing to be dense clusters of many tiny fruits (e.g., a raspberry) (p. 222); compare 'multiple fruit'

alternate: attached singly, neither paired nor whorled (p. 220); compare 'opposite,' 'whorled'

angiosperm: a plant with ovules/seeds enclosed in an ovary/fruit; a flowering plant, member of the Magnoliophyta; compare 'gymnosperm'

annual ring: the wood laid down in a single year, visible (in cross-section) as a ring because of alternating layers of earlywood and denser latewood (p. 13)

anther: the pollen-bearing part of a stamen (p. 17)

arboretum [arboreta]: a place where trees and other plants are cultivated for their beauty and for scientific and educational purposes (see appendix, p. 216)

aril: a specialized covering attached to a mature seed (p. 222)

armed: bearing prickles, spines or thorns (p. 220)

ascending: oriented obliquely upwards (p. 12)

axil: the angle between an organ (e.g., a leaf) and the part to which it is attached (e.g., a stem) (p. 15)

axis [axes]: the main stem or central line of a plant or plant part

bark cambium: see 'cork cambium'

bark: the protective outer covering of the trunks and branches of a woody plant, composed of dead, corky cells and produced by the cork cambium; in the broadest sense, bark includes all tissue from the phloem outwards (pp. 13, 15)

bast: see 'phloem'

berry: a fleshy fruit developed from a single ovary and containing one to several seeds (p. 223)

bisexual: with both male and female sex organs; also called 'perfect'; compare 'unisexual'

blade: the broad, flat part of an organ (e.g., of a leaf or petal) (p. 225)

bloom: a whitish, waxy powder on the surface of some leaves and fruits

board foot [board feet]: a cubic measure for lumber, equivalent to that of a board measuring 12 inches by 12 inches by 1 inch (2.36 dm³)

bole: the section of a trunk below the crown (p. 12)

bract: a small, specialized leaf or scale (p. 221)

Compound leaves

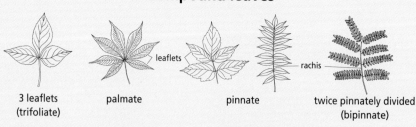

3 leaflets (trifoliate)

palmate — leaflets

pinnate — rachis

twice pinnately divided (bipinnate)

Simple leaves: lobes and teeth

teeth

lobes

palmately lobed

lobes

teeth

pinnately lobed

bud: an undeveloped stem, branch, leaf or flower, usually covered by protective scales (pp. 15, 224)

bur: a barbed or bristly fruit (or compact cluster of fruits) designed to stick to passing animals (p. 222)

callus: a small, firm thickening or protuberance

calyx [calyxes, calyces]: the outer (lowermost) circle of floral parts composed of separate or fused segments called sepals, which are usually green and leaf-like (p. 17); compare 'corolla'

cambium: a thin layer of cells responsible for producing new xylem and phloem cells or new bark cells (see 'cork cambium') and thereby controlling stem growth (p. 13)

canopy: see 'overstorey'

capsule: a dry fruit produced by a compound ovary and splitting open at maturity (p. 222)

carpel: the female unit of reproduction in a flower, formed from a modified leaf and consisting of a stigma, style and seed-bearing ovary; compare 'pistil' (p. 222)

catkin: a dense spike or raceme of many small, unisexual flowers that lack petals but usually have a bract (pp. 221, 222)

chlorophyll: the green pigment that allows plants to manufacture carbohydrates through photosynthesis

ciliate: edged with cilia, fringed

cilium [cilia]: a tiny, eyelash-like structure, usually part of a fringe

clone: all of the offspring produced vegetatively (asexually) by a single individual

compound: composed of two or more smaller parts, such as leaves consisting of several leaflets (p. 218), flower clusters consisting of smaller groups, ovaries consisting of two or more carpels, or substances formed by the chemical union of two or more ingredients; compare 'simple'

cone: a reproductive structure with overlapping scales or bracts arranged around a central axis, usually woody when bearing seeds and non-woody when bearing pollen (pp. 16, 221)

conifer: a cone-bearing shrub or tree

coniferous: cone-bearing (e.g., coniferous trees); or composed of coniferous trees (e.g., coniferous forests)

cork cambium: thin layer of living cells located on the inner side of the bark and responsible for producing new bark cells (p. 13)

corolla: the circle of floral parts second from the outside, composed of separate or fused segments called petals; usually conspicuous in size and color but sometimes small, reduced to nectaries or absent (p. 17); compare 'calyx'

corymb: a flat- or round-topped, branched flower cluster in which the outer (lower) flowers bloom first (p. 221)

cotyledon: a leaf of the developing plant (embryo) within a seed; a seed leaf

Leaf shapes

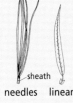

needles   linear   linear-oblong   oblong   lance-shaped, widest above midleaf (oblanceolate)   lance-shaped (lanceolate)   ovate   ovate, widest above midleaf (obovate)

sheath   single teeth

elliptic   oval   round (orbicular)   heart-shaped (cordate)   broadly triangular (deltate)   triangular

double teeth

Glossary

cross-pollination: the transfer of pollen from the anthers of one flower to the stigma of another flower on a different plant; compare 'self-pollination'

cross-section: a slice or fragment cut and viewed at right angles to the main axis (p. 13); compare 'long-section'

crown: the leafy head of a tree or shrub (p. 12)

cultivar: a cultivated plant variety with one or more distinct differences from the species; e.g., *Acer platanoides* is a botanical species, of which 'Crimson King' is a cultivar distinguished by maroon leaves

cuticle: a waxy layer covering the outer surface of a stem of leaf

cyme: a flat- or round-topped flower cluster in which the inner (upper) flowers bloom first (p. 221)

DBH: trunk diameter at breast height, or diameter at 1.3 m from the ground (p. 12)

deciduous: shed after completing its normal function, usually at the end of the growing season; compare 'persistent'

dehiscent: splitting open along slits or via pores to release seeds

dioecious: with male and female flowers or cones on separate plants (p. 221); compare 'monoecious'

disjunct: separated, referring to plant or animal populations located a significant distance from all other populations of the same species

double-toothed: edged with large teeth bearing smaller teeth (p. 219); compare 'single-toothed'

drupe: a fruit with an outer fleshy part covered by a thin skin and surrounding a hard or bony stone that encloses a single seed, e.g., a plum (p. 223)

dwarf shoot: see 'spur-shoot'

earlywood: pale, relatively large-pored wood produced by rapid growth early in the growing season (p. 13); also called 'springwood'

ellipsoid: a three-dimensional form in which every plane is an ellipse or a circle

embryo: an immature plant within a seed

endangered: threatened with immediate elimination through all or a significant portion of a region

evergreen: always bearing green leaves

extinct: describes a species no longer existing anywhere

extirpated: formerly native to a region, now no longer existing there in the wild but still found elsewhere

family [families]: a group of related plants or animals forming a taxonomic category ranking below order and above genus

fertile: describes plants capable of producing viable pollen, ovules or spores; describes soil rich in nutrients and capable of sustaining abundant plant growth

fetid: with a strong, offensive odour

filament: the stalk of a stamen, usually bearing an anther at its tip (p. 17)

fleshy: succulent, firm and pulpy; plump and juicy

flora: the plants that are representative of a certain region or period; or a comprehensive treatise or list that includes all such plants

flower: a specialized shoot of a plant, with a shortened axis bearing reproductive structures (modified leaves) such as sepals, petals, stamens and pistils

follicle: a dry, pod-like fruit, splitting open along a single line on one side (p. 222)

fruit: the seed-bearing organ of an angiosperm, including the ripened ovary and any other structures that join with it as a unit (pp. 222, 223)

Leaf/branch attachment

whorled

spiralled

opposite

alternate

thorns

armed

functionally unisexual: having both male and female parts (sometimes appearing bisexual), but with organs of only one sex maturing to produce reproductive cells

generic name: the first part of a scientific name, denoting the genus to which the species belongs; e.g., *Abies* in *Abies balsamea*

genus [genera]: a group of related plants or animals constituting a category of biological classification below family and above species

germinate: to sprout

girdle: to remove a ring of bark and cambium around a trunk, thereby stopping the transport of water and nutrients and killing the tree

gland: a bump, appendage or depression that secretes substances such as nectar or oil (p. 225)

glandular-hairy: with gland-tipped hairs

glandular-toothed: with gland-tipped teeth (p. 225)

gymnosperm: a plant with naked ovules/seeds (i.e., not enclosed in an ovary); a conifer, a member of the Pinophyta; compare 'angiosperm'

hardwood: a broad-leaved, deciduous tree (occasionally evergreen elsewhere) belonging to the angiosperms or Magnoliophyta; compare 'softwood'

haw: the fruit of hawthorns, a small, berry-like pome containing 1–5 bony nutlets (p. 223)

heartwood: the darker, harder wood at the centre of a trunk, containing accumulations of resin and other compounds and therefore unable to transport fluids (p. 13)

herbarium [herbaria]: a large collection of dried plant specimens that have been mounted, labelled and filed systematically (see appendix, p. 217)

husk: the dry, often thick, outer covering of some fruits (p. 222)

hybrid: the offspring of two kinds of parents (usually parents from different species)

hybridization: the process of creating a hybrid

hypanthium [hypanthia]: a ring or cup around the ovary formed by fused parts of the sepals, petals and/or stamens

imperfect: see 'unisexual'

introduced: brought in from another region (e.g., Europe), not native

key: see 'samara'

latewood: the relatively small-pored wood produced by slow growth towards the end of the growing season (p. 13); also called 'summerwood'

layering: a form of vegetative reproduction in which branches droop to the ground, root and send up new shoots

leader: the uppermost shoot of a tree

leaf scar: the mark left on a stem where a leaf was once attached (pp. 15, 224, 225)

leaflet: a single part of a compound leaf (p. 218)

Cones and flower/fruit clusters

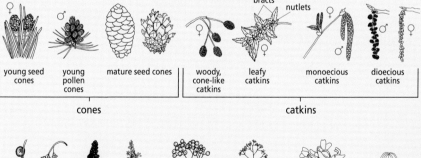

cones — young seed cones / young pollen cones / mature seed cones

catkins — woody, cone-like catkins / leafy catkins (bracts, nutlets) / monoecious catkins / dioecious catkins

racemes / panicles / corymbs / cymes / umbels / pseudanthium

Glossary

legume: a pod-like fruit characteristic of the pea family (Fabaceae or Leguminosae), typically splitting down both sides (p. 222)

lenticel: a slightly raised pore on root, trunk or branch bark (p. 15)

lobe: a rounded division, too large to be called a tooth (p. 218)

long-section: in full, 'longitudinal section'; a slice or fragment cut and viewed parallel to the main axis (p. 224); compare 'cross-section'

membranous: in a thin, usually translucent sheet; like a membrane

midvein: the middle vein of a leaf (p. 225)

monoecious: with male and female parts in separate flowers or cones on the same plant (p. 221); compare 'dioecious'

multiple fruit: a dense cluster of many small fruits, each produced by an individual flower (e.g., a mulberry) (p. 222); compare 'aggregate fruit'

naked: exposed, not covered by scales, hairs or other appendages

native: indigenous to a region, having evolved there as part of an ecosystem over a long period of time; compare 'naturalized,' 'introduced'

naturalized: well established in the wild, but originally introduced from another area; compare 'adventive,' 'native'

nectar: the sweet liquid secreted by a nectary, usually serving to attract pollinators

nectary: a nectar-secreting gland, usually in a flower

net-veined: with a network of branched veins; also called 'reticulate'

node: the point where a leaf or branch attaches to a stem; a joint (p. 224)

nut: a dry, thick-walled, usually one-seeded fruit that does not split open when mature (p. 222)

nutlet: a small, nut-like fruit (p. 221)

opposite: situated directly in front of one another (e.g., stamens opposite petals) or directly across from each other at the same node (describes leaves, branches) (p. 220); compare 'alternate,' 'whorled'

ovary: the organ containing the young, undeveloped seed(s), located at the base of the pistil and maturing to become all or part of the fruit (p. 17)

overstorey: the uppermost stratum of foliage in a forest, the forest canopy; compare 'understorey'

ovoid: with a three-dimensional, egg-shaped form that is broadest below the middle

ovule: an organ that develops into a single seed after fertilization (p. 17)

palmate: with three or more lobes or leaflets arising from one point, like fingers of a hand (p. 218); compare 'pinnate'

Fruits

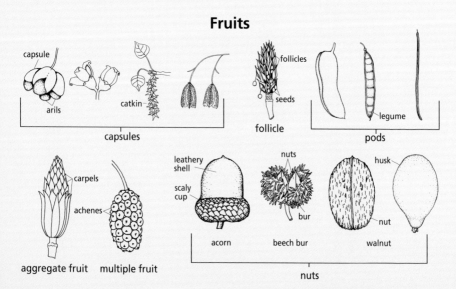

capsule · arils · catkin — capsules

follicles · seeds · follicle · legume — pods

carpels · achenes — aggregate fruit · multiple fruit

leathery shell · scaly cup — acorn · nuts · bur — beech bur · husk · nut — walnut — nuts

panicle: a branched flower cluster in which the lower blooms develop first (p. 221)

perfect: see 'bisexual'

perianth: a flower's petals and sepals collectively

persistent: remaining attached after its normal function has been completed; compare 'deciduous' (p. 223)

petal: a segment of the inner whorl (corolla) of the perianth, usually white or brightly coloured (p. 17)

phloem: a thin layer of vascular tissue located between the bark and the wood, responsible for transporting nutrients (e.g., sugars) produced by the tree to its living tissues (p. 13); also called 'bast'

photosynthesis: the process by which plants manufacture carbohydrates using chlorophyll, carbon dioxide, water and the energy of the sun

pinnate: with branches, lobes, leaflets or veins arranged on both sides of a central stalk or vein, feather-like (p. 218); compare 'palmate'

pioneer species: a colonizer of sites in the early stages of succession (e.g., sites that have been burned, cleared or otherwise disturbed)

pistil: the female part of a flower, composed of single or fused carpels (p. 17)

pith: the soft, spongy centre of a stem or branch (pp. 15, 224)

pod: a dry fruit that splits open to release seeds (p. 222)

pollard: a tree with a small, dense crown produced by cutting branches almost back to the trunk; or to prune a tree in this severe manner

pollen: tiny, powdery grains containing the male reproductive cells that fertilize the ovule

pollen cone: a cone that produces pollen, i.e., a male cone (p. 221); compare 'seed cone'

pollination: the transfer of pollen from male to female reproductive organs, leading to fertilization

pome: a fleshy fruit with a core (e.g., an apple); comprises an enlarged hypanthium around a compound ovary (p. 223)

pseudanthium [pseudanthia]: a compact cluster of tiny flowers and associated bracts resembling a single large flower (p. 221)

raceme: an unbranched cluster of stalked flowers on an elongated central stalk, in which the lowest flowers bloom first (p. 221)

rachis [rachises]: the main axis of a compound leaf or flower cluster (p. 218)

rare: existing in low numbers and/or in very restricted areas in a region

ray: a ribbon-like group of cells visible as a radial line in wood (viewed in cross-section), responsible for transporting water and nutrients across trunks or large branches

respiration: the act of taking in oxygen and producing carbon dioxide through oxidation

rib: a prominent, usually longitudinal vein

runner: a slender, prostrate, spreading branch, rooting and often developing new shoots and/or plants at its nodes or at the tip

Fruits

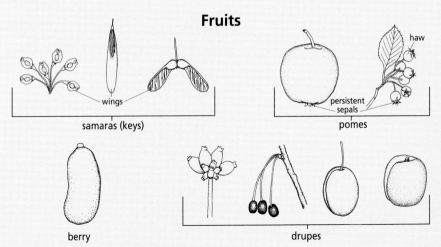

samaras (keys)

wings

pomes

haw

persistent sepals

berry

drupes

Glossary

samara: a dry, winged, one-seeded fruit that does not split open at maturity; may be single (e.g., ashes) or paired (e.g., maples) (p. 223); also called 'key,' especially for the ashes and maples

sap: the mineral- and sugar-containing solution that circulates through a plant via the xylem and phloem

sapwood: the paler, softer, outer wood of a trunk, still capable of transporting fluids (p. 13)

scale: a small, flat structure, usually thin and membranous (pp. 15, 16)

scar: the mark left on a stem by a fallen leaf, scale or fruit (pp. 15, 224, 225)

scurfy: covered with tiny scales

seasonality: the timing of biological events (e.g., leaf growth, flower development) during the year

seed: a fertilized ovule, containing a developing plant embryo along with nourishing tissue (usually) and a protective covering or seed coat (pp. 16, 222)

seed cone: a cone that produces seeds, i.e., a female cone (p. 221); compare 'pollen cone'

self-pollination: the transfer of pollen from the anthers to the stigma of the same flower, or from one flower to another flower on the same plant; compare 'cross-pollination'

sepal: a segment of the outer whorl (calyx) of the perianth, usually green and leaf-like (pp. 17, 223)

sexual reproduction: producing offspring through the union of female and male cells, as in the fertilization of the egg cell in an ovule by a pollen grain; compare 'vegetative reproduction'

sheath: a tubular organ surrounding or partly surrounding some part of a plant (e.g., the base of a bundle of pine needles) (p. 219)

shrub: a perennial, woody plant, usually less than 4 m tall and bushy with several small (typically less than 7.5 cm wide) main stems originating at or near the ground; compare 'tree'

simple: in one piece, undivided; describes leaves not divided into separate leaflets (though sometimes deeply lobed); describes fruits derived from a single ovary; compare 'compound'

single-toothed: edged with simple teeth, that is, teeth not bearing smaller teeth (p. 219); compare 'double-toothed'

softwood: a needle-leaved, coniferous, normally evergreen tree (deciduous in larches) belonging to the gymnosperms or Pinophyta; compare 'hardwood'

species [species], abbreviated **sp.** [spp.]: the fundamental unit of biological classification; a group of closely related plants or animals ranked below genus and above subspecies and variety

specific epithet: the second part of a species' scientific name, distinguishing that species from other members of the same genus; e.g., *balsamea* in *Abies balsamea*

spreading: diverging widely from the vertical, approaching horizontal (p. 12)

springwood: see 'earlywood'

spur-shoot: a short, compressed branch, developing many closely spaced nodes (p. 224); also called a 'dwarf shoot'

stamen: the male organ of a flower, usually comprising a pollen-bearing anther and a stalk called a filament (p. 17)

staminate: with stamens

sterile: lacking viable pollen, ovules or spores

stigma: the tip of the female organ (pistil) of a flower, designed to catch and hold pollen (p. 17)

stipule: a bract-like or leaf-like appendage at the base of a leaf stalk (p. 225)

stoma, stomate [stomata]: a tiny pore in the plant 'skin' (epidermis), bounded by two guard cells that open and close the pore by changing shape; gas exchange takes place through a plant's stomata

Twig parts

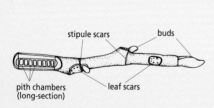

stipule scars   buds

pith chambers   leaf scars
(long-section)

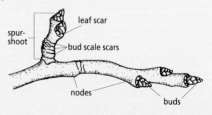

spur-shoot   leaf scar

bud scale scars

nodes   buds

stone: the tough, bony centre of some fruits (e.g., drupes), enclosing and protecting a seed

style: the narrow middle part of a pistil, connecting the stigma and ovary (p. 17)

subspecies, abbreviated **ssp.:** a naturally occurring, regional form of a species, often geographically isolated from other subspecies but still potentially interfertile with them; a ranking between species and variety in biological classification

succulent: fleshy, soft and juicy; also refers to a plant that stores water in fleshy stems or leaves

sucker: a vertical vegetative shoot growing from an underground runner or from spreading roots (p. 12)

summerwood: see 'latewood'

synonym: an alternative name for a plant; usually a scientific name that has been rejected because it was incorrect or was misapplied

taproot: a root system with a prominent main root that extends vertically downwards and bears smaller side roots (p. 12)

taxon [taxa]: a taxonomic group or entity (e.g., a genus, species or variety)

taxonomy: the orderly classification of organisms based on similarities and differences believed to reflect natural evolutionary relationships; or the study of these systems of classification

tepal: a sepal or petal, when these structures are not easily distinguished

terminal: located at the tip

threatened: likely to become endangered in a region unless factors affecting its vulnerability are reversed

tooth [teeth]: a small, often pointed lobe on the edge of a structure such as a leaf (pp. 218, 219, 225)

tree: an erect, perennial, woody plant with a definite crown reaching over 4 m in height, and with a trunk (or trunks) reaching at least 7.5 cm in diameter; compare 'shrub'

trifoliate: divided into three leaflets (p. 218)

trunk: the main stem of a tree or shrub, composed mainly of dead, woody cells covered by a thin layer of living tissues under a protective covering of bark (pp. 12, 13)

umbel: a round- or flat-topped flower cluster in which several flower stalks are of approximately the same length and arise from the same point, like the ribs of an inverted umbrella (p. 221)

understorey: the lower stratum of foliage in a forest, located below the forest canopy; compare 'overstorey'

unisexual: with one set of sex organs only, either male or female; also called 'imperfect'; compare 'bisexual,' 'functionally unisexual'

variety, abbreviated **var.:** a naturally occurring variant of a species; a ranking below subspecies in biological classification

vascular: pertaining to the conduction of substances such as sap or blood within the body of an organism; see also 'vein,' 'xylem,' 'phloem'

vegetative reproduction: producing offspring from asexual parts (e.g., rhizomes, leaves) rather than from fertilized ovules (seeds); compare 'sexual reproduction'

vein: a strand of conducting tubes consisting of xylem and phloem, especially if visible on the surface (e.g., on a petal or leaf) (p. 225)

vein scar: the mark left on a stem where a vein was once attached (p. 15)

whorl: a ring of three or more similar structures (e.g., leaves, branches or flowers) arising from one node

whorled: arranged in whorls, verticillate (p. 220); compare 'alternate,' 'opposite'

wing: a thin, flattened expansion on the side(s) or tip of an organ (e.g., on a fruit or twig) (pp. 16, 223)

wood: the tough, fibrous material forming the greater part of the trunks, branches and roots of trees and shrubs; composed mainly of cellulose and lignin

xylem: a vascular tissue, consisting mainly of tubes of hollow dead cells joined end to end, that conducts water and minerals and provides support; makes up the wood in trees and shrubs (p. 13)

Leaf parts

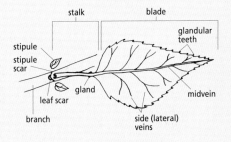

References

Argus, G.W., K.M. Pryer, D.J. White and C.J. Keddy, eds. 1982–87. *Atlas of the Rare Vascular Plants of Ontario.* Four parts. National Museum of Natural Sciences, Ottawa.

Argus, G.W., and D.J. White. 1977. *The Rare Vascular Plants of Ontario.* Botany Division, National Museum of Natural Sciences, Ottawa.

Argus, G.W., and K.M. Pryer. 1990. *Rare Vascular Plants in Canada: Our Natural Heritage.* Canadian Museum of Nature, Ottawa.

Beck, A., and K. Renwald. 2001. *Tree and Shrub Gardening for Ontario.* Lone Pine Publishing, Edmonton, Alberta.

Blackburn, B. 1952. *Trees and Shrubs in Eastern North America.* Oxford University Press, New York.

BONAP. n.d. [cited 2001]. *A Synonymized Checklist of the Vascular Flora of the United States, Canada, and Greenland* [online]. Biota of North America Program of the North Carolina Botanical Garden, and Museum Informatics Project, University of California, Berkeley. <http://www.mip.berkeley.edu/query_forms/browse_checklist.html>.

Brayshaw, T.C. 1996. *Trees and Shrubs of British Columbia.* UBC Press, Vancouver, British Columbia.

Brickell, C., T. Cole and J.D. Zuk, eds. 1996. *Reader's Digest A–Z Encyclopedia of Garden Plants.* Reader's Digest Association (Canada), Montreal.

Brownell, V.R., C.S. Blaney and P.M. Catling. 1996. Recent discoveries of southern vascular plants at their northern limits in the granite barrens area of Lennox and Addington County, Ontario. *Canadian Field-Naturalist* 110(2): 255–259.

Campbell, C.S., F. Hyland and M.L.F. Campbell. 1975. *Winter Keys to Woody Plants of Maine.* University of Maine Press, Orono, Maine.

Catling, P.M., M.J. Oldham, D.A. Sutherland, V.R. Brownell and B.M.H. Larson. 1997. The recent spread of autumn-olive, *Elaeagnus umbellata,* into southern Ontario and its current status. *Canadian Field-Naturalist* 111(3): 376–380.

Chambers, B., K. Legasy and C.V. Bentley. 1996. *Forest Plants of Central Ontario.* Lone Pine Publishing, Edmonton, Alberta.

Core, E.L. and N.P. Ammons. 1958. *Woody Plants in Winter.* Boxwood Press, Pittsburgh, Pennsylvania.

COSEWIC. 2000. Committee on the Status of Endangered Wildlife in Canada [online database]. <http://www.cosewic.gc.ca>.

Edlin, H. 1978. *The Tree Key: A Guide to Identification in Garden, Field and Forest.* Charles Scribner's Sons, New York.

Elias, T.S. 1989. *Field Guide to North American Trees.* Grolier Book Clubs, Danbury, Connecticut.

Farrar, J.L. 1995. *Trees in Canada.* Fitzhenry and Whiteside, Markham, Ontario, and Canadian Forest Service, Natural Resources Canada, Ottawa.

Fernald, M.L. 1950. *Gray's Manual of Botany.* 8th ed. Van Nostrand, New York.

Flint, H.L. 1983. *Landscape Plants for Eastern North America.* John Wiley and Sons, New York.

Foster, S., and J.A. Duke. 1990. *Field Guide to Medicinal Plants: Eastern and Central North America.* Houghton Mifflin, Boston.

Gleason, H.A., and A. Cronquist. 1991. *Manual of Vascular Plants of Northeastern United States and Adjacent Canada.* New York Botanical Garden, Bronx, New York.

Grimm, W.C. 1962. *The Book of Trees.* Stackpole, Harrisburg, Pennsylvania.

Hole, L. 1997. *Lois Hole's Favorite Trees and Shrubs.* Lone Pine Publishing, Edmonton, Alberta.

Hosie, R.C. 1969. *Native Trees of Canada.* Canadian Forest Service, Ottawa.

ITIS. 2000. Canadian version (ITIS*ca) of the Integrated Taxonomic Information System [online]. Agriculture and Agri-Food Canada, Ottawa. <http://sis.agr.ca/itis/>.

References

Kock, H. 1996. Tree identification tips for atlassers: spring. *Ontario Tree Atlas Project* 1(2): 2–3.

Lauriault, J. 1992. *Identification Guide to the Trees of Canada*. Canadian Museum of Nature, Ottawa.

Legasy, K., S. LaBelle-Beadman and B. Chambers. 1995. *Forest Plants of Northeastern Ontario*. Lone Pine Publishing, Edmonton, Alberta.

Little, E.L. 1980. *The Audubon Society Field Guide to North American Trees: Western Region*. Alfred A. Knopf, New York.

Little, E.L. 1996. *The Audubon Society Field Guide to North American Trees: Eastern Region*. Alfred A. Knopf, New York.

Looman, J., and K.F. Best. 1979. *Budd's Flora of the Canadian Prairie Provinces*. Canadian Government Publishing Centre, Hull, Quebec.

Mitchell, A., and J. Wilkinson. 1982. *The Trees of Britain and Northern Europe*. Wm. Collins, Sons and Co., London.

Moss, E.H. 1983. *Flora of Alberta*. University of Toronto Press, Toronto.

ONHIC. 1997. *NHIC List of Ontario Vascular Plants* [online]. Ontario Natural Heritage Information Centre, Ontario Ministry of Natural Resources. <www.mnr.gov.on.ca/MNR/nhic/nhic.html>.

Ontario Ministry of Natural Resources. 1991. *Common Pests of Trees in Ontario*. Queen's Printer, Toronto.

Peterson, L.A. 1977. *A Field Guide to Edible Wild Plants of Eastern and Central North America*. Houghton Mifflin, Boston.

Phillips, D.H., and D.A. Burdekin. 1992. *Diseases of Forest and Ornamental Trees*. 22nd ed. Macmillan Press, London.

Phillips, R. 1978. *Trees of North America and Europe*. Pan Books, London.

Phipps, J.B., and M. Muniyamma. 1980. A taxonomic revision of *Crataegus* (Rosaceae) in Ontario. *Canadian Journal of Botany* 58: 1621–1699.

Reader's Digest. 1981. *Field Guide to the Trees and Shrubs of Britain*. Reader's Digest Association, London.

Rehder, A. 1947. *Manual of Cultivated Trees and Shrubs Hardy in North America*. Macmillan, New York.

Rosendahl, C.O. 1955. *Trees and Shrubs of the Upper Midwest*. University of Minnesota Press, Minneapolis.

Rowe, J.S. 1972. *Forest Regions of Canada*. Canadian Forest Service Publication 1300. Information Canada, Ottawa.

Sargent, C.S. 1908. *Crataegus* in Ontario. *Ontario Natural Science Bulletin* 4: 11–98.

Scoggan, H.J. 1978–79. *The Flora of Canada*. National Museum of Natural Sciences, National Museums of Canada, Ottawa.

Soper, J.H. 1949. *The Vascular Plants of Southern Ontario*. University of Toronto Department of Botany and Federation of Ontario Naturalists, Toronto.

Soper, J.H., and M.L. Heimburger. 1961. *100 Shrubs of Ontario*. Ontario Department of Commerce and Development, Toronto.

Soper, J.H., and M.L. Heimburger. 1982. *Shrubs of Ontario*. Royal Ontario Museum, Toronto.

Spangler, R.L., and J. Ripperda. 1977. *Landscape Plants for Central and Northeastern United States Including Lower and Eastern Canada*. Burgess Publishing Company, Minneapolis.

Stokes, D.W. 1981. *The Natural History of Wild Shrubs and Vines: Eastern and Central North America*. Harper and Row, New York.

Trelease, W. 1931. *Winter Botany*. Dover Publications, New York.

Voss, E.G. 1972. *Michigan Flora. Part I. Gymnosperms and Monocots*. University of Michigan Herbarium, Ann Arbor, Michigan.

Voss, E.G. 1985. *Michigan Flora. Part II. Dicots (Saururaceae–Cornaceae)*. University of Michigan Herbarium, Ann Arbor, Michigan.

Index to French Names

Index to French Names

Index to French Names

Index to Common and Scientific Names

Index to Common and Scientific Names

Index to Common and Scientific Names

Index to Common and Scientific Names

Index to Common and Scientific Names

Index to Common and Scientific Names

Index to Common and Scientific Names

Index to Common and Scientific Names

Index to Common and Scientific Names

Index to Common and Scientific Names